Victimology: A New Focus

Volume IV

Violence and Its Victims

Victimology: A New Focus

Volume IV
Violence and Its Victims

Edited by
Israel Drapkin and Emilio Viano

Lexington Books
D.C. Heath and Company
Lexington, Massachusetts
Toronto   London

Library of Congress Cataloging in Publication Data

International Symposium on Victimology, 1st, Jerusalem, 1973
    Violence and its victims.

    (Victimology: a new focus, v. 4)
    Includes primarily papers presented at the symposium.
    1. Victims of crime—Congresses. 2. Crime and criminals—Con-
gresses. 3. Violence—Congresses. I. Drapkin Senderey, Israel, 1905-
ed. II. Viano, Emilio, ed. III. Title.
HV6030.I54 1973 vol. 4   364s [364]   74-14830
ISBN 0-669-95752-6

International Standard Book Number, vol. iv 0-669-95752-6
International Standard Book Number, *set*, 0-669-95778-x

Library of Congress Catalog Card Number: 74-14830

In memory of all victims,
of genocide and mass violence,
of tyranny and injustice,
of exile and neglect.

Contents

Preface

If any single set of books can succeed in making "victimology" profession-ally respectable and intellectually serious, then the volumes in this series, *Vic-timology: A New Focus*, will do it. The five volumes of the series, remarkable for the variety and breadth of their content, are: *Theoretical Issues in Victim-ology*; *Society's Reaction to Victimization*; *Crimes, Victims, and Justice*; *Violence and Its Victims*; and *Exploiters and Exploited: The Dynamics of Victimization*.

While this is not the first publication in the field of victimology, it is a truly comprehensive presentation of the best current work originated in the inter-national scholarly community. Victimology, a relatively new development within the study of crime and deviance, is experiencing a rapid and vigorous development. Although the founders of criminology were well aware of the important role that the criminal-victim relationship plays in the dynamics of crime, it was not until recently that a systematic and sustained effort to study the victims of crime developed. Von Hentig's paper entitled, "Remarks on the Interaction of Perpetrator and Victim" (1941) and his book, *The Criminal and His Victim* (1948); Mendelsohn's paper, "New Bio-psycho-social Horizons: Victimology" (1947); and Ellenberger's study on the psychological relationship between the criminal and his victim (1954) are among the seminal works that spurred research on the subject of the criminal-victim relationship. Since then, many scholars and criminal justice professionals have focused their attention on this dimension of the criminal situation. As a consequence, a respectable body of literature has emerged.

At the same time, practitioners and reformers became interested in restoring to the victim some of the recognition and rights that he had enjoyed in antiquity. Margery Fry, the late English penal reformer, led the movement asking for revival of the victim's importance and for the institution of more effective remedies for victims other than the traditional tort procedure in the civil courts (1955). This movement made some inroads as New Zealand established the first crime compensation tribunal in 1963, followed by England in 1964. In the United States, the first state to acknowledge the need to compensate the victims of crime was California (1965); followed later by New York (1966); Hawaii (1967); Massachusetts (1967); Maryland (1968); Nevada (1969); New Jersey (1971); Alaska (1972); and Washington (1974). Several efforts undertaken at the federal level have been unsuccessful to date.

Other experts have suggested a different approach for the compensation of

crime victims: insurance. For example, insurance protection is now reportedly
offered in the United States to corporate clients against kidnapping and ransom
demands. Meanwhile, other important facets of the victim's situation have come
under scrutiny and have spurred people into action. Students and professionals
in the criminal justice system have become increasingly aware that a victim of
a criminal becomes—more often than not—also the victim of the criminal justice
system. Once the victim reports his victimization to the police—the gateway to
the criminal justice system—he or she is routinely faced by postponements,
delays, reschedulings, and other abuses. All this means loss of earnings, waste of
time, frustration, and the painful realization that the system does not live up to
its ideals and does not serve its constituency, but instead serves itself and its
underlings. As a consequence, many innovative proposals have been advanced,
such as the creation of central citizens' complaint and service bureaus; witness
coordinators at police stations, courthouses, district attorneys' offices, and
defenders' offices; participation of the victim in plea bargaining by prosecutors;
reports, at some point, by police to victims on whether they are making progress in investigating and solving their cases; the provision of the services of an
ombudsman who would assist the victims of crime by intervening in the crisis,
acting as a community facilitator, and referring the victims to the community's
and other resources.

This ferment of ideas, research, and reform efforts in the area of victimology has now reached a significant momentum. The First International Symposium on Victimology held in Jerusalem in 1973 gave the area of victimology
international recognition as a distinct focus of inquiry within criminology.
With the Symposium, victimology has entered its mature stage and will, hope-
fully, bear fruits from the point of view of theoretical insights, research break-
throughs, and practical implementation.

The major papers in the English language presented and discussed during
the Symposium are published in these five volumes. A few other papers, not
read in Jerusalem, have also been included because of their relevance to the
development of victimology. In this sense, these volumes are an accurate
reflection of the current work undertaken by the international community of
scholars and professionals on the subject of victims of crime.

The principal aims of the Symposium were to facilitate the exchange of
ideas and to stimulate more and improved research in victimology, the potential
of which has not yet been well mined. The value of the Symposium for the
participants consisted in the pooling of topics, in learning what particular
problems interest various people, and then receiving the stimulation of others
to pursue problems in one's own work. To date, the field has been one in which
individual scholars have contributed as individuals, with little, if any, of the
work reflecting the cumulative effort of groups of scholars. These volumes aim
at providing new data, theoretical inputs, and analyses that will encourage the
building of ideas and the development of intellectual dialogues in the field of

victimology. In particular, these volumes seek to contribute to a discourse within the international community of scholars, and to bring together scholars whose paths may not easily cross, in spite of their common interest.

While the papers published in these volumes reflect the wide scope and diversity of pursuits in the field of victimology, they have been organized as follows:

Theoretical Issues in Victimology consists first of all of papers discussing "The Notion of Victimology," that is, the definition of the concept of victim, the locus of victimology in the realm of the social sciences and in relation to criminology, and future directions of development. The second part of the volume, "Victim Typology," debates the issues of victim definition and classification, and their impact on empirical research. In particular, the offender-victim relationship is examined and discussed.

Society's Reaction to Victimization consists first of seven papers on "Prevention and Treatment of Victims of Crime," dealing with the ways and means which society might adopt to come to the aid of victims in distress and also to effectively prevent victimization. Then, a series of papers discuss "Compensation and Restitution to Victims of Crime" as representing the restoration of the social equilibrium in all its aspects, individual and collective, following the disturbance by the criminal act.

Crimes, Victims, and Justice discusses problems related to the treatment of the victim at the hands of the criminal justice system. The case of the falsely accused person and a closer look at the offender as the victim are also examined. Moreover, past and current research being conducted in the area of victimology is described and important methodological questions about victimization surveys are raised.

Violence and Its Victims and *Exploiters and Exploited: The Dynamics of Victimization* pursue the themes developed in the previous volumes by applying them to the analysis of specific situations. The collection of papers in *Violence and Its Victims* is divided in three sections: Homicide and Suicide, Mass Violence and Genocide, and Children's Victimization. The volume *Exploiters and Exploited* addresses the issues of Sex Offenses and Rape, White Collar Crime, Institutional Victimization, Traffic Offenses, and Related Victimization.

We are grateful to the authors of the various papers for granting us permission to publish their contributions. We feel indeed privileged in being able to bring their work to the attention of the international scholarly community for the first time being certain, as we are, that they will be favorably received. We also feel that they will spur further debate, research, and innovative thinking in the area of victimology. At Lexington Books, we would like to thank Mr. Mike McCarroll, Director, and Ms. Barbara Levey, former Editor-in-Chief, for their generous understanding and encouragement; Ms. Shirley End and the production staff for their careful aid in editing and preparing the manuscript for publication; and Ms. Judy Zelin for her skillful efforts to bring these volumes to the attention of scholars and of the general public.

References

Ellenberger, H.
1954
"Psychological Relationships between the Criminal and his Victim." *Revue Internationale de Criminologie et de Police Technique* 2: 103-121.

Mendelsohn, B.
1947
"New Bio-psycho-social Horizons: Victimology." Unpublished communication read to the Roumanian Society of Psychiatry in Bucharest.

Von Hentig, H.
1941
"Remarks on the Interaction of Perpetrator and Victim." *Journal of the American Institute of Criminal Law and Criminology* 31 (March-April) 303-309.

Von Hentig, H.
1948
The Criminal and His Victim: Studies in the Socio-biology of Crime. New Haven: Yale University Press.

Introduction

Remarks read by Professor Israel Drapkin, Chairman of the Organizing Committee, at the Opening Ceremony of the First International Symposium on Victimology held in Jerusalem on September 2, 1973.

The scholars gathered here in Jerusalem today have come with the purpose of discussing with their Israeli colleagues the basic issues of a topic that is as old as mankind but comparatively new as a scientific endeavor. We refer, obviously, to "victimology," an expression usually accepted to have been coined in 1947 by Mr. B. Mendelsohn here with us tonight, to whom I should like to pay respect on behalf of all of us.

From the simple etymological point of view, "victimology" derives from the Latin word "victima" and the Greek root "logos." "Victima" has two basic meanings: one implies the living creature sacrificed to a deity, or offered in performance of a religious rite. The second meaning is that used in criminology and related fields. It refers to the person suffering, injured or destroyed by the action of another—which may be due to some uncontrollable quality in himself—in pursuit of an object or purpose, in gratification of a passion, or as a result of events or circumstances. In other words, "victimology" basically refers to the study of the victim. It is precisely this plural definition which creates the possibility of studying the subject from quite a number of different, and even antagonistic, points of view.

In 1948, the famous German criminologist Hans Von Hentig dealt with the subject in an extensive way. Since then, a good number of works have come to the fore, both of a philosophical and a scientific nature. In spite of their importance, however, they lack a common foundation. Each researcher acted more or less as a freelancer, without paying too much attention to the personal points of view of his colleagues working in the same subject. What was lacking was an international platform on which to interchange ideas and results, to compare methodology and techniques, and to facilitate coordination and cooperation in order to try to reach a consensus on basic issues already developed or on matters to be studied in the future. Just this, and nothing else, is the basic purpose of this First International Symposium on Victimology.

Sir Peter Medawar has properly stressed the point that all advances of scientific understanding, at every level, begin with a speculative adventure, and imaginative preconception of what might be true; a preconception which always, and necessarily, goes a little, or even a long way beyond anything in which we have logical or factual authority to believe. The conjecture is then exposed to criticism. Scientific reasoning is therefore, at all levels, an inter-action between two episodes of thought, the one imaginative and the other critical; a dialogue, if you like, between the possible and the actual; between proposal and disposal; conjecture and criticism. In this conception of the scientific process, imagination and criticism are integrally combined. Imagination without criticism may burst out into a comic profusion of grandiose and silly notions. Critical reasoning alone is barren.

If some of you might be inclined to believe that the Greek philosophers went too far in their speculative exercises, there are others who are convinced that present-day science pays too much respect to statistical checking and counter-checking. Excessive play with theoretical hypothesis, lacking appro-priate critical control, is as dangerous as excessive worship at the altar of statistics, without the benefit of the imaginative mind. It is the adequate blending of these two approaches—the pragmatic and sometimes even distasteful eclecticism—that will bring us nearer to our ultimate and common goal.

In ancient civilizations, the victim of forbidden acts or omissions was always a paramount figure on the stage of the criminal setting. Compensation and "wergeld" were the means by which humanity moved slowly from the practice of private revenge to that of public justice. Then, with state and government taking justice into their own hands, the offender gradually became the central figure of the criminal drama, and the victim was almost entirely forgotten. The last thirty years have witnessed a rebirth in the care for the victim.

Ecclesiastes stresses the fact that for everything there is a season: a time for every purpose and for every work; a time to keep silent and a time to speak. We are convinced that the time has come to speak and to work for the rights of the victim, with the aim of mobilizing public opinion in benefit of this excessively neglected subject.

We are living in a technological and materialistic era, controlled by eco-nomic rules, competitive antagonism, and blatant aggressiveness among human beings; a world torn by bitterness and hatred, where the right of force prevails rather than the force of right; a world which seems to forget that violence does not finish with the problems but with the solutions; a world in which honesty is almost considered to be a pathological anomaly; a world which lives dangerously without trying to avoid unnecessary victimization. In this world, all kinds of alienation become the natural and frequent outcome.

Technology, as any other human conquest, has a price to be paid, a price that seems to be a frighteningly high one. The time has come to start thinking of the means to control the dreadful might we have created, and this can only be achieved by returning once more to the eternal moral human values. Let us

hope that this modest Symposium may become our common contribution to
facilitate the dawn of a new era, where mankind will start again to forgive and
to love; an age of hope, brotherhood and peace, dignity and freedom, mutual
respect and trust; an era of justice and righteousness.

This is perhaps the most important reason why we have to stop treading
the old paths of our prejudices; we have to start daring and risking, leaving
part of our own selves on every one of the stepping stones marking the way
of our future. If there is a future for our endeavors, it will only be possible
if all, or at least some of us, become iconoclasts and destroy those unworthy
idols still worshipped by mankind. If this means being called 'extremist',
'revolutionary', 'anti-establishment', 'nonconformist' or any other of the
infinite variety of today's slogans—more used than understood—let us not be
afraid of it. Like new crusaders, our fight should not be based on religious
grounds, but on working for a better future for tomorrow, the world of our
children and of our children's children.

The declared purposes of this Symposium can be summarized as follows.
We will try, first, to reach an agreement regarding the scope of victimology:
should it cope only with victims of crime or should it include all kinds of
victims, no matter the source, nature or degree of their victimization? Once
this crucial point has been settled, as we hope it will be, agreement on the
problems of methodology and other research matters may then be easily
arrived at. Secondly, we have to consider the possibilities of establishing
a valid typology of victims, an indispensable tool for future developments.
Thirdly, it will be necessary to analyze the role of the victim, both in the
juridical and judicial settings, in order to improve the present situation as
much as possible. Our fourth aim is the analysis of the offender-victim
relationship, particularly with regard to the main categories of criminal
offense. And, finally, the problem remains of how to improve society's
reaction towards victims, be it by means of compensation, insurance, prevention, or treatment.

Besides these five main objectives, it is of the utmost importance to avoid
two frequent pitfalls in this slippery field of victimology. On the one extreme,
we can overdo the emphasis on the role of the victim and reach the opposite
conclusion, namely that the victim is the real criminal and the criminal a mere
victim of his victim. On the other extreme, we should abstain from being
involved in what could be called the "conspiracy of silence." The vast majority
of us acquiesce with silence when the process of victimization starts in the
highest echelons of the power structure of our respective societies, no matter
what their political flavor is. It is time for us criminologists to become
vociferous when government, high-placed authorities, or the so-called "Establishment" victimizes members of the community outside the criminal law
framework.

With all this in mind, victimology might be properly shaped here. It will not be an easy task, but it is certainly possible. Every first experience is difficult, sometimes even painful, like all kinds of creative endeavor. We cannot foresee the impact that the guidelines established here might have on the course of immediate and future orientations in this new field. We accept this historical responsibility with a great amount of trepidation, but no fear, and we leave to the social scientist and historian of the future the evaluation of our work here. But on an occasion like this, when an important milestone is reached, there is cause for a common and justifiable pride.

Our personal pride and confidence stems from the fact that this First International Symposium on Victimology takes place here in Israel, the new nation of the Jewish people. We belong to an old people that has been discriminated against and persecuted by its fellow men through the ages, for numberless generations, and in spite of all this, or perhaps because of it, we have a deep understanding for all kinds of victim; we never understood nor believed in the existence of the impossible; we have always been in the forefront of change, running away from frozen ideologies; we have been able to sum up the sufferings, deceits, and disillusionments of twenty centuries, not in a tremendous failure, but in a resounding success; we are a people who, for the third time in our history, have come back to the land of our biblical ancestors, to rebuild our capital here in Jerusalem, the City of Peace, as the Kings of Israel called it 2500 years ago, and from where we extend to all and every one of you our most cordial Bruchim Ha-Baim, Welcome, Soyez Les Bienvenus, Bienvenida.

We cannot possibly finish these opening remarks without expressing our most sincere gratitude and deepest appreciation for the so many organizations, colleagues, and friends that have contributed so much to the crystallization of our dream: this First International Symposium on Victimology. Without their assistance and stimulation it could never have taken place. We should like to mention the various authorities of the government of Israel; the International Society of Criminology, represented here tonight by its vice president; and the Hebrew University of Jerusalem by its president. They are the sponsors of the Symposium, with the cooperation of the Universities of Tel Aviv and Bar Ilan, the Israel Academy of Sciences and Humanities, and the Van Leer Jerusalem Foundation that have so kindly opened their doors for our meetings. We should also like to express our happiness at having with us here the representatives of the Council of Europe; of the International Penal and Penitentiary Foundation; and of the British Council. They have all contributed to the success of this Symposium. Our esteem goes also to the distinguished members of our International Advisory Board, which so much influenced many of our decisions; to the members of our National Organizing Committee, who worked with us from day to day; to the distinguished colleagues who have so unselfishly accepted the responsibilities of being the chairmen and rapporteurs of the various sections into which this Symposium has been divided; to the members of our Steering Committee; to Mr. Justice Chaim Cohen, who will deliver the opening lecture; and to the academic staff and secretariat of our Institute of Criminology, who so devotedly and anonymously have taken the major part of the organizational burden; to those of you particularly that have come from abroad, despite certain doubts and fears regarding the safety of modern international traveling. To all and every one of you, my personal gratitude for all you have done to make this project possible and successful.

Introduction to Volume IV

Popular concepts and the adversary nature of the criminal justice process alike presuppose that there is a clear and identifiable distinction between the offender and the victim. Many believe that the role of the criminal and the role of the victim are completely different, and find in such difference the justification for their claims that the victim be compensated and the offender be punished. However, there is growing evidence that such a conceptual model must be revised to reflect more realistically the many possible varieties of the relationship between the victim and the offender. The victim's behavior can be categorized on a continuum anchored with the polar adjective pair "innocent-guilty." A series of scale positions could be designed to measure the innocence and/or guilt of the victim, from one pole—completely innocent—to the other pole—completely guilty.

One of the founders of victimology, Hans von Hentig, in his paper "Remarks on the Interaction of Perpetrator and Victim" (1941), was among the first scholars to focus on the interaction between what he called "the penal couple." He discussed, "the scale of graduated inter-activities between perpetrator and victim which elude the formal boundaries set up by our statutes and the artificial abstractions of legal science." Beniamin Mendelsohn (1956) also constructed a six-part typology that is predicated on the amount of guilt a victim contributes to the event.

In his work, "Towards a Criminological Classification of Victims," Ezzat Abdel-Fattah (1967), outlined a rather complicated scheme which has five major categories of victims and eleven subgroups. The five major types are labeled as: non-participating, latent, provocative, participating, and false victims.

Thorsten Sellin and Marvin Wolfgang, in their book *The Measurement of Delinquency* (1964), offered a typology envisioning five possible categories of victimization: primary, secondary, tertiary, mutual vicitimization, or no victimization.

Thus, it appears that in order to reach a valid evaluation and assessment of responsibility in a criminal situation, it is imperative that both parties, their personalities, their interrelationship, and their interaction be examined, and that the role each has played before and during the commission of the crime be studied. The thirteen papers published in this volume represent the most recent works of victimologists in this delicate area of inquiry. These works have been grouped into three parts, according to the major offense which the writer investigates.

In Part I–"Homicide and Suicide," papers by Pawel Horoszowski, Stephen Schafer, Klaus Sessar, Stuart Palmer, and Neville Avison discuss the offender-victim relationship in cases of homicide.

In Part II–"Mass Violence and Genocide," Bruno Cormier, Chanoch Jacobsen, Vahakn Dadrian, and E. L. Quarantelli and Russell Dynes discuss in their respective contributions the theme of mass deviance, multicide, and genocide.

In Part III–"Children's Victimization," issues and research related to the "battered" child and to the child victim of a sex offense are discussed in the papers prepared by Emilio Viano, Susan Harlap and Israel Drapkin, LeRoy Schultz, and J.E. Hall Williams.

**Part I
Homicide and Suicide**

1

Homicide of Passion and Its Motives
Pawel Horoszowski

Introduction

The basic problems of victimology are rather substantial facts concerning the results of criminological research investigations dealing with the victim of crime, and especially with the victim-doer[a] relationship. This paper deals with such problems in connection with a given kind of crime—"homicide of passion."

My research, which is described below in a detailed way has been published in several articles before World War II and in a monograph in 1947. Those publications are in Polish and therefore basically unknown to criminologists of other countries. Nevertheless, it is interesting that similar studies dealing with the victim of crime, especially with the victim-doer relationship have been made in connection with homicide in Poland and twenty years later in the United States (of course, independently). I refer especially to the very well-known Wolfgang study, which is based on police records in one big city (Philadelphia), whereas mine is based on court cases from rural and urban places in Poland.[1] In spite of the differences in economic, socio-cultural, and political structures (although Poland, at the time of my investigation was a capitalistic country), differences in legislations, law enforcement, industrialization and urbanization (more than 50 percent of Poland's population was at that time agrarian), some results of both studies are similar.

The intent of my paper is not a comparison of results concerning homicides in America with "homicide of passion" in Poland. I believe that some parts of my research, especially concerning the concept of "motive," can be useful to

---

[a]Who among criminologists "is credited [let me use Reckless' formulation] with having made the first criminological identification of the victim-doer relationship?"[2] As I already mentioned, I don't believe—contrary to Reckless and other authors—that this can be established without doubt. Anyway, I do not pretend to take away from anybody the delusive conviction of being the inventor, discoverer or creator of a completely "new, original" idea of "the victim-doer relationship." Nevertheless, in two of my publications which are the basis for the present paper, there is a chapter entitled: "Data concerning the victim." It consists of four subdivisions, entitled: 1. "Sex of the victim," 2. "Age of the victim," 3. "The victim's profession," and 4. "The victim-doer relationship." In another chapter dealing with the problem of "The motives of homicide of passion," there are two subdivisions, entitled: 1. "Motives and victim-doer relationship," and 2. "Motives and the victim's sex."[3] I do not pretend to priority in "having made the first criminological identification of victim-doer relationship"; I quote in my prewar research some earlier publications which started to consider a number of characteristics of the victim of crime.

any criminologist and particularly those interested in the problem of victimology, chiefly because motive is still very unclear and confusing—although it is a factor important for understanding any individual case of criminal behavior, especially directed against a person.

From a detailed semantical and psychological analysis it follows that we have to differentiate between the direct purpose of our action and the "motive" for it. The decision to act in a particular way is called by the legislator "criminal intent"; it is something other than motive, which indicates a kind of a causal factor for the decision. The term motive has the most ambiguous meanings in psychology, as well as in other branches of science, and in common use. After a thorough, multilateral analysis I defined motive as *an idea* (or thought of a given state of facts—in the past, present or future) *under the influence of which we make our decision to act in a given way.* The motive—based on right, or illusionary perceptions of facts, and other correct or incorrect mental processes— is only one of many more of less conscious, temporary or permanent psychic factors (related to our personality features) which influence our behavior. It is neither the only nor the most important causative factor, especially in cases of homicide of passion. As it is commonly accepted by behavioral sciences, our intellectual processes (to which the motives belong, according to the above indicated definition) would be inefficient without the stimulating power of the emotion, which is the incentive or the *impulsion* of our decision. The *impulsion* is, therefore, *the emotion which accompanies the motive in the process of making the decision.*[4]

It is very difficult, if not impossible, to establish in an exact way the type, strength, and developmental stages of an emotion which was the impulsion to commit a homicide. We call such an emotion "affect" (or—not exactly—"passion"), if it is a vehement, overpowering perturbation of "normal" emotional processes.

The court can more easily assume what was the motive, if it takes into consideration witness testimony, circumstantial evidence, expert opinions, and the perpetrator's explanations. That was the reason why the investigation of the motives of homicide was the basic idea of my research.

Research Results

Neither police statistics nor police records nor court statistics seemed to me sufficient for my study. Police statistics as well as court statistics present data in a formal way, and do not permit an analysis of individual cases. In the case of police records we have to do with incompetent qualifications. Such records include a substantial number of cases which the court does not consider homicide at all. It is not the duty of the police to make decisions replacing the court trial. The police are often prone to a kind of professional exaggeration, and jump to premature conclusions on the basis of quite often insufficient evidence and without a multilateral analysis of all available facts. Felonious homicide is not what the police say but what the court establishes in its sentencing procedure.

My study is based on an analysis of 330 separate, mostly voluminous court files concerning 330 cases of homicide of passion and, for comparative reasons, 100 court cases of "ordinary" homicide. The research results were published before World War II as a separate monograph. My paper basically presents, in a summarized way, the research results of the 330 homicides of passion. I quote only for some comparisons the results of the other study. The collected material includes cases terminated with conviction in the years 1932 to 1936, in eight district courts located in different geographic areas in Poland. Each of such courts exercized, before World War II, its jurisdiction over several counties. In six of these district courts, all cases for the years mentioned were taken into consideration, and in the remaining two courts a great majority of the cases were considered.

In the 330 cases there were 340 offenders, *263 male* (77.3 percent) and *77 female* (22.7 percent)—or 29.3 female offenders per 100 male offenders. Among the 77 female offenders 39 killed their children, of whom only two were older than a few weeks. These cases are very similar to infanticide treated by the Polish Penal Code 1932 in a separate article. If we eliminate these cases, we get a rate of 14.4 female offenders per 100 male offenders. This proportion can be reduced to 12.9, if we consider the sex relation in the districts taken into account (according to the census of 1931—4,250,420 males and 4,643,010 females, or 47.79 percent male and 52.21 percent female). In cases of ordinary felonious homicide female participation was even smaller. Roesner (1933) established a similar relation of passion homicides (Affektbetonte Morde) in Germany.[5] Nevertheless this male-female rate varies in different countries.

It may be mentioned here that (according to Hacker 1935) in international comparisons, unfortunately made by him in a most uncritical way, the rate of felonious homicide per 100,000 population ranged from 0.2 (England and Wales, and Norway) up to 22.3 (Bulgaria); the rate for all kinds of homicide was 7.3 in Poland, and 3.0 in the United States.[6]

The fiction and even nonsense of such as Hacker's international statistics is obvious. According to his statistics concerning serious crimes in different countries, the totals of these crimes ranged in the early 30's from 5,951 (South African Union) per 100,000 population down to the country which had the lowest rate in the world—55 per 100,000 population. This country was the USA.[7] As I indicated in a critical review (1937) and in my textbooks of criminology, Hacker mixed up police, court, and correctional statistics; felonies, misdemeanors, and even transgressions; rates per 100,000 of the whole population and only of the age of penal responsibility.[8] His two publications (1931 and 1935) confirmed again how unreliable are international crime statistics, and this conclusion is still valid. Brearley (1932) was of the opinion that the amount of homicides committed in the United States is approximately three times higher than recorded in the official police statistics.[9] According to the Uniform Crime Reports, the rate of murder and nonnegligent homicide per 100,000 population in the United States is now approximately 9.[10] In Poland in the later postwar period there was a sharp drop in the homicide rate.

In my 330 cases there were 358 victims. Since committed and attempted homicide are treated by the Polish Penal Code (1932) in the same way, I included both in the research. Of course, it could be questioned whether the attempted cases were in reality attempted homicides and not eventually aggravated assaults. But such an objection does not have much validity. We may ask with the same degree of justification, if in the committed homicides the offender had in reality the intent to commit this crime. It would be naive if somebody believed that the court's decision always corresponds with reality. Neither can a highly qualified psychologist often answer the question, what was the real intent of the offender? This is obvious even without examples of constructive criminal intent, plea bargaining, and similar procedures. Paraphrasing Thomas Aquinas, we may say *Quod est in actis est in mundo.* Anyway *quod est in actis* of the court is much closer, in this regard, to reality than what is in the police records.

As a result of the offenders action 214 (59.8 percent) victims died. Among the victims of male offenders 56.4 percent died, whereas among victims of female offenders 71.8 percent died. Nevertheless, if we eliminate children below one year of age, the percentage of victims who died as a result of homicide committed by females drops to 41.7 percent. Of course, a presentation of etiological problems of the aforementioned rate can not be included in the framework of this paper.

The age of 340 offenders showed that the age group 20-29 exceptionally high, and the age group 30-39 was still substantially higher among offenders than among the population. These groups made together more than 65 percent of the offenders—compared with 34 percent in the population.

From the analysis of professions it could be concluded that except in seven cases the professions of all male and female offenders were typical for the lower class; many of the offenders did not have a profession at all, and at least three-quarters of all offenders were persons living in poor economic conditions. With a few exceptions, all the offenders were uneducated persons (most of whom did not graduate from elementary school.)

In a country in which religion played and still plays a very important role in social life, it was interesting to establish these relations among the offenders. Roman Catholics, Greek Catholics, and Orthodox were represented in a higher percentage among the offenders than in the population; on the other hand Protestants were two times less often among offenders than in the population, and

Jews—even less often than 4.5 times. Not discussing etiological explanations I may only mention that, as in cases analyzing other variables, responsible for these differences is not, of course, one factor (like religion) per se.

Poland in the prewar period was a country of very slight physical mobility and only limited social mobility. Nevertheless it could be established that the majority of the offenders belonged to people whose birthplace and place of residence were not the same. Such an alienating factor may have contributed more or less directly to conflicting, provocative situations.

Taking the relative ratio of urban and rural population, we may say that in homicide of passion, per 100 urban offenders there were 90 rural offenders. But in the district of Warsaw, the Polish capital, there were almost 115 rural offenders per 100 urban offenders. The latter difference is substantially higher in cases of ordinary homicide.

The official records of convictions (filed in a special department of the Polish Ministry of Justice) showed that the rate of formerly convicted offenders was almost 22 percent among males and almost 12 percent among females. None of the offenders had been formerly convicted for a serious crime against a person. In the cases of ordinary homicide there were over 38 percent of formerly convicted offenders, mostly more than one time, and often for crimes against a person.

Among victims of male offenders (in passion homicide) there were 217 males, 60 females, and 3 young children. Among victims of female offenders there were 30 males, 3 females, and 45 children. It follows that among adult victims only one in every five was a female. In ordinary homicide the ratio was even more favorable for women. As is known, this ratio is not similar not in all countries.

When both sexes are combined, 65 percent of the adult victims are in the age group 21-40; this is close to the age distribution among the offenders. It was similar also in cases of ordinary homicide.

With the exception of 18, all the victims had professions typical for the lower social class; many of them, especially female victims, did not have any profession. Among the 18 victims with middle-class professions, the majority were superiors, employers, or landlords of the offenders. A similar conclusion has been drawn from the analysis of the ordinary homicide cases.

Analyzing the *relationship between victim and offender,* I am omitting 9 victims, because their relationship to the offender could not be established in an exact way, although there were indications that they did not belong to the category "stranger." Among 271 victims of the male offenders 111 (53 males and 58 females) were members of the offender's family, his relatives, and similar close persons. The remaining 160 victims (157 males and 3 females) basically were close acquaintances with whom the offender was in different kinds of relationship and in frequent contact. Here are examples of such relationships: neighbor, tenant, subtenant, roomer, landlord, companion, friend, lease-holder, employer or former employer (14), the wife's paramour (8), the mother's or sister's paramour, rival, suitor and the husband of the offender's mistress.

The 53 male victim-members of the male offenders family and relatives were the following: brother-in-law (15), father-in-law (8), brother (7), father (3), son (2), stepfather (2), stepson (2), and other relatives. Except for 3 acquaintances, all remaining 58 female victims of male offenders were their following family members, relatives, or other close relationships: wife (16), mistress, fiancé, or girl-friend (24), mother-in-law (9), sister-in-law (3), and other relatives (6).

In the cases of female offenders 41 victims were the offenders' children. Among the remaining victims were 31 male victims whose relation to the offender was such as: paramour, fiance (18), husband (7), son-in-law (2), son (1), and other relatives (3).

Apart from 2 female victims who were acquaintances of the female offenders, the remaining 3 female victims were: daughter (2—older than the 41 child victims), sister-in-law (1).

In a general way it may be stated that among 210 male victims of male offenders there were 25.2 percent family members, relatives, and others close to them; whereas among 61 female victims of male offenders 95.1 percent were their family members, relatives, and others close to them. It means that every fourth male victim of male offenders, and almost all female victims of male offenders are members of the offender's family, relatives, or similar close persons.

In the cases of female offenders, female victims constitute an unsubstantial part, and all male victims are members of the offender's family, relatives, and similar close persons. I omitted here the 41 child victims of the female offenders; independently of their sex and illegitimacy (in all cases) they are, of course, members of the offender's family.

It may be concluded that basically all victims of the opposite sex to the offender's sex are his or her members of family, relatives, or similar close persons. Apart from kiling an illegitimate child, the most common victim of a female offender is her paramour, fiancé, or husband. Similarly, among female victims of male offenders the great majority are the mistress, fiancé, or wife. Even not including the illegitimate children, we may establish that 47.4 percent of the victims of crimes of passion are the offender's family members, relatives, and similar close persons. In the cases of ordinary homicide this percentage is lower (28.3 percent). But frequency of acquaintanceship and close relationship between victims and offenders in the cases of ordinary homicide is very high. A better understanding of this relationship, as well as in cases of homicide of passion, follows from the given below enumeration of motives.

An almost identical percentage (48) of victims—family members, relatives, and similar close persons was established by Lorentz in his 286 cases of man-slaughter.[11] Exner showed that almost all victims of "passion murder" (Leidenschaftsmord) were relatives and other very close persons (paramours and similar).[12] Höpler found a very high incidence (42.9 percent) of relatives in his murder cases.[13] Krämer showed that in the majority of "passion" and "conflict murders" the victim was in some way related to the offender.[14] Gast established that among 721 murders committed by women in only 84 cases the victim was not a relative of the offender.[15] Similar facts have been established by von Hentig.[16] If we also consider as strangers in Wolfgang's classification victims enumerated by Wolfgang as "innocent bystanders," police officers, and prostitutes (which Wolfgang enumerates together with paramours and mis-tresses), there will be approximately 25 percent of victims related to the offender, and at least 55 percent acquaintances and close friends.[17] Wolfgang also found that "the Philadelphia data clearly show that close and intimate relationships— particularly those of a spouse—are much more common among the victims of female offenders than of male offenders."[18] Nevertheless, before Pollak (as quoted by Wolfgang) expressed such "belief," there were available objective data concerning this problem (according to the aforementioned research inves-gations). Pokorny accepted, in his Houston study, the Philadelphian classifi-cation introducing some changes; unfortunately his group "other categories" is exceptionally high (22.7 percent). But out of the total 100 percent of vic-tims approximately 70 percent are in family relationship, friends, or acquain-tances of the offender.[19] Of course these results are similar to the results of the prewar research investigations.

From data concerning the place where the crime had been committed, as well as from additional circumstances, it follows that female offenders act more often than male offenders in conditions enabling the concealment of the deed. Such behavior, of course, is not typical for an action following from an outburst of a vehement emotion.

The research results concerning weapons and methods of inflicting injuries (including their body location) showed that in this regard there was a very basic difference between committed and attempted homicide. In committed homicides firearm had been used in only 35 percent of the cases, whereas in attempted homicide cases firearms had been used in 80 percent of the times. Our analysis led to the conclusion that the court qualifies the crime as attempted homicide or only as an assault especially according to the kind of weapon, the bodily location of the injury, and the result of the inflicted injury. But shooting was for the court an indication of attempted homicide even if there was no bodily harm at all.

As I indicated before, the basic idea of my research investigation was to elaborate, not only theoretically, but also from the practical point of view, the problem of the *motive,* which is so important in victimology and in other branches of criminology. For this purpose I used, as an example, the practical applicability of the *motive* (as defined after a thorough analysis of the available publications and jurisprudential sources) to homicides of passion. I indicated that for an analysis of the motives we must, first of all, understand its meaning in a uniform way. Of course, we cannot accept either the court's classification or, especially, the ones used by the police. It does not make sense to use the term *motive* to indicate any kind of physical and psychic facts, or any kind of circumstances and events of any nature. Therefore, I proposed the definition of a motive as only an intellectual act in the would-be criminal's mind when he is making the decision to act. After a thorough analysis of my 430 homicide cases (passion and ordinary homicides), I established the existence of the following groups of motives, in which we take into consideration facts:

1. of an economic nature (*economic motives*);
2. of an erotic nature (*erotic motives*);
3. connected with endangering of our safety or honor (*safety-honor motives*);
4. connected with an interest of another person (*solidarity motives*);
5. of a mixed nature (combination of the enumerated motives).

With indicated exceptions, the motives are the offender's thoughts of actions or behavior attributed to the would-be victim, and directed, first of all, against himself, the would-be offender. This is mostly the case; nevertheless there are some exceptions, indicated below, in which the offender did not attribute to the victim the facts which he took into consideration as the motive for his decision. Quite often the offender acts also, as indicated especially in the separate group of solidarity motives, when the would-be victim's action is directed against other persons and not directly toward the would-be offender. Sometimes even the very existence of the would-be victim, as in the case of illegitimate children, contributes to the arising of a motive, and to the decision to commit a homicide. Nevertheless, in the great majority of cases it is obvious that the would-be offender considers the action of the would-be victim, or even some specific circumstances (which are the basis for the origin of the motive), as a specific provocation.

A detailed enumeration of the motives, separated by cases of male offenders and female offenders is presented in the Appendix; the following considerations refer to the motives enumerated there.

In brief, it may be stated that in 250 male offender cases there were four basic groups into which we divided the 276 motives; the additional fifth group, the "mixed" motives, has not been considered in the presentation of percentages, as this group is basically comprised of a mixture of the foregoing four kinds of motives. The mentioned groups of motives are the following: (1) economic—50 (21.2 percent); (2) erotic—36 (15.3 percent); (3) safety-honor—120 (50.8 percent); (4) solidarity—30 (12.7 percent). There were 40 cases of mixed motives (fifth group).

As it follows from the specification given in the Appendix, the safety-honor and solidarity motives basically are very similar, the only difference is that in the former group of motives the offender considers that the action is directed against himself, whereas in the latter group he assumes that an action is directed, first of all, against some persons who are close to him. In the safety-honor and solidarity group there are together (in male offender cases) 150 motives (63.6 percent). This means that in three-fifths of male passion homicides we have mostly such motives as beating, insulting, assaulting, threatening, and similar acts—understood by the would-be offender as directed against himself, or against persons with whom he identifies in some regard. Slightly over one-fifth of the male offenders are making their decisions taking into consideration economic motives; and only less than one-sixth of decisions are based on erotic motives.

Omitting the cases of 41 illegitimate children (and one additional, similar case concerning a legitimate child), we could establish the following 37 motives of 35 female offenders: (1) economic—0; (2) erotic—13; (3) safety-honor—15; (4) solidarity—3; (5) mixed—6. There were no cases of female offenders with purely economic motives; nevertheless in all mixed motives, as well as in basically all omitted child-victim cases, an economic component (an additional motive) was obvious. Not taking into consideration the child victims and the mixed motives we may state that safety-honor and solidarity motives together account for almost three-fifths of all motives (similar to the male offender cases); the remaining over two-fifths are erotic motives (relatively almost three times more often than in the cases of male offenders). Of course, the indicated differences are connected with the (still existing) very specific woman's status prevalent all over the world.[20]

In the cases of ordinary homicide the safety-honor and solidarity motives together are also approximately three-fifths of all motives; but there are more economic motives (approximately one-third), and fewer erotic motives (approximately one-tenth) in ordinary homicide than in homicides of passion. Basically all kinds of motives which we met in homicides of passion were also present in ordinary homicides. We must agree with Holtzendorff, who said (one hundred years ago) that we find the same motives in both murder and manslaughter.[21] Nevertheless in our cases there were the following additional motives in ordinary homicide which we did not find in the homicide of passion: robbing the victim (9 cases), to inherit property (from the victim—1 case), and receiving money for killing the would-be victim (1 case).

The general conclusion from this part of the motive analysis was the following: "the popular opinion that the erotic motive is typical for homicide of passion is wrong; similarly wrong is the opinion that the typical motive of ordinary homicide is robbing the victim or another economic motive."[22]

The *kind of motive, and victim-offender relationship* has been established separately for male offenders and for female offenders. In the cases of male offenders it seemed most advisable to ask the question: what will be the number of relatives and other close persons per 100 unrelated persons—separately in each group? The answer was: economic motives—63; erotic motives—278; safety-honor motives—39; solidarity motives—52. It follows from these data that close persons are victims of homicide of passion in the erotic motive group almost three times more often than among victims unrelated to the offender. At the same time we may conclude that in all other groups of motives victims related to the offender (and similar persons) are much less frequent than victims unrelated to the offender.

The victims of 36 female offenders were in 34 cases related to the victim (and similar persons). Even if we do not take into consideration the illegitimate children, we may say that the victims of female offenders are basically only their family members, relatives or similar close persons. From the analysis of female offender motives (belonging, with a few exceptions, only to the safety-honor and erotic groups) and from all the circumstances established in the court records, it follows that female offenders are acting in situations in which the degree of provocation by the victim is mostly much higher than in the case of male offenders. In cases of female offenders their violent reaction can be explained, to a certain degree, by situational factors. Especially in the safety-honor group we have mostly to do with a reaction against permanent mistreatment by a husband or paramour—usually a dangerous alcoholic.

As I mentioned before, it is difficult to compare "motives" defined and presented in my study with the "motives" presented by Wolfgang. Nevertheless, he came to a conclusion similar to mine.[23]

The *relation between motive and the victim's sex* can be clearly seen, if we present separately the four categories of motives in 100 cases of male victims, and separately in 100 cases of female victims (not taking into consideration the child group).

In 100 male victims there were involved the following motives: safety-honor—55, economic—18, solidarity—15, and erotic—12. In 100 cases of female victims the motives were: erotic—45, safety-honor—25, economic—21, solidarity—9. Therefore, it can be concluded that in over one-half of male victims the motives belonged to the safety-honor group; but only one-fourth of these motives belonged to this group in the cases of female victims. The erotic motives were represented only in one-tenth of male victims, but in almost one-half of female victims. In the frequency of other motives there were no substantial differences in regard to the sex of the victim. It follows, therefore, that in approximately every second case of male victims the offender's motive of killing was safety-honor; and in approximately every second case of female victims the offender's motive was of an erotic nature.

Taking into account the proportion of the number of female victims in relation to the number of male victims (in the presented court cases) we may compare how many female victims are represented in comparison with 100 male victims in each group of motives. The appropriate calculations show that per 100 male victims there were: in economic motives—approximately 29 female victims, in erotic motives—96, in safety-honor motives—approximately 11.5, and in solidarity motives—approximately 16.5; a female victim, therefore, is represented as often as a male victim only in erotic motives. In economic motives she is represented over three times less frequently; and a woman considered by the would-be offender for passion as endangering his or a related person's safety or honor is an exception.

The number of the studied cases is, of course, too small for definite conclusions regarding the problem of *"motive and age."* Nevertheless, if we establish the average age of male offenders as 31.4 years, we receive the following average ages for five groups of motives (the mixed included): solidarity—27.2, erotic—29.9, safety-honor—30.6, mixed—33.8, and economic—35.7. Male offenders over the age of 39 are represented (among all male offenders) in the following percentages: economic motives—34.1, safety-honor—15.7, erotic—9.1, and in solidarity motives—only 6.5 percent. Therefore, even in regard to the question "age and motive" the results seem not to be accidental. The proposed classification of motives also seems to have a useful practical applicability here.

The female offender's average age was 28.1 years. The figures for female offenders are too small for a classification into five groups. But we may mention that the youngest, most frequent age (about 25 years) was represented among female offenders who killed their illegitimate children. Marginally it may be added that this age seems to be high in comparison with contemporary sex standards. Nevertheless, this result has to be considered from the sex-moral standards existing in a typical Catholic country four decades ago.

Our sample is not large enough for categorical statements concerning the question of motives and urban-rural distribution. Nevertheless, as a result of the research investigation it could be established that in 140 rural offender cases and in 95 (mostly big-) city offender cases the distribution of motives does not seem accidental. Making a very close approximation we may say that out of 100 rural cases of passion homicide there were the following motives: safety-honor—60 percent, economic—a little less than 20 percent, erotic and solidarity—slightly over 10 percent each. On the other hand, out of 100 urban cases there were these motives: safety-honor—almost 40 percent, erotic—almost 30 percent, economic—almost 20 percent, and solidarity—15 percent. Therefore, economic and solidarity motives are approximately distributed in the same way in the urban and rural areas. In the case of the remaining kinds of motives there are substantial differences. The safety-honor motive is 1½ times higher in the rural area than in the urban area, and the erotic motive is 2½ times more frequent in the urban area than in the rural area. We may conclude that our results are in agreement with the patterns of the so-called, in Poland, "rural stable boys" subculture; this term refers to the still persistent aggressive and violent way of solving conflicts arising between villagers of a young age.

If we take into consideration the cases of killing illegitimate children, not included in the aforementioned figures concerning the urban-rural distribution of passion homicide, and compare them with other homicides committed by women, we may say the following: whereas children victims of homicides occur in 80 percent of all female rural homicides, in a big city killing an illegitimate child constitutes only 34 percent of homicides committed by women. These results do not seem accidental.

Much attention has been paid in my investigation to a detailed analysis of the court's attitudes toward homicide of passion. This analysis has taken into consideration the dependence of the court's decision upon several factors which seemed to be most influential.

Investigating the severity of the sentence we have to take into consideration that the legislator considers killing another human being, even under influence of passion, as a very serious felony. Nevertheless the penal code left to the court (consisting of three professional judges in felony cases) a very large discretionary power. In homicide of passion cases the penalty could be from six months to ten years imprisonment. The average penalty should, therefore, vary somewhere between four and five years imprisonment. After eliminating 4 cases of juveniles who have been sent to a juvenile institution, in 366 cases taken into consideration the sentences mostly were not in the indicated range. Penalties under four years imprisonment have been applied in over 74 percent of all cases, and penalties above six years imprisonment in less than 5.5 percent of all cases. In over 60 percent the prison sentence was under two years. The obvious conclusion is that the court showed an exceptionally lenient attitude toward persons accused of committing homicide under the influence of passion. This lenient attitude is even more characteristic for the appeal court which reconsidered 191 sentences (163 instigated by the sentenced person and 28 by the public prosecutor, or by both the prosecutor and the sentenced person). In 10 cases (approximately 5 percent) the appellant has been acquitted, and in over 30 percent the court commuted the sentence.

Not taking into consideration the very mildly treated cases of female offenders who killed their illegitimate children, we may draw the following conclusion: out of 10 offenders sentenced for homicide under the influence of passion only 3 have been punished by more than three years imprisonment. This lenient attitude of the court toward persons sentenced for such serious crimes is also characteristic in cases of ordinary homicide. Punishment for these crimes is substantially higher than for homicide of passion, because the court's discretionary power is foreseen, in ordinary homicide, between a minimum of five years imprisonment and the maximum, which is the death penalty.

The Polish Penal Code (1932) indicates clearly that the absence of a felonious result of a criminal action should not be considered as a mitigating circumstance. Not the result but the social danger revealed in the attempted crime should be the basis for the court's sentence. Nevertheless, in the analyzed cases it turned out that the *fatal or non-fatal result* was one of the most substantial factors influencing the severity of the sentence. In committed homicides only less than 5.5 percent of the offenders have been sentenced to imprisonment for one year and less, whereas in attempted homicide more than 40 percent of the offenders have been treated in such a lenient way. Prison sentences of over two years have been applied in approximately 75 percent of all committed homicides, and in only approximately 20 percent of all attempted homicides. Almost one-fourth of all offenders who committed homicide of passion have been sentenced to more than five years imprisonment. But none of the offenders who attempted homicide has been sentenced to imprisonment for more than five years, and only a small percentage of them for more than three years. A positive correlation between seriousness of the objective result and the length of the prison term has been established also in ordinary homicide cases.

Although the number of *recidivists sensu largo* (punished previously for any kind of crime) was relatively small; nevertheless it could be found that among the most severely punished offenders the substantial majority were persons with previous sentences. The same conclusions could be drawn from the analysis of ordinary homicides. Such facts have been established for murder by von Hentig (1928) and other authors.[24]

Another factor which indicated a difference in treatment by the court is sex of the offender. Of course, similarly to other factors, it is not sex per se which influences the attitude of the court. But it is not our purpose here, as has been indicated before, to consider all these complicated causative problems. In committed homicide of passion male offenders have been sentenced in over one-fourth of all male cases to prison for over five years; whereas among women the appropriate fraction is approximately one-eighth. In attempted homicide almost one-fourth of the male offenders has been sentenced to imprisonment for over two years, whereas the appropriate fraction in female offender cases was only about one-twentieth.

For the analysis of the relation between the offender's motives and the severity of punishment all the cases have been divided into two basic groups: attempted homicide and committed homicide. In both these groups male and female cases have been treated separately. This has been done in view of the aforementioned substantial influence of such factors on punishment. In order to get a clear picture we divided the male offender cases (197) into the following three groups: (a) lenient punishment (six months to three years inclusively, in committed homicide; six months to one year inclusively, in attempted homicide); (b) intermediate punishment (over three years to five years inclusively, in committed homicide; over one year to three years inclusively, in attempted homicide); (c) severe punishment (over five years, in committed homicide (it is more than the minimum punishment in ordinary homicide); over three years, in attempted homicide).

Lenient punishment was almost the same (40 out of 100 in each group)

in erotic, safety-honor and solidarity motives; only in economic motives was
the appropriate percentage approximately 20. Therefore, it may be stated that
even in homicide of passion the court considers the economic motive mostly
as a circumstance not deserving lenient treatment.

The highest amount of intermediate punishment (over 55 percent) was
connected with economic motives, and the lowest (30 percent) with erotic
ones. The second highest percentage of intermediate punishment (over
45 percent) was related to safety-honor motives. The solidarity group was
almost the same (over 30 percent), as the erotic group—in intermediate
punishment.

Severe punishment for two groups of motives (economic and solidarity)
was almost the same, approximately 25 percent. In erotic motives the severe
punishment was higher than in the cases of the remaining motives. It is contrary to common belief that killing in connection with erotic motives is treated
by the court in the most lenient way. The lowest amount of severe punishment
(only 10 percent of all cases in this group) is connected with safety-honor
motives. As it follows from the analysis of the court records, such cases were
considered by the court as psychologically very close to self-defense. The
court often has taken into consideration the provocative behavior of the would-
be victim, and the offender's reaction to this behavior. It may be added that
the attitude of the court was similar in some cases of economic motives. In
such cases deserving lenient treatment, the court attributed provocative behavior
to the would-be victim, and considered the action of the offender as an excessive
defense of his property.

The *aggravating circumstances* enumerated by the court in all the analyzed
cases are worth listing here in a literal translation: "causing a serious damage
(a fatal or other serious result of the deed, more than one victim, depriving the
husband, orphaning children); previous convictions; premeditation; being cruel
to the victim; being a troublemaker; being a person of ill-repute; setting a trap;
lack of repentance; lack of serious or logical reason; social danger of the
perpetrator; mean reason; close family relationship of the victim."[25] Nevertheless, such aggravating circumstances have been very often superseded or over-
balanced by the aforementioned factors.

It may be added here that drunkenness and alcoholism have not been
treated in a uniform way by the court, if the judges paid attention to these
factors at all; especially drunkenness has been mentioned in many cases as a
mitigating circumstance. The attitude of the court in such cases, as well as in
many others, has deserved much criticism. I indicated, quoting among others,
Milovanic's research, that drunkenness and alcoholism of the victim is often a
causal factor in manslaughter and murder. The quoted author used 214 autopsies
for his conclusion. He found that among victims of murder only 9 percent had
been under the influence of alcohol during the incident, whereas among the

victims of manslaughter there were over 70 percent of such persons. The drunk would-be victims were represented among males over six more often than among females.[26]

The *mitigating circumstances* enumerated by the court were the following characteristics of the accused person, or situations in which he acted: "good reputation, former unpunishability, a quiet person, destitution or extreme poverty, very strong affect, hysteria, irritability, limited ability to direct his own behavior, drunkenness, young and old age, low intelligence."[27] Let me add here, verbatim: "among the most common mitigating circumstances, enumerated by the court, provocation of the incident by the would-be victim took the first place"; this provocation has been commented on by the court mostly by using such descriptive terms as: "tormenting, harassment and mal-treatment of the offender by the would-be victim, causing of severe harm by the victim, rowdiness."[28]

It may be added that the court formulated its opinion quite often in accordance with psychiatric expert-testimonies (which are applied in Poland in a very substantial percentage of cases, especially connected with homicide).

Omitting a detailed presentation of *additional conclusions* drawn from the analysis of court records, proposals *de lege lata* and *de lege ferenda*, it may be stated, in a general way, that qualified as ordinary homicide were basically such cases in which there were, at the same time, at least a few substantial aggravating circumstances; nevertheless, sometimes even only one factor (example given, killing a policeman) influenced the court's decision that the act was murder—independently of the existing affect (as it was obvious from the analysis of some court records). On the contrary, qualified as homicide under the influence of passion were such cases in which "there exists usually a large amount of mitigating circumstances, like: good reputation of the accused person, provocation by the victim, considerable harm inflicted by the would-be victim on the perpetrator, and similar."[29] The court's awareness of the victim's role and contribution to the crime, as well as the clearly expressed attitude toward offenders whose crime was a reaction to the would-be victim's provocation, is very interesting from the victimological point of view, particularly because it was clearly formulated several decades ago.

Appendix

Motives of Homicide of Passion

In cases in which it was possible to establish clearly the existence of more than one motive, they were indicated separately, and not in the group of mixed motives.

The motives (289) of 263 male offenders (totals):

Group of Motives	Number	Percentage (out of 236 cases)
1. economic	50	21.2
2. erotic	36	15.3
3. safety and honor	120	50.8
4. solidarity	30	12.7
5. mixed	40	–
unknown	13	

In the five enumerated groups there were the following 276 motives (the mixed ones included):

1. *Motives of economic nature*   50

   - theft, taking some goods   12
   - not fulfilling some financial obligations (by the would-be
     victim)   9
   - dismissal from job   8
   - damaging property (basically of agricultural nature)   8
     laying claims to land   5
   - eviction from the farm (resulting from a legal action)   4
   - refusal to move from the apartment (in the offender's house)   2
   - damaging and not permitting the use of a part of the house
     (owned by the offender and would-be victim)   1
   - the victim (daughter) a financial burden to the offender   1

2. *Motives of erotic nature*   36

   - breaking off, threatening to break off, not reciprocating   14
     love (by wife, mistress, etc.)
   - unfaithfulness (wife, mistress, etc.)   7
   - seducing (the wife, mistress, etc.)   7
   - refusal (by the victim's parents) to marry (the would-be victim)   5

and one of each of the following:

   - encouraging (by the would-be victim, the offender's mother-in-
     law) his wife to unfaithfulness
   - interfering in (the offender's) relationship with his mistress (the
     victim—the offender's wife)
   - seduction and making the offender's wife pregnant

3. *Motives connected with endangering of safety or honor*   120

- beating   47
- insults, insults and threats, insults and beating   21
- approaching with hostile intent   8
- assault   8
- intrusion (in the offender's house)   4
  permanent molestation and threats   3

the following two cases each:

- permanent insulting and attacking (throwing stones)
- throwing stones
- not permitting to use a path
- permanent vexation and insulting
- beating up and approaching with hostile intent
- blustering and challenging behavior

one of each of the following:

- threats
- abusive language and making fun (of the offender)
- threats and taking away a knife
- ˉ abusive language and permanent claims
- resistance (against the offender who tried to take back some goods stolen by the would-be victim)
- permanent mistreatment
- refusing entrance to a dance hall
- throwing stones and beating
- hitting with a thrown bottle
- beating and imminence of injury
- reproaches and vexations by associates (victim the offender's illegitimate child)
- beating and permanent vexations
- arrest (for poaching) and weapon seizure
- suspicion of theft
- attempt to kill
- having caused a long prison term
- threatening to report a theft to the police.

4. *Motives referring to solidarity with close persons (behavior directed against those persons)*   30

- beating   16

- insults   4
- permanent brutal treatment   3
- killing the father (of the offender) in one case (contrary to reality)   2

and one of each of the following:

- killing the brother (the would-be victim's paramour)
- gossiping
- eviction from an apartment
- threats to kill and permanent brutal treatment (of the victim's family)
- pain and suffering (the victim a close person to the offender)

5. *Motives of mixed nature*   40

- financial claims and beating   5
- insults, beating and unfaithfulness   4
- depriving or attempt to deprive of family and property   3
- vexation and attempting to cause dismissal from job   3

the following two cases each

- unfaithfulness and taking away some goods
- theft and beating
- beating the offender and his sister
- destroying property and insulting

one of each of the following:

- insults and refusal to leave the tenancy in spite of the court's decision
- breaking off and taking away some goods
- mistreating the would-be offender and his family
- knife-attack on the would-be offender and mistreatment of his sister
- beating and disturbing during sex intimacy
- seducing the wife and taking away goods
- seducing the wife, threats and blackmailing
- laying claims on land and intrusion (in the house)
- permanent vexation of the offender and his wife
- beating the offender and his mother
- seducing the wife and making fun of him

- breaking off by the mistress and refusal to support (the offender)
- unfaithfulness and threat to kill
- unfaithfulness and throwing out from home (by the offender's wife)
- seducing the wife, beating, and insults
- gossiping to the employers, and insults
- theft and insults

Apart from the groups of above presented motives, there was in female offender cases an additional specific group of motives in cases of killing one's own child. Altogether they numbered 42; apart from 41 mothers of illegitimate children, one mother killed her child because she was unable to provide for him, and considered him as a hindrance. These motives (of mixed nature—economic and honor) were eliminated as they are incomparable with the motives of male offenders. Among the remaining 37 motives of 35 female offenders there were:

Group of Motives	Number
1. economic	0
2. erotic	13
3. safety and honor	15
4. solidarity	3
5. mixed	6

1. *Motives of economic nature*	0
2. *Motives of erotic nature*	13
• breaking off (husband, paramour, fiancé)	9

and one of each of the following:

- unfaithfulness (paramour)
- unfaithfulness and refusal to marry
- taking away the husband
- forcing to abnormal sex relations

3. *Motives connected with endangering of safety or honor*	15

- permanent mistreatment (by husband or paramour) (in one of these cases there was an accidental killing of her own child instead of the intended person)   11 and one of each of the following:

- insults
- threats (to inform her parents about her immoral behavior)
- gossip (about her immoral behavior)
- attempt to rape

4. *Motives referring to solidarity with close persons*   3

one of each of the following:

- serious illness (of the would-be victim)
- the child-victim's destitution (the offender-mother attempted suicide)
- deserting the offender's daughter by her husband (the would-be victim)

5. *Motives of mixed nature*   6

- mistreatment and refusal to support (husband, paramour)   2

and one of each of the following:

- mistreatment and taking money
- unfaithfulness and refusal to support
- unfaithfulness, mistreatment and taking money (paramour)
- to get relief for her and her daughter from supporting the daughter's husband

Notes

1. M.E. Wolfgang, *Patterns in Criminal Homicide* (Philadelphia: University of Pennsylvania Press, 1958).
2. W.C. Reckless, *The Crime Problem,* 5th ed. (New York: Appleton-Century-Crofts, 1973), p. 91.
3. P. Horoszowski, "Zabójstwo z afektu w świetle 330 spraw sadowych." (Homicide of passion—investigated in 330 court cases), *Archiwum Kryminologiczne,* 1939, Warszawa; *Zabójstwo z afektu* (Homicide of Passion), Warszawa 1947. Theoretical considerations concerning semantical, psychological, juridical, and criminological questions of the motivation, as well as concerning some additional investigations have been presented particularly in my following publications: "Motyw a pobudka" (The motive and the emotional incentive), *Wspólczesna Myśl Prawnicza,* Nr. 8-10, Warszawa 1937; "Motywy

zabójstwa z afektu" (The motives of homicide of passion), *Archiwum Kryminologiczne,* Warszawa 1937; "Zabójstwo w świetle akt sadowych" (Homicide-investigation of court cases), *Przeglad Policyjny,* Nr. 2-3, 1939; Narzedzie przestepstwa i okoliczności czynu w 100 przypadkach zabójstwa z afektu (The tools and circumstances of the crime in 100 cases of homicide of passion), Czasopismo sadowo-lekarskie, 1937.

4. A short description of my above mentioned analysis of motive and impulsion—including a review of many contemporary American psychological, socio-psychological, and psychiatric publications—has been presented by me at a meeting of the American Society of Criminology, New York, November 2-6, 1973, in a paper entitled "The 'Motive' of Homicide—Some semantic and Psychological Suggestions."

5. As quoted in my above mentioned monograph *Zabójstwo z afektu* (Homicide of Passion), p. 79.

6. Ibid., pp. 71-72.

7. Ibid.

8. Ibid.

9. Ibid.

10. In 1972 it was 8.9 according to *Crime in the United States 1972.* Uniform Crime Reports, released August 1973.

11. According to my quoted monograph, pp. 99-100.

12. Ibid.

13. Ibid.

14. Ibid.

15. Ibid.

16. H. von Hentig, *The Criminal and His Victim* (New Haven: Yale University Press, 1948), p. 392.

17. Wolfgang. *Patterns in Criminal Homicide,* pp. 203-221.

18. Ibid., p. 218.

19. A.D. Pokorny, "A Comparison of Homicides in Two Cities," *Journal of Criminal Law, Criminology and Police Science* 56, 4 (1971).

20. See, among others, P. Horoszowski, "Woman's Status in Socialistic and Capitalistic Countries," *International Journal of Sociology of the Family,* 1, 1 (1971) and 1, 2 (1972).

21. Quoted in my monograph, p. 117.

22. Ibid., p. 117.

23. Wolfgang, *Patterns in Criminal Homicide,* p. 218.

24. Quoted in my monograph, p. 131.

25. Ibid., pp. 134-35.

26. Ibid.

27. Ibid.

28. Ibid.

29. Ibid., p. 142.

2 Changing Victims of Changing Homicide
Stephen Schafer

Victimology, as a social-structural way of viewing law and crime, and criminal and victim, provides challenging insights when the analysis of crime rates and crime situations is employed in the mirror of social change. In our particular study we have investigated the fluctuating features of homicide from 1934 to 1964 in Massachusetts in the United States of America, with special attention to the offender and his victim and their relationships. While we are not certain how "social change" can accurately be defined in order to use it as a reliable methodological instrument, somewhat arbitrarily we decided for the following key years: 1934, characterized as one of the peak years of economic depression; 1939, seen as a relatively peaceful and happy year when the majority of Americans were hoping to avoid their involvement in the visible beginnings of world conflict; 1944, the year when America was most deeply involved in the world war; 1949, the time when veterans and prisoners of war returned, and a long peaceful and prosperous era was hoped for; and 1964, three decades after our first research year, when violence and crime in general started to increase to an unparalleled rate, aggression had begun to be a style of negotiations, and a variety of social movements got under way toward a number of societal changes.

In these years changes in the profile of homicide occurred on several levels. Among others, we could observe that:

1. The rate of homicide increasingly changed. For example, while in these three decades the population increased only by 12 percent, the cases of homicide increased by 300 percent.

2. The more homicide crimes were committed, the less severe was the disposition practice of the courts. For example, plea bargaining has become not only more frequent, but also more successful for the advantage of the offender.

3. While there was no significant change in the status position of victims (giving an emphasis to occupation and education in speculating about what status really means), offenders who were occupants of relatively low-status positions decreased, and the number of offenders in relatively high-status positions almost doubled.

4. General unemployment or economic depression does not appear to be a decisive factor for guiding to homicide. For example, in 1934 only some 20 percent of the homicide offenders and victims were unemployed, and this rate proved to be only slightly higher than the overall unemployment rate at

25

that time in Massachusetts. In all the other years studied the unemployment rate among offenders and victims was 50 percent or more.

5. The contention, proposed by Wolfgang's homicide study, that both offenders and victims of homicide most often belong to generally low-status groups, should perhaps be revised in view of the relative nature of status categories. In 1934, for example, to be unemployed was not really a symptom of low-status position since at that time being unemployed was a largely common situation.

6. Profit as a homicide motive did not vary much in the course of the studied three decades, and it appeared always in a small percentage of homicide cases. For example, in 1934, when the depressed economic situation would have indicated an increased number of profit motivated homicides, unemployed homicide offenders most often killed victims of similar status to themselves, usually friends.

7. "Altercation" as a springboard of homicide clearly dominated all the years in the explanation of crime. Altercation about money or sex gradually decreased from 1934 to 1964, and at the end most of the angry disputes between a criminal and his victim were centered around various other causes, not rarely petty issues.

8. Similarly, significant alcohol consumption on the part of the offender strongly decreased throughout the studied thirty years. A noticeably high rate of alcohol use was observed in 1934, that is, shortly after the prohibition period came to its end.

9. By comparing the median age in the general population with the median age of the homicide population, the offenders appeared to be the same age or younger than the larger population. In contrast, however, the victims were older than the median in the general population; in other words in all of the years studied the criminal usually killed someone older than himself, and the data indicated the age difference of five to ten years.

10. Offenders were predominately male, while in each year the victims were up to one-half female. But, in the course of the studied thirty years the number of female victims decreased by 11 percent. In all of the years, except in 1964, the female victims were predominantly "family-females," that is victimized by a male member of the family, usually for some family reasons. In 1964, however, the "miscellaneous-females" have shown an increased rate; in this year more females were victimized outside the family, and for reasons other than family matters, such as profit.

11. In terms of race, comparing the percentage of blacks and "others" in homicide situations with blacks and "others" in the general population, an over-representation of blacks among both criminals and victims appeared to be clear, however, while the rate of black homicide offenders from 1934 to 1964 increased by 300 percent the number of black victims has shown a reversed trend.

12. By creating "disjunctive status categories," such as people with "low education and high occupation," "low education and low occupation," "high education and low occupation," and "high education and high occupation," another challenging profile emerged. The "high education and high occupation" category has always been a very small percentage of all the cases, except in the year of depression (that is, in 1934) when a relatively high proportion of the killers came from this group. For the first four key years (that is, 1934, 1939, 1944, and 1949) practically no offenders appeared in the "high education and low occupation" category, but in 1964 a significant number of criminals appeared in this class, mainly among those who in spite of their high education have descended from high to low occupational position. The "low education and high occupation" group is practically not represented in the studied homicide cases. The "low education and low education" class had shown in all of the studied years the highest participation in homicide offenses, yet their proportion in the total was much lower in 1964 than in any of the other years.

13. A disproportionate number of widowed and divorced killers appeared in all of the studied years: 20 to 50 percent each year, significantly higher than the state average. The proportion of single offenders increased in 1964, while in the general population the proportion of married increased. Likewise, for victims the increase in the proportion of single people contradicts the population trends.

14. In all of the studied years most homicides occurred between persons who knew each other, but in 1964 homicides between strangers increased. The proportion of family homicides was always relatively high, but from 1934 to 1964 it has been trebled. Homicide-resulting tensions were observed mainly in those families where the head of the family was in a disjunctive status position.

15. The geographical closeness of the victim's residence to the killer's residence, one of my suggestions several years ago, has been proved correct throughout the studied three decades. Moreover, moving from 1934 to 1964 this closeness (one to ten miles, or living at the same place) has gradually narrowed down to a closer-and-closer proximity.

16. Seasonal variations have been observed between the studied years, no less than those between Wolfgang's Philadelphia study and my Florida project ten years ago. Although Florida, Pennsylvania, and New England have different climates, and this explains one kind of variation, the differences within New England are not well understood, and probably heavily sociological factors should be summoned for a better understanding.

Generally speaking, the mentioned examples of our research results are meaningless in themselves, without analyzing them in a conceptual structure. Currently I am working with these data for a book manuscript. I do not believe in the popular quantitative, almost mechanical method which alone is aimed at measuring human behavior, and I do not subscribe to the assumption that the statistical and methodological skill, however excellent it might be, can lift up a sociologist—as some sociologists seem to delude themselves with this idea— to the pedestal of a scholar or a scientist. The good research material is not enough; fantasy and life-giving breath of imaginative passion is needed for the understanding of the recorded data.

Also, this inquiry is only an investigation of Massachusetts homicides. Much more is needed to make this research valuable. I have taken the liberty of presenting to you some of the raw material I found in the hope that at least some of the participants of this International Symposium will join forces for cross-cultural studies, as far as this research is concerned, on the impact of social change in criminal-victim relationships.

3

The Familiar Character of Criminal Homicide
Klaus Sessar

In this paper we want to present some considerations to the relationship between the offender and the victim in criminal homicide. Of course, this topic is not new; besides von Hentig's great merit, to have "detected" the importance of the doer-sufferer relation quite generally, he also seems to be one of the first to have studied comprehensively the contacts of the victim to his slayer under its various aspects.[1] Since then, numerous investigations in this respect have been carried out, the most important of which is Wolfgang's *Patterns in Criminal Homicide.*[2]

In many of these studies one outstanding aspect attracts the attention of the criminologist, giving grounds for the following remarks: this is the phenomenon that criminal homicides occur decidedly often among people who know each other at the time of the crime, moreover, who are closely related to each other, such as family members or close friends.

For example, in Wolfgang's homicide investigation, 65 percent, and in a study of the Baltimore Criminal Justice Commission, 45 percent of all offender-victim relationships were of such an intimate nature. Roesner found relatives and close friends rated 46 percent among the killers of his studied victims, Blühm counted 52 percent and Krause 67 percent of victims who had been killed by people from their immediate environment.[3] Similar results can be found in English, Danish, and French investigations. This conformity is highly remarkable, as the various investigators had used quite different sources (police or court statistics), they included different degrees of the crime commission in their data (attempted and completed or only completed homicides), and, with respect to the American legal system on the one side and the continental legal systems on the other, they based their studies on quite different legal definitions of what is meant by "criminal homicide."

It is the purpose of this article to look for some criminological and perhaps legal consequences which might result from the fact that the occurrence of murder and manslaughter is especially drawn to intimate social relationships. These primary group relationships include spouses, parent-child relations, relatives, fiancés, and close friends, the latter referring, in accordance with Wolfgang, to people with frequent, direct, personal, and intimate contacts which are consistently maintained until the time of the crime.[4] They are contrasted to nonprimary group relationships including, for example, casual friends, acquaintances, and strangers. The point of this distinction is that in the first group intense interactions exist, founded, at least at the beginnings, either on strong affections (love, passion) or on group solidarity, as in families, in which one partner depends (or up to the time of the crime depended) somehow on the other, each moulding and shaping the other in a manner that determines (or determined) their way of life. Therefore only these family members are included in the first group who fit into this picture, and a boy who tried to kill his former girlfriend because of jealousy, being definitely separated from her for months, belongs in the second group as well.

The study has been based on the court statistics of Baden-Württemberg, one of the eleven states of Germany (Federal Republic) with about 8.9 million inhabitants; it consists of the whole population of cases being brought to the attention of the courts in 1970 and 1971, including cases in which the offender was acquitted because of insanity, excluding cases in which he was acquitted because of lack of evidence (six offenders). The court sentences used are those giving minute description of the offender's family and social background, of the history of the offense including all details of the offender-victim relationship if it was necessary for the understanding of the deed.

The studied crimes are murder (§211) and manslaughter (§212), as defined by the German Penal Code. Both types of crime presuppose the intention to kill; the distinction between them is that manslaughter is the "plain" killing of a human being with intent, whereas murder must be committed under aggravated circumstances (malicious or cruel proceedings, acting out of greed, etc.).[5] As attempted crimes are treated legally like completed crimes (though the punishment is usually milder) they are included in the study; the fact that the victim— mostly accidentally—survived has no impact on the evaluation of the offense, but might be important considering his role as a possible agent of social control.

One hundred and seventy victims were killed by 142 offenders; the total number of interpersonal relationships is 176.[a] When these figures are divided up with respect to primary and nonprimary group relations, 69 offenders have (almost) killed 79 victims (82 relationships), whereas in the secondary group, 91 victims have (almost) been slain by 73 offenders (94 relationships); this means that 49 percent of the offenders, 46 percent of the victims, and 47 percent of all relationships belong to the primary group (because 5 offenders killed members of the primary group and of the nonprimary group as well, the percentages differ slightly); the general experience that criminal homicide occurs decidedly often among people in close contact with one another is therefore supported by the present findings. The interpretation of the data reveals that in 18 percent of all cases the victim was a spouse; in 14 percent a child had been attacked by one of its parents; in 5 percent one of the parents, in another 5 percent, some relatives, and in 6 percent, close friends were the victims of a

---

[a]When two assailants attacked two victims, four relationships were counted. This is commendable, because motives, type of crime, or type of interpersonal relationship might vary among the four partners.

fatal attack. As to secondary relations, acquaintances or casual friends accounted for 27 percent and strangers for 25 percent of all relationships.

Three points will be discussed in this article; the first concerns the general and ever present problem of the reliability of the data with respect to the hidden criminality in close relationships; the second point refers to some qualitative differences of homicide between primary and nonprimary relationship; the third point indicates briefly some legal consequences of these differences.

Reliability of Data with Respect to Hidden
Criminality in Close Relationships

Any criminological study using official statistics has to stand up to the question whether its data are representative or not, or, more precisely, whether the study is biased because the quality of the material is not only determined by those who constitute criminality, i.e., the offenders, but also by those who control or should control it, for example, the law enforcement authorities. (We must neglect the fascinating question, whether criminality is only constituted by those who control it; according to a new movement in sociological criminology, a crime which is not labeled as such is like an unobserved or unreported falling star in the heavens—it is not a fact.[6]) In other words, *to what extent* are the figures of our statistics, the main sources of our investigations, reliable in terms of (a) the problem of dark figures, and (b) the problem of the prosecuting policy of the agents of social control. As to the second point, the representativeness of the present study is doubtful in some respects; it is based on court statistics, which reflect a kind of negative selection of cases, because they were left over after a long weeding out process in which the majority of cases were sorted out (about 80 percent; the mortality of these cases from the time of their notification until the final decision of the district attorney or the judge will be the object of a further study).

However, we are mainly concerned with the first point and want to ask, if, with regard to the intimate character of interrelations between the offender and his victim, the latter or third persons will contribute to the notification of criminal homicides.

The role of the victim as an informal agent of social control is recognized,[7] since some field surveys have been carried out, in order to fill the gap between the official and the real criminality. People were questioned with regard to their possible criminal victimization; for example, in a survey of the National Opinion Research Center of the University of Chicago (NORC) members of households were asked whether they or anyone in their family had been a victim of a murder, aggravated assault, forcible rape, burglary, robbery, auto theft, or larceny (over $50). The result was that the figures of the survey were about two times greater than those of the official police statistics, the Uniform Crime Reports,

varying considerably, however, according to each crime type.[8] The value of
victim surveys seems to be recognized today and is recommended as "a contin-
ually necessary supplement to police figures."[9]

However, in terms of criminal homicide, this type of survey must fail. The
NORC study indicated lower homicide rates than the police statistics. The
reason is obviously the fact that homicide is mainly a matter of people living
in the same household (in 74 percent of our primary relationships, the victim
was slain in his and the offender's apartment; not surprisingly this was the
case in only 9 percent of the secondary relationships); to ask someone for a
homicidal victimization might mean asking the possible offender, who would
most likely prefer to suppress his participation in the crime.[10] But even if
the interviewee is the victim who had survived the attack, he might refuse to
mention the act to the interviewer—as he had omitted to report it to the police.
As we will see below (p. 33), homicides among family members or close friends
very often reflect ambivalent mutual feelings much more than unambiguous
hostile sentiments; therefore it might happen that an attempted homicide is
forgiven or even forgotten when the interviewer appears.

In other cases, the fear of provoking a second violent attack might lead
to the denial of those previous experiences. But when no victim can be asked
because he did not survive the fatal attack or because he is too young to understand it, can a criminal homicide really remain unknown to the police? Is not
this most serious act the object of wide public attention, the network of social
controls being woven in a way that no such crime can pass unobserved? Sellin
and Wolfgang assume that criminal homicide has a high reportability, which
means that this "offense has a great likelihood of being reported to the police,"
so that these offenses "will come closer to the reality of delinquency than do
offenses with low reportability."[11]

This assumption overlooks the intimate character of criminal homicide
which, quite to the contrary, might hinder rather than encourage its notification to the police. And this intimacy does not only prevent the victim—if there
is still one alive—from exercising his role as an agent of social control, but also
third persons being closely linked to the offender-victim relationship.

For example, when an individual dies, the cause of his death is certified
by a physician. He is another agent of social control because his judgment
decides about the further fate of the dead body: permission for immediate
interment or previous autopsy, should there be some clues to a violent death.
Those diagnoses are not necessarily reliable because they depend on many
factors, medical ones as well as those which have to do with the physician's relation to the dead man and his family. According to medical sociologists, a diagnosis is a kind of communication means in the interaction of physician and
patient, the social function of which is sometimes more important than the
medical statement. Therefore the elements of this interactional pattern might

determine the diagnosis in a way which has not much to do with medical experiences.[12]

This situation is especially valid when the physician plays a somewhat familiar role vis-à-vis to his patients; this "Hausarzt" type knows more about the personal background of the family in his care than would be necessary for the treatment. How does he react when he detects some injuries on the body of the deceased patient whose family has been treated by him for years, while knowing about steady domestic quarrels?

An excellent example in this respect is the battered child problem; "more children are injured in or near the home than in any other settings. What should be the safest and least stressful environment is, in fact, the most dangerous."[13] According to some collected German and American newspaper reports, about one hundred children were not only injured, but killed in Germany (Federal Republic) in 1971 as a result of abusive treatment, either by their parents or other persons who were supposed to care for them. New York's respective death rate is 52, and in Boston, 10 children were known to have been killed in that way. The dark figures for battered children are estimated to be quite high; hence it follows that many more children are abusively battered, resulting in death, than are known to the law enforcement authorities. (It is interesting that the present study does not contain one single case of a child who had been killed or almost killed following ill-treatment. Wolfgang's study is more or less silent on this point.) The only person who could report such events as presumable crimes to the police is the physician, but, as was said, much depends on his relation to the family in which the offense occurred.

Thus, it can be assumed that a certain amount of hidden murders and manslaughters will always exist, due to the fact that the intimacy of the relationships prevent them from being reported. (Of course, the extent of the dark figures depends on whether attempted homicides are included, as in many European countries, or practically excluded, as in the United States, where the offender is charged with criminal homicide only when the victim has died.)

Some Qualitative Differences of Homicide
Between Primary and Nonprimary Relationships

In all legal systems, murder is one of the most abominable crimes, which is punished severely, either by death or life-long imprisonment. Perhaps under the influence of Cain's deed of slaying his brother Abel—incidentally the first murder which occurred in a primary group relationship—mankind developed a picture of the murderer as a sanguinary monster who kills pitiless for the sake of greed or lust. Only the more recent recognition that to each offender belongs a specific victim, that this victim has quite specific contacts with the offender, and that the act can often be analyzed only by investigating these contacts, contributes gradually to a different understanding of murders and murderers. It was Sir John Macdonnell, Master of the Supreme Court, who wrote more than sixty years ago after the study of the English crime statistics of 1886 to 1905:

> "... I am inclined to think that this crime (murder) is not generally the crime of the so-called criminal classes but is in most cases rather an incident in miserable lives in which disputes, quarrels, angry words and blows are common. The short history of the large number of cases which have been examined might be summed up thus: —Domestic quarrels and brawls; much previous ill-treatment; drinking, fighting, blows; a long course of brutality and continued absence of self-restraint. The crime is generally the last of a series of acts of violence."[14]

These were important insights, confirmed by many other studies since that time, and also by the present one. Some more remarks will deepen the problem.

Von Hentig classified criminal homicides according to their underlying motivation in "Gewinnmord" (murder for profit), "Konfliktmord" (murder because of conflict), "Deckungsmord" (murder to cover up a crime), and "Sexualmord" (sex-murder).[15] Applying these categories to our cases, and defining conflict roughly either as an emotionally based, mutually destructive relationship between two or more individuals or as the psychological inability of an individual to solve personal problems, we found that the conflict type of homicide dominates the whole study. In 81 percent of all relationships the conflict between some individuals or the personal conflict of one individual was the reason for the murder; however, whereas in the nonprimary group 67 percent conflict crimes occurred—the remainder were mostly crimes for profit and those committed in order to cover up another offense—the primary group accounts for 98 percent of crimes committed through conflict. For the better understandings of this kind of conflict, the introduction of sex variable is needed.[b]

Table 3-1 shows the general distribution of both sexes in the whole population and in both groups. The figures confirm the general experience that criminal homicide is an act committed mainly by males; but whereas the second category is almost exclusively dominated by males, a considerable number of females were

---

[b]Another variable is "culture." Due to an excessive over-employment, about 2.5 million foreigners are actually working in Western Germany, mostly coming from southern European countries. They are often accompanied by their families, living mostly among themselves, their culture being distinct from their cultural environment. These "Gastarbeiter" are underrepresented with respect to the general criminality, but they contribute disproportionately to violent crimes relative to their quota in the overall population (7%). About one-fourth of all offenders in this study are foreigners who are more or less equally distributed in both groups.

Table 3-1

Sex of Offender and Victim in Criminal Homicide, by Type of Interpersonal Relationship

Offenders	Total % (N)	Primary Group %(N)	Nonprimary Group %(N)
Male	91 (129)	84 (58)	97 (76*)
Female	9 (13)	16 (11)	3 (2)
Total	100 (142)	100 (69)	100 (78*)
Victims			
Male	59 (100)	35 (28)	79 (72)
Female	41 (70)	65 (51)	21 (19)
Total	100 (170)	100 (79)	100 (91)

*In these figures, five offenders are included who appear also in the primary group category, because they killed members of both groups.

offenders in the first category (16 percent of the offenders in this group, or 85 percent of all female offenders).

The sex distribution among victims is much more striking. More than two-fifths of all victims are women, but they clearly outnumber the men in the first group by representing about two-thirds of the victim, compared to one-fifth in the second group.

The cross-tabulation of the offender's sex with the sex of the victim reveals the clear *intrasexual* character of homicide in the secondary group (78 percent) and the equally clear *intersexual* character in the group with intimate personal relationships (69 percent) (see table 3-2)[c]; the differences are statistically significant.

Appropriate to the high involvement of women in the killing, the reasons that played a role in the act were often typically due to the sexual ambivalence of the conflict, for example, faithlessness (founded or not) with 26 percent, and separation with 41 percent of all intersexual relationships in the primary group, after the exclusion of those with small female children.

In looking for the "motives" of the act in the primary group quite generally, some distinct patterns can be found. Beside the above mentioned male-female conflict, which had roughly to do with the further existence of the relationship threatened by one of the partners, domestic quarrels, either between wife and

[c]The intersexual character in the primary group does not change, but would be even slightly strengthened, if all small children were excluded, their sex not being decisive in the act. There are ten boys and eight girls among the victims.

Table 3-2
Sex of the Offender by Sex of the Victim in Criminal Homicide, by Type of Interpersonal Relationship in percentage (N)

Offenders	Primary Group			Nonprimary Group			Both Groups		
	Male	Female	Total	Male	Female	Total	Male	Female	Total
Male	26 (21)	58 (48)	84 (69)	78 (73)	20 (19)	98 (92)	53 (94)	38 (67)	91 (161)
Female	11 (9)	5 (4)	16 (13)	2 (2)	–	2 (2)	6 (11)	2 (4)	9 (15)
Total	37 (30)	63 (52)	100 (82)	80 (75)	20 (19)	100 (94)	60 (105)	40 (71)	100 (176)

$X^2 = 39.51$; df = 1; p < 0.01.

husband or between two male members of the same family, prevail; they were seldom merely trivial, but often the result of a deep-rooted tension between the partners (the victim was the superior of both, dominating the offender; or he was a steady provocation in the family). In a third category, all those cases are included in which the offender, out of despair, intended to commit suicide by taking the victim with him; the victims were babies, but sometimes also the husband or the wife, whose slayers survived the attempted suicide or lost the courage to accomplish their plan. Despair or pity were the motivations in some other cases; being unable to find a way out of common difficulties, the offender believed in the fatal solution of these problems, the victims being again often children, husbands, or wives.

The motives to kill were different in the secondary group. As has already been mentioned, crimes out of greed or to cover up another crime played an important role (30 percent; only 3 percent were sex-murders); in the "conflict cases," the killing of the sex rival, of a casual homosexual partner, of a drinking fellow in a bar or restaurant or of an individual who damaged the self-respect of the offender, were the most common patterns; the first and the last group are typical offenses with foreigners involved.

These observations lead to a first important point. Not only did we find 23 percent of the cases in the group with close relationships in which the victim was killed because of pity or despair—one can say that the crime had been committed *for* the victim—but also were those cases in which something like aversion, hostility, hatred or anger governed the act, more ambivalent in the first than in the second group. When the offender killed a drinking fellow following an argument in a bar, he nearly always acted out of some hostile sentiments, because the whole situation was determined by hostility. If, on the other hand, the girlfriend intended to separate and was killed after many attempts on the part of the offender to change her mind, the sentiments of hostility and destruction had often been accompanied by the feeling of not having been able to keep the loved person and to maintain the hitherto existing relationship.

These contradictory motivations are accurately discussed in all our sentences. They are the object of intense studies of Coser, who interprets Georg Simmel's and Sigmund Freud's theories on this topic. He writes:

> We note that, like Simmel, Freud derives ambivalence of feelings from the intimacy of the relationship within which it occurs. He traces the simultaneity of feelings of love and hate to the numerous occasions for conflict to which intimate relations give rise. This would mean that there is more occasion for the rise of hostile feelings in primary than in secondary groups, for the more the relationship is based upon the participation of the total personality—as distinct from segmental participation—the more it is likely to generate both love and hate.[16]

As could be observed in the present cases, the distinction between primary and secondary groups is in fact one between intricate links of positive and negative sentiments on one side and a dominance of negative sentiments on the other side (in cases other than those determined by conflict, the sentiment of indifference prevails; the offender regards the victim only as an obstacle to be removed, see table 3-3).

Coser mentions the total personality being involved in primary group conflicts. This touches another point. Primary group relationships are total in that they embrace both partners in most segments of their existence. Moreover, because most of these relationships are legally protected and socially controlled, they possess a kind of inescapability. Both partners do not or cannot always separate without more ado when their relations are becoming worse or are about to break down; legal norms, social impediments, habits, or the authority of one partner force them to live together, at least outwardly; a kind of hothouse atmosphere generates with rising conflicts, stirred up often by both sides and affecting third persons, mostly the children, the fatal clash being the culmination of these conflicts.

Again, the situation in nonprimary groups is different. These relationships are never very close and can be solved at anytime. The offender and the victim *come* together, whereas in the primary group, they *are* together; their clinch does not have this dreadful aspect of inevitability in the former case as it has in the latter.

What do these observations mean to us? When we are aware that we can

Table 3-3
Emotional Attitude of the Offender by Type of Interpersonal Relationship. (in percentage)

Emotional Attitude	Primary Group	Nonprimary Group
Hostility (hatred, anger, dislike, etc.)	76	65
Pity, Despair	23	—
Indifference	1	35
Total	100	100

only speak of some principle features, we might state that in the primary group the crime emerges from the offender-victim relationship itself which is a kind of *conditio sine qua non* for the deed. Consequently, *this* victim is meant. In the secondary group the relations are not close enough to be so decisive, which means that the particular personality of the victim is of minor importance; the crime is linked much more to a particular situation. This distinction means further that in secondary groups, the victim is interchangeable because the actual situation moulds the act more so than a particular person; in primary groups the crime is mostly unthinkable without the specific victim involved.[17] Finally it signifies that because of the interchangeability of situations and consequently of victims, the crime is likely to recur among strangers or acquaintances more than among friends or family members. "Relation" on one side and "situation" on the other are first clues for an easier distinction between the two types of homicides which require more and more a different criminological—and legal—evaluation.

Some Legal Consequences of these Differences

The legal point is worthy of some final observations. It can be assumed that the offender type in the first group is different from the one in the second group. Extraordinary life circumstances and conflict situations are often the only determinant of the deed in the first category; Göppinger calls this phenomenon "krimineller Übersprung," which means that in spite of a normal social conformity, the singularity of an event might induce a law-abiding individual to commit a serious crime.[18]

Should official conviction records be reliable sources of information, then this assumption is confirmed. When we exclude foreigners, because we know nothing about their home records, 65 percent of all offenders in the primary group (three missing observations), but only 26 percent in the secondary group (five missing observations) had not been convicted previously; 11 percent of the primary group offenders, but 44 percent of the offenders in the secondary group had been convicted because of violent crimes, which will be considered as a criterion for dangerousness (see table 3-4). No offender in the first, but five offenders in the second category even had a previous record with respect to the commission of a homicidal act.

There are some indications that the courts take the different types of homicide into account. The present study reveals 25 percent offenders in the primary group and 41 percent in the nonprimary group who were convicted because of murder or its attempt. This distribution has of course to do with the lack of "Gewinnmorden" and "Deckungsmorden" in the first group; another reason is the fact that some features of aggravation in the killing, like malice (see note 5), interpreted as the exploitation of the victim's unawareness or defenselessness, are not attributed to the offender when he acted out of despair or pity; jealousy is not considered to be a "base motive" when it originates from humiliation or disappointments; and so on. In such cases, which are distinctive of primary group relationships, the crime is not murder, but manslaughter.

Table 3-4

Previous Record (Convictions) of Offender by Type of Interpersonal
Relationship (Foreigners excluded. No petty traffic offenses.)
(in percentages)

Previous Record	Primary Group	Nonprimary Group
No record	65	26
record because of violent crimes	11	44
record because of nonviolent crimes	24	30
Total	100	100

But it is not only the type of homicide, but also the punishment policy
which differs in accordance with the offender's place in the one or the other
group. If we take all sane adult offenders who have committed a completed
murder, only two out of seven offenders in families or friendships (29 percent),
but thirteen out of seventeen offenders being acquainted or unknown to their
victims (76 percent) were sentenced to life imprisonment. The only possibility
of reducing this punishment is by acknowledging extenuating circumstances
in terms of mental disorder. Seventy-seven percent of the murderers in our
primary group were considered to have acted with diminished responsibility,
compared to 29 percent in the nonprimary group (attempted crimes are
included). These figures do not signify a higher number of psychopathic
personalities in close relationships than in others, but the efforts of the courts
to reduce the punishment by assuming that the emotional and psychological
involvement of the offender in interpersonal conflicts diminished temporarily
his responsibility. (Although alcohol is often the cause for partial responsibility,
it is present in the homicide situation more in the secondary group (69 percent)
than in the primary group (51 percent).)

In terms of manslaughter, it is more often possible to take extenuating
circumstances into consideration.[19] The courts make considerable use of it
(in 83 percent of the cases), but again, the offenders in close relationships
received a milder punishment (89 percent) than other offenders (76 percent);
probation was granted to eight offenders of the first and to two offenders of
the second group.

What is acknowledged by jurisdiction could one day find a legislative
expression, which would then take the differences between both types of homicide into account. Much depends on whether the deed and the actor are considered isolatedly, or if the offender-victim relationship receives central attention. We agree therefore with Sigg, who suggests we abandon the evaluation
of the isolated subjective antisocial attitude of the offender, because the criteria

for the social disapproval is to be found in the relation of the offender, the victim, and the offense.[20]

Notes

1. H. von Hentig, *The Criminal and his Victim. Studies in the Sociology of Crime* (New Haven: Yale University Press, 1948), pp. 390-98.
2. M.E. Wolfgang, *Patterns in Criminal Homicide* (Philadelphia: University of Pennsylvania Press, 1958), pp. 203-268.
3. Ibid., p. 206; *Criminal Homicides in Baltimore,* Maryland, 1960-1964, an analysis prepared by the Criminal Justice Commission. Baltimore, 1967, p. 50; E. Roesner, "Mörder und ihre Opfer," in *Monatsschrift für Kriminologie und Strafrechtsreform* 29 (1938): 161-85; 209-228; H. Blühm, *Die Kriminalität der vorsätzlichen Tötungen* (Bonn,1958), p. 45; R. Krause, "Die vorsätzlichen Tötungen und vorsätzlichen Körperverletzungen mit tödlichem Ausgang," dissertation, University of Hamburg, 1966, p. 139.
4. Wolfgang, *Patterns in Criminal Homicide*, p. 205.
5. *§211. Murder*
   1. Murder shall be punished by confinement in a penitentiary for life.
   2. Anybody who kills a human being out of murderous lust, or to satisfy a sexual urge, or out of agreed or from other base motives, maliciously or cruelly, or by means endangering the public, or in order to commit or cover up another punishable act, is a murderer.
   §212. Manslaughter
   1. Anybody who intentionally kills a human being in a manner not amounting to murder shall be punished for manslaughter by confinement in a penitentiary for a term of not less than five years.
   2. In especially serious cases the punishment shall be confinement in a penitentiary for life.
   (Translation by G.O.W. Mueller and Th. Buergenthal, in *The German Penal Code of 1871* (South Hackensack and London, 1961), p. 113).
6. See W.C. Reckless, *The Crime Problem*, 3rd ed. (New York: Appleton-Century-Croft, 1961), p. 23.
7. G. Kaiser, "Viktimologie," in *Kleines Kriminologisches Wörterbuch* (Freiburg Br.: Herder Verlag, 1974), p. 380-86.
8. P.H. Ennis, *Criminal Victimization in the United States: A Report of a National Survey* (Washington: U.S. Government Printing Office, 1967), p. 9.
9. D. Glaser, "Victim Survey Research: Theoretical Implications," in *Criminal Behavior and Social Systems,* Contributions of American Sociology, ed. by A.L. Guenther, (Chicago: Rand MacNally, 1970), p. 139.
10. Ibid., p. 142; Ennis, *Criminal Victimization in U.S.*
11. T. Sellin and M.E. Wolfgang, *The Measurement of Delinquency* (London: Wiley, 1964), pp. 126-27.

12. M. Pflanz, *Sozialer Wandel und Krankheit*. Ergebnisse und Probleme der medizinischen Soziologie (Stuttgart: Enke Verlag, 1962), p. 321. See, addressed to this whole problem, W. Heinz, "Bestimmungsgründe für die Anzeigebereitschaft des Opfers. Ein kriminologischer Beitrag zum Problem der differentiellen Wahrscheinlichkeit strafrechtlicheɪ Sanktionierung," Dissertation, University of Freiburg/Br. 1972, pp. 31-37.

13. *Report to the President. White House Conference on Children, 1970* (Washington, D.C.: U.S. Government Printing Office, 1970), p. 211.

14. See E.R. Calvert, *Capital Punishment in the Twentieth Century*, 5th ed. (London: Putnam, 1936), p. 32.

15. H. von Hentig, *Zur Psychologie der Einzeldelikte*. II. *Der Mord* (Tübingen: J.C.B. Mohr Verlag, 1956), p. 45.

16. L. Coser, *The Functions of Social Conflict*: An examination of the concept of social conflict and its use in empirical sociological research (New York: The Free Press, 1964), p. 62.

17. H. Göppinger, *Kriminologie* (München: Verlag C.H. Beck, 1973), p. 309.

18. Ibid., p. 219.

19. *§213. Manslaughter Under Extenuating Circumstances*. If the person charged with manslaughter was provoked into a fit of anger, without fault of his own, by battery or serious insult, committed by the deceased against the defendant or one of his relatives, and the defendant was prompted instantly to commit the deed, or if other extenuating circumstances are present, the punishment shall be imprisonment for a term of not less than six months. (For the translation, see note 5.)

20. F.A. Sigg, *Begriff, Wesen und Genese des Beziehungsdelikts* (Zürich: Polygraphischer Verlag, 1969), p. 238.

4

Characteristics of Homicide and Suicide Victims in Forty Non-Literate Societies

Stuart Palmer

This is essentially a report of selected characteristics of homicide victims, offenders and acts and of suicide victims and acts in forty non-literate societies. Data on various conditions of the social systems of those societies as they are related to questions about victimology are also presented. While in the main, this is an empirical, exploratory study, certain theoretical ideas, especially those having to do with social integration, are drawn upon.

Method

The forty geographically diverse societies that constitute the sample used here were chosen in the light of requirements of a larger research project on various forms of aggression around the world (Palmer 1970b). That project drew upon findings about child training and crime by Whiting and Child (1962) and by Bacon, Child, and Barry (1963). The forty societies analyzed in this paper are those within the larger samples of the two studies just mentioned for which adequate homicidal and suicidal victimology data were available.

All data were taken from the Human Relations Area Files (Murdoch et al. 1950). Ratings of the incidence of homicide, suicide, and of degrees of social integration in the forty societies were made by a panel of three judges working independently of each other. This method is described elsewhere (Palmer 1970b). In contrast, characteristics of homicidal victims, offenders, and acts and of suicidal victims and acts were established by two research assistants working together. They were instructed to resolve any differences in interpretation of the data as they proceeded. They were told, that is, to attempt to reach common judgments. Judges and research assistants were furnished with detailed instructions, including operational definitions of all terms.

Criminal homicide is defined as the killing of one person by another which is not accidental and is not in the course of socially prescribed duty. The general definition of suicide employed is that set forth by Durkheim (1951, 44): "death resulting directly or indirectly from a positive or negative act of the victim himself, which he knows will product this result." Definitions of social integration have varied widely (Douglas 1967; Durkheim 1951; Gibbs

Research supported in part by several grants from the Central University Research Fund of the University of New Hampshire.

and Martin 1964; Maris 1969; Powell 1958). In the present study social integration is defined in terms of the extents to which five basic groupings of social roles involve reciprocity or unreciprocity. (The role groupings are familial, economic, educational, political, and religious.) Reciprocity refers to the degree to which role-players mutually facilitate each other's performances toward the end of meeting social expectations. Unreciprocity has to do with the degree to which role-players mutually block each other's performances toward that same end. The greater is reciprocity, the higher is social integration. The greater is unreciprocity, the lower is social integration. (For further detail, see Palmer 1970a, 1972. For discussion of reciprocity per se, see Gouldner 1960; Homans 1961; Mauss 1954.)

Age, Sex, and Social Prestige of Homicidal
Offenders and Victims

In regard to these three variables—age, sex, and prestige—judgments were made as to whether the proportions of the total volume of homicidal victims and of offenders in a given society were approximately equal to, higher than, or lower than the proportion of the society's population in the given age, sex or prestige category. For example, if a society were composed of about 50 percent males and 50 percent females and two-thirds of the victims were male, then "high" was assigned to the male category and "low" to the female category. If, on the other hand, about 50 percent (45 to 55 percent) of victims were males and 50 percent females, the word "moderate" was used to describe the proportion of victims in both sex categories.

Age was divided into three groupings: pre-adult (under twenty years), young adult (twenty to forty years), older adult (over forty years). Prestige was also judged on the basis of three categories: low (manual workers and their families); medium (technical workers, overseers, and their families); and high (professionals, e.g., shamen, "educators," rulers, and sub-rulers). The manner of categorizing proportions of victims and offenders was the same as that just described in regard to sex.

Table 4-1 presents the results. In general, the findings on homicide victims parallel strikingly those for literate societies (Palmer 1972; Wolfgang 1958; Wolfgang and Ferracuti 1967). There is a definite tendency for homicide victims to be young adults. At the same time, older adults are victims far more often than pre-adults. The proportions of pre-adult victims are somewhat lower than for literate societies. Regarding sex, the preponderance of male victims mirrors reasonably closely the findings for literate societies.

Turning to prestige, persons of low prestige were most often the victims of homicide, as is true in literate societies. Those of medium prestige were relatively seldom homicide victims. However, there was a rather pronounced

Table 4-1

Proportions of Homicidal Offenders and Victims by Age, Sex and Social Prestige in 40 Non-Literate Societies, in Percentages of Societies

	Age			Sex		Prestige		
Proportions of Homicidal:	Pre-Adult	Young Adult	Older Adult	Male	Female	Low	Medium	High
Victims								
High	5.0	60.0	32.5	35.0	15.0	42.5	7.5	32.5
Moderate	12.5	30.0	27.5	47.5	35.0	35.0	30.0	30.0
Low	82.5	10.0	40.0	17.5	50.0	22.5	62.5	37.5
Total	100.0	100.0	100.0	100.0	100.0	100.0	100.0	100.0
Offenders								
High	20.0	62.5	5.0	40.0	12.5	35.0	10.0	32.5
Moderate	45.0	30.0	35.0	45.0	32.5	30.0	72.5	60.0
Low	35.0	7.5	60.0	15.0	55.0	35.0	17.5	7.5
Total	100.0	100.0	100.0	100.0	100.0	100.0	100.0	100.0

tendency for high prestige persons to be homicide victims. This last finding is the major divergence between the data in table 4-1 and data for literate societies insofar as homicide victims go. Subjective perusal of the Human Relations Area Files suggests two main explanations for the findings about victims in the non-literate societies: persons of power and prestige are killed by others of power and prestige in order to gain further power and prestige or to retain power and prestige. Individuals of low prestige murder those of high prestige because of feelings of having been mistreated. (While there are definite differences in prestige among members of the societies analyzed here, seldom are there relatively distinct social classes as is so often true of literate societies.)

Turning now to homicide offenders: Table 4-1 indicates a preponderance of offenders in the young adult category, considerable in the pre-adult group, and few among older adults. As with victims, offenders are predominantly male. Here, too, we see close similarity with findings about literate societies (Palmer 1972; Wolfgang 1958, Wolfgang and Ferracuti 1967). However, a considerable proportion of offenders tend to be of high prestige. As was true with victims, this departs from that which typifies literate societies. As indicated above, it would appear that persons of power and prestige kill each other to increase or retain those attributes.

Situational Factors and the Homicidal Act

Four situational factors were considered: time and place of the homicidal act, means of committing it, and frequency of victim-precipitation. Data were available for forty societies for the first three factors and, regarding victim-precipitation, for twenty-nine societies.

In 71 percent of the societies, homicide was committed predominantly (more than half the time) during darkness. In 20 percent, it was committed half the time or less during hours of darkness. This conforms roughly to findings for moderate societies (Palmer 1972; Wolfgang 1958, Wolfgang and Ferracuti 1967). It was not possible to gain information systematically on other time periods, e.g., seasons, etc. In two-thirds of the societies, homicide was committed outdoors rather than indoors more than half of the time. This runs counter to data for literate societies (Palmer 1972; Wolfgang 1958; Wolfgang and Ferracuti 1967). Probably the explanation lies in the fact that most non-literates are "outdoors" people whose interaction occurs outside of dwelling places much more than is true among literates.

The predominant means of committing homicide was by use of a hunting weapon or some form of club-like instrument in 68 percent of the societies. Hands or feet were the usual means in 24 percent of the cases, and "other" means—for example, strangling with some form of rope, poisoning, pushing off a cliff, etc.—in the remaining 8 percent. In a sense this parallels findings for literate societies (Palmer 1972; Wolfgang 1958; Wolfgang and Ferracuti 1967) if one recognizes that firearms are seldom readily available in non-literate groups and if one equates hunting weapons, which were used more often than clubs, with firearms.

The findings on victim-precipitation are of special interest. The nature of the information available made it necessary to define victim-precipitation in terms of how usual it was for the victim to make the first aggressive move physically, orally or by gesture during the homicidal encounter. Victim-precipitation was more usual than unusual; it was judged to occur in over half of the homicidal encounters in each of fifteen of the twenty-nine societies for which data were available. One analysis of criminal homicide in the United States found the percentage of cases in which victim-precipitation was present to be 26 percent (Wolfgang 1958). There, victim-precipitation was confined to those cases where the victim made a physical attack upon the offender before the homicidal attack. If in that study oral and gestural aggression had been included as forms of victim-precipitation, probably the percentage of victim-precipitated cases would have been considerably greater than 26 percent. (For general discussion see Schafer 1968.)

Age, Sex, and Social Prestige of Suicide Victims

The same approach was used here as with homicidal offenders and victims.

Judgments were made as to whether the proportion of the total volume of suicide victims in a society was higher than, lower than, or approximately equal to (termed moderate), the proportion of the society's population in the particular age, sex or prestige category. The results, as set forth in table 4-2, are rather similar to those for literate societies (Gibbs 1968; Gibbs and Martin 1964; Palmer 1972). Quite definitely, the older the population, the greater the volume of suicide. Among the non-literate societies, suicide is more a male than a female phenomenon although definitely not as much so as in literate societies. As for prestige, the patterns that emerge in this research are again aligned with those for literate societies: suicide occurs among persons of low or high prestige much more than among those of moderate prestige. Unfortunately, it was not possible in the analysis of the non-literate groups to gain a measure of social mobility. While downward mobility and the threat of it have been found in a number of studies to be positively associated with suicide (Breed 1964; Wood 1961), we do not know whether this is the case among the non-literates in the present sample.

Situational Factors and Suicide

Four situational factors surrounding suicide were investigated: time of day, place, means, and major precipitants. Also, the question of "suicidal victim-precipitation" was given brief attention. In a vast majority of the forty societies, thirty-two, suicide was more often than not committed during daylight hours. In thirty-three of those societies, the place more often than not was outdoors. The first finding corresponds to data for literate societies, while the second does not (Gibbs 1968). The latter is, again, probably explained in part at least by the outdoor life-style of most of the non-literates.

Means of commission of suicide were classified into three categories. The first included those where the individual killed himself with weapons, such as knives, spears, and firearms; and (the second) those where suicide was committed without weapons, by such means as hanging, poisoning, drowning, or jumping from high places. A third category—where the individual had another person kill him—was also used. Raw data were sufficient to make judgments in the cases of thirty-five societies. Weaponless suicide was far more usual than suicide by weapon. In eighteen societies, weaponless suicides were usual and suicide by weapon rare. The two broad categories were found about equally in ten socieites. Only in five societies were weaponless suicides rare. In the remaining two societies, neither of these categories applied; it was usual, rather, for the individual to have someone else kill him. As to the specific method used, hanging was definitely the most prevalent. As might be expected, these findings are somewhat at odds with those for literate societies. Poison or firearms are the predominant means in many literate societies (Dublin 1963).

Table 4-2

Proportions of Suicide Victims by Age, Sex and Social Prestige, in Percentages of Societies

Proportions of Suicidal Victims:	Age			Sex		Prestige		
	Pre-Adult	Young Adult	Older Adult	Male	Female	Low	Medium	High
High	2.5	17.5	62.5	30.0	17.5	45.0	17.5	42.5
Moderate	12.5	50.0	25.0	52.5	52.5	27.5	25.0	30.0
Low	85.0	32.5	12.5	17.5	30.0	27.5	57.5	27.5
Total	100.0	100.0	100.0	100.0	100.0	100.0	100.0	100.0

(As noted regarding homicide,) while firearms were not unknown in most of the nonliterate societies, in few were they readily available (Palmer 1971).

Major precipitants fell into three broad types: social failure or loss in some form; hostile actions of others; and cultural prescriptions for suicide under specified circumstances (the last being similar to forms of altruistic suicide as defined by Durkheim 1954). Failure or loss was the dominant precipitant in twenty-one of the forty societies, others' hostile actions in fourteen, and cultural prescriptions in the remaining five societies.

The suicidal person is generally assumed to be his own victim. Hence little attention is given to what may seem upon initial consideration the superfluous ideas of victim-precipitation in suicide. At the same time, it is reasonable to suggest that where self-condemnation of the suicidal person before the suicidal act appears to be greater than condemnation by others, what might be termed suicidal victim-precipitation will not obtain. In nineteen of the forty societies, self-condemnation was judged usually (over half of the time) to be greater than condemnation of others. In the remaining twenty-one societies condemnation by others was judged to be greater. Thus one can suggest that, according to the above reasoning, suicidal victim-precipitation was more prevalent than not in almost half of the societies. This question of victim-precipitation is touched upon again at a later point.

Survivors of Suicidal Persons as Victims

What commonly in a society are the consequences of suicide for those persons, relatives and friends, who were close to the suicidal person? Do they blame themselves, harm themselves physically, blame others, harm others physically, seem relatively "untouched" by the suicide, or find reward in it? These responses of others to suicide were judged in terms of usual or unusual. Usual meant that in over half of the suicides one or more persons appeared to manifest the given behavior. Unusual meant that one or more persons did so in half or less of the cases of suicide.

As will be evident, the attempt here is to gain rough measures of the extent to which others are or are not "victimized" when suicides occur. Table 4-3 presents the results. Blaming others was the most "usual" response in 55.0 percent of the societies. Those others were sometimes spiritual as well as living enemies of the suicidal individual. Blaming the self was the next most usual response; this occurred in 42.5 percent of the societies. Harming the self or others physically and experiencing reward were highly unusual. Seeming to be "untouched" by suicide was usual in but 12.5 percent or five of the forty societies. These were the same societies (five in number) in which cultural prescriptions were the major precipitating factors in suicide. Those prescriptions appear, then, to immunize individuals to the effects of suicide by friends and relatives.

Social Integration, Homicide and Suicide

It will be useful to look briefly at the degrees of social integration of the non-literate societies as they are related to incidence of homicide and suicide and extent of victim-precipitation. As stated earlier, social integration is conceived in terms of reciprocity and unreciprocity in the playing out of a number of key roles in a society. Reciprocity refers to mutual facilitation of performances by role-players while unreciprocity pertains to mutual blockage of performances by role-players. (A 21-point scale was used where 21 indicated maximum reciprocity and 1 maximum unreciprocity.)

Table 4-3
Responses of Relatives and Friends to Completed Suicides, in Percentage of Societies

Response:	Usual	Unusual
Blame Self	42.5	57.5
Harm Self Physically	10.0	90.0
Blame Others	55.0	45.0
Harm Others Physically	7.5	92.5
Seem "Untouched"	12.5	87.5
Experience Reward	5.0	95.0

Table 4-4

Numbers of Non-Literate Societies Above and Below Median Scores for
Reciprocity-Unreciprocity in Role Relationships and for Incidence of
Homicide and Suicide

	Homicide			Suicide		
	Below Median	Above Median	Total	Below Median	Above Median	Total
Reciprocity (Above Median)	14	6	20	7	13	20
Unreciprocity (Below Median)	7	13	20	13	7	20
Total	21	19	40	20	20	40

Table 4-4 presents the findings in simplified form. Of the nineteen societies
above the median for rates of homicide, thirteen were below the median for
reciprocity-unreciprocity, that is, tended to be unreciprocating; and six were
above the median—were reciprocating societies. Of the twenty-one societies
below the median for homicide, fourteen were above the median for reciprocity-
unreciprocity (tended to be reciprocating) and seven were below (unreciprocating). In regard to suicide, the opposite tendency obtained. Of the twenty
societies above the median for rates of suicide, thirteen were also above the
median for reciprocity-unreciprocity; seven were below that median. Of the
twenty societies below the suicide median, thirteen were below the reciprocity-
unreciprocity median and seven above. Hence, suicidal societies were found to
be characterized by role reciprocity, an indicator of high social integration.
Homicidal societies were characterized by role unreciprocity, indicative of low
social integration.

To raise again, but now in relation to degrees of social integration, the
question of homicidal and suicidal victim-precipitation, unusual though the
concept may be in regard to suicide. Earlier, homicidal victim-precipitation
was considered to occur when the victim made the first aggressive move physically, orally or by gesture during the homicidal encounter. Suicidal victim-
precipitation was said to obtain when self-condemnation by the suicidal person
prior to the suicide was greater than condemnation by others.

The twenty-nine societies for which data on extent of homicidal victim-
precipitation were available were divided into two groups: those above the
median score for victim-precipitation and those below it. As for victim-precipitation in suicide, all forty societies were divided into two groups: those
nineteen where self-condemnation was more usual than condemnation by
others and those twenty-one where it was not.

Table 4-5
Numbers of Non-Literate Societies Above and Below Median Scores for Reciprocity-Unreciprocity in Role Relations and Homicidal and Suicidal Victim-Precipitation

	Homicidal Victim-Precipitation			Suicidal Victim-Precipitation		
	Low (Below Median)	High (Above Median)	Total	Low (Other-Condemnation Usual)	High (Self-Condemnation Usual)	Total
Reciprocity (Above Median)	11	3	14	6	14	20
Unreciprocity (Below Median)	3	12	15	15	5	20
Total	14	15	29	21	19	40

Table 4-5 shows the following results: of the fifteen societies above the median for homicidal victim-precipitation, a large majority, twelve, were below the median for role reciprocity-unreciprocity and but three were below it. Of the fourteen societies below the victim-precipitation median, eleven were above the reciprocity-unreciprocity median and three below. This is strong indication of homicidal victim-precipitation in these non-literate societies being positively associated with unreciprocity (low social integration) and negatively associated with reciprocity (high integration).

Concerning suicidal victim-precipitation, the findings were clearly in the opposite direction (table 4-5). Fourteen of the nineteen societies where victim-precipitation (self-condemnation) was usual were above the median for role reciprocity-unreciprocity; five were below that median. Of the remaining twenty-one societies ("condemnation by others" usual) fifteen were below the median for reciprocity-unreciprocity and six above. Thus suicidal victim-precipitation was positively related to reciprocity and high social integration; and it was negatively related to unreciprocity and low social integration.

Summary

Findings regarding characteristics of homicide victims, offenders and acts and suicide victims and acts in the forty non-literate societies were, broadly speaking, similar to those in literate societies. A major difference was the tendency for homicidal victims and offenders in the non-literate societies to be of high as well as of low prestige.

In about half of the non-literate societies, physical or psychological victim-precipitation in homicidal cases was more usual than not. Similarly, in half of the non-literate societies, "suicidal victim-precipitation," as measured by self-condemnation, was more usual than unusual. Both homicidal victim-precipitation and sheer incidence of homicide were inversely related to the degree of social integration of the non-literate societies. In contrast, "suicidal victim-precipitation" and incidence of suicide were each positively related to degree of social integration.

References

Bacon, Margaret K.; Irvin L. Child; and Herbert Barry III. "A Cross-Cultural Study of Correlates of Crime." *Journal of Abnormal and Social Psychology* (April 1963): 291–300.

Breed, Warren. "Occupational Mobility and Suicide." *American Sociological Review* 28 (1964): 179–88.

Douglas, Jack D. *The Social Meanings of Suicide*. Princeton, N.J.: Princeton University Press, 1967.

Dublin, Louis I. *Suicide: A Sociological and Statistical Study*. New York: Ronald, 1963.

Durkheim, Emile. *Suicide*. Glencoe, Illinois: Free Press, 1951.

Gibbs, Jack P. *Suicide*. New York: Harper and Row, 1968.

Gibbs, Jack P. and Walter T. Martin. *Status Integration and Suicide*. Eugene, Ore.: University of Oregon Press, 1964.

Gouldner, Alvin. "The Norm of Reciprocity." *American Sociological Review* 25 (1960): 161–77.

Homans, George C. *Social Behavior: Its Elementary Forms*. New York: Harcourt, Brace and World, 1961.

Maris, Ronald W. *Social Forces in Urban Suicide*. Homewood, Ill.: Dorsey Press, 1969.

Mauss, Marcel. *The Gift*. Trans. by I. Cunnison. Glencoe, Ill.: Free Press, 1954.

Murdock, George P. et al. *Outline of Cultural Materials*. New Haven, Conn.: Human Relations Area Files, 1950.

Palmer, Stuart. *Deviance and Conformity*. New Haven, Conn.: College and University Press, 1970a.

Palmer, Stuart. "Aggression in 58 Non-Literate Societies: An Exploratory Analysis." *Annales Internationales de Criminologie,* 1er semestre 1970b, pp. 57-69.

Palmer, Stuart. "Characteristics of Suicide in 54 Non-Literate Societies." *Life-Threatening Behavior* (Fall 1971): 178-83.

Palmer, Stuart. *The Violent Society*. New Haven, Conn.: College and University Press, 1972.

Powell, Elwin H. "Occupation, Status and Suicide." *American Sociological Review* (April 1958): 131-39.

Schafer, Stephen. *The Victim and His Criminal*. New York: Random House, 1968.

Whiting, John W.M. and Irvin L. Child. *Child Training and Personality: A Cross-Cultural Study*. New Haven, Conn.: Yale University Press, 1962.

Wolfgang, Marvin E. *Patterns in Criminal Homicide*. Philadelphia, Pa.: University of Pennsylvania Press, 1958.

Wolfgang, Marvin E. and Franco Ferracuti. *The Subculture of Violence*. New York: Barnes and Noble, 1967.

Wood, Arthur Lewis. "Crime and Aggression in Changing Ceylon: A Sociological Analysis of Homicide, Suicide and Economic Crime." *Transactions of the American Philosophical Society* (Dec. 1961), Philadelphia, Pa.

5 Victims of Homicide
Neville H. Avison

Introduction

Scotland is a small country of some five million inhabitants, forming part of Great Britain. In international journals and in conference papers it is frequently assumed that descriptions of the incidence and type of crime in England and Wales apply equally to Scotland: such an assumption is false. Furthermore Scotland has a separate and different system of criminal law and of administration of justice. Under Scottish law, murder is, speaking broadly, the deliberate killing of a self-existent individual, the assault being intentional and the death being at least the probable consequence of the offender's act. Seen as less heinous, but still criminal because the killing was not intended in a legal sense, is culpable homicide, which may be compared with the English crime of manslaughter. During the last fifteen years English criminal law has absorbed some Scottish concepts, such as diminished responsibility, and has abandoned the doctrine of constructive malice, never a feature of the Scottish law of homicide. However, in Scotland there is no crime comparable to the English infanticide: if the offender is proceeded against, corresponding actions in Scotland are defined as murder, but by administrative practice they are usually dealt with as culpable homicide.[1]

The present paper draws for illustrative purposes upon the results of research designed to explore the nature of Scottish homicide, but it is suggested that the issues discussed here, and specifically those relating to the victims of such crimes, have wider implications and are likely to be of relevance beyond the confines of Scotland and even of Great Britain.

Published *Criminal Statistics* reveal that compared with England and Wales, Scotland has twice the recorded incidence of homicide per 100,000 of the population, and while in England there is a high proportion of depressive homicide, in which the offender commits suicide after murdering close relatives,[2] such crimes are infrequent in Scotland. On the other hand, Scotland shows a higher proportion of homicides arising after drunken quarrels, and also of violence committed by groups of young men, loosely organised on a territorial basis into violent gangs.

The period chosen for study was 1950 through 1968, and during this time more than six hundred homicides—unlawful killings—were recorded in the Scottish statistics. Unlawful homicide does not, in Scotland, include suicide, and this was excluded from the survey except when it was preceded by acts of homicide. In addition cases of causing death by dangerous driving were omitted. On the other hand, the researcher revealed that some incidents in which people were killed were recorded in the statistics under other legal classifications, and further, that some incidents which had been investigated by the police with a view to tracing an offender who could be charged with homicide, were *not* included in the official statistics at all. Both these categories were, however, included in the present research, which deals altogether with 968 incidents of homicide and 1,027 victims.

It is not intended here to give an account of these incidents, nor of the victims, but rather to draw on these data to illustrate an approach to victimology in relation to homicide which may offer new insights to those concerned with the criminal process and with the treatment of offenders. While victim precipitation is a factor common to most murders, the legal process is almost exclusively concerned with the question of guilt; usually it is only where the defense is one of provocation that the role of the victim plays a part in the proceedings. It is well known that apart from a handful of important exceptions the study of the victim in criminology has lagged behind the study of the adjudged offender. Yet, today few criminologists could be persuaded to agree with Mendelsohn when he suggests that victimology is not a branch of criminology, but rather a science parallel to it.[3] In studying the role of the victim we must not lose sight of that of the offender: they are intertwined in a socio-cultural nexus and to study one in isolation from the other is to miss the truth about each. In searching for an understanding of the role of the victim one must turn first to a consideration of the offender, his intentions and his motives.

Classification of Intent and Motive

Intent is an important concept in criminal law. It is frequently confused with motive—the intention of reaching a specific goal is confused with the reasons for wanting to do so.[4] Some offenders plead "accident" or "no intention to kill" but, if there is sufficient evidence of *mens rea* in other respects, their homicide is still treated as culpable. The difficult subjects of legal intention, knowledge of the consequences of actions, carelessness, and recklessness will not be considered here.

Rather what will be attempted is a discussion of intent and motive from a sociological point of view, using the words not in a legal but in a "taken for granted" context. Here, intention is taken to mean the degree of intention on the part of the offender to cause the death of his victim—ranging from a clear intent to kill to no intent to kill. Motive is used to mean the reason for the social interaction between the offender and his victim seen from the offender's point of view—motives include, for example, the perpetration of a sexual offense, robbery, or the settling of an argument. Obviously, any attempt to impute a motive, or an intention, to a person subsequently defined as a homicide offender is fraught with difficulty. In the present research, the classifications were deduced from a study of contemporary documents and trial transcripts. In only a few cases were offenders interviewed and asked about the reasons for their actions at the time of the offense. Responses to such questions are themselves unreliable, colored by the prisoner's attitude to his sentence, and subject to post hoc rationalization. Accordingly, it is impossible to be sure that the imputed motive was a primary or even a subsidiary motive for the attack. As Bohannan points out,[5] motive itself has two meanings: the reason in the mind of the individual, and cause assigned to it by other members of society.

Despite all the difficulties, the attempts made to understand the reasons for the crimes allow additional insights into the nature of homicide and, if it is borne in mind that there are areas of uncertainty and overlap in the categories, these classifications may provide a useful tool for analytical purposes. The offender may be said to have broad reasons for carrying out his actions, and these lie behind the immediate motives. One broad reason which must be singled out allows a division of types of homicide into two classes: homicides which can be seen primarily as problem-solving actions, and those having a more complicated interaction between victim and offender.[6]

Problem-solving homicides occur when the offender decides that the victim must die, as his continued survival poses too great a threat to the way of life of the offender. Victims in these cases are almost always powerless to intervene in the interaction leading to their death. The commonest type of problem-solving homicide involves the death of a new-born child where the offender is usually the mother and only rarely is the father directly involved. The motives for such killings are particularly hard to ascertain and it may well be that some are the result of postpartum depression. Where there is no evidence of mental disturbance it might be argued that the child is killed because of the threat its continued existence causes to the mother in terms of her domestic circumstances. This may be equally true of married or unmarried women and the only element of victim participation involved lies in the child's very existence. Similarly the mere existence of the victim may be relevant at the other end of the life-cycle and parents or grandparents may be killed by their children for no better reason than having lived beyond the span which is regarded by the offender as convenient. Even here, of course, the victim may well have contributed very directly to the causation of intra-familial tensions, but a study of the cases in the Scottish survey suggests that deliberate parricide of a problem-solving variety does not occur in the course of more direct victim participation. Other cases of problem-solving homicide occur when the victim of a sexual assault is slain so that she is then unable to identify the offender, or when a night-watchman is killed so that a robbery can take place without his intervention. So far as sexual homicides are concerned, it is evident that there may well

be a degree of victim participation in the *sexual* offense. However, the point
stressed here is that once the sexual assault is completed, in a few cases the
offender then kills his powerless victim to avoid subsequent identification:
such cases must, of course, be distinguished from those sexual murders in which
the murder is *itself* an integral part of the sexual act. Again, as will be seen later,
victims of robbery may participate to some extent in the crime.

It is important to distinguish these problem-solving homicides from other,
more frequent, incidents in which death occurs as a result of the victim playing
a more important role in the situation.

Precipitation or Participation

By definition, acts of aggression culminating in homicide involve an interaction between participants; homicide is a social relationship. A study of the
nature of such interaction, its degree and extent, suggests that the role of the
victim is not restricted to precipitation of the crime as set out in the now classic
description given by Wolfgang, in which he applies it to cases involving the victim
inducing his death *through his own* menacing actions.[7]

The victim can contribute in many different ways to the interaction preceding
the aggressive behavior, and it may be more meaningful to consider such involvement on a continuum ranging from participation (which may involve little more
than the mere *presence* of the victim in a given situation) through varying degrees
of provocation, and culminating in active precipitation by the victim. Such a
perspective focuses on the behavior of the victim in relation to the behavior of
the offender, and insofar as it provides a clearer picture of the nexus between
them, allows a better understanding of the background of homicide. Without
such an understanding any analysis of murder in sociological terms is meaningless. In particular, it highlights the infrequency with which an "innocent" victim
is killed: such victims seems to be largely confined to incidents characterized as
"problem-solving" homicides.

While recognizing such a continuum of victim participation, for the purposes
of this discussion it is convenient to describe three main categories of involvement. Firstly crimes in which there is no victim involvement, or at least only
minimal participation; secondly a much larger group where some degree of participation is involved, and thirdly a small group of cases where it is possible to
discern a clear responsibility on the part of the victim for the aggressive action
of his attacker.

Clearly, as with imputing motive and intent to the offender, any attempt to
assess the degree to which a victim precipitates his own death is necessarily open
to criticism on the grounds of subjectivity. Furthermore, the accuracy of such
assessments will be very dependent upon the availability of reliable documentation. The following attempt to discuss homicide in these terms must therefore

be regarded as highly tentative and is made simply in the hope that it will stimulate further study and discussion.

Incidents with Little or no Victim Participation

Incidents involving no victim participation may best be exemplified by those cases where the victim is accidentally killed in circumstances where there is no possibility of interaction with the offender; in the absence of such inter-action where can be no participation in the sense that is implied above.

The role of the "accidental" victim can also be seen in some cases in which robbery was the presumed motive; thus a man who is passing along a street may be attacked from behind, robbed, and killed. He has little or no opportunity to react to the assault. On the other hand, such an example raises very complex issues, the solution of which involves the need to have detailed knowledge of the precise circumstances of the attack before assessing victim participation; had the assault been made from the front it is possible that the specific mode of response used by the victim might have contributed by converting a crime where the intent was robbery into a homicidal incident. In other words, the defensive action, or even the offensive retaliation of the victim, may have played a major part in his own death.

Nor is this situation confined to individual offenders; groups may attack passers-by who are total strangers, and here, too, the initial reaction of the victims may be a key factor in the escalation of the violence to a level at which death is a certain, or at least probable, outcome. The importance of cultural determinants of behavior must be considered here: no doubt the best thing to do if an ordinary member of the public is attacked by strangers in the street might be to lie down with his back to the wall, adopt a fetal position, and cover his head with his arms. However, in Scottish lower-class urban culture, such a response is totally alien to any one who is attacked. The victim would see this supine response as an act of supreme cowardice, and more "manly," and in the event almost suicidal responses, have tended to be the immediate reaction of many who are attacked in this way.

Again, when the death of a woman or girl occurs after a sexual assault, similar problems arise regarding degrees of participation. There are, for example, instances where a female, an apparent stranger to the attacker, is ravished and killed and where, in the absence of contemporaneous observa-tion, it is impossible to know anything about the role of the victim. In such cases there tends to be an assumption that there was no victim participation, yet there is some reason for believing that in many such cases the victim, if not deliberately contributing to her death, at least selects herself to be at risk.

Equally, it is usually argued that a child who accepts a lift in a car from a total stranger is in no way participating in what may culminate in a homicidal killing. However, Gibbens and Prince have pointed out that there is a "participating" group of child victims of sexual offenses who show little maladjustment, but are simply submissive, seductive girls ready to participate in any relationship at a superficial level.[8] More recently, Lindy Burton has suggested that this group includes some girls who are sexual delinquents, in the so-called "latency" period of development.[9] In either case, there is clear evidence that such crimes frequently involve a degree of participation on the part of the victim which allows the offender to infer acquiescence if not agreement on the part of the child. If the offense escalates—from whatever cause—to the point at which the child dies, it is difficult to argue that there was no victim participation.

From the foregoing discussion it is apparent that apart from most problem-solving homicides and those that are purely accidentally determined, it is difficult to discern groups of homicides in which there are no circumstances of victim participation. Obviously there are difficulties involved in using information collected after an event for the purpose of interpreting the behavior of those involved. However, where detailed information is lacking it would seem likely that a proportion of the cases involved a degree of victim participation: that it is so difficult to find instances of minimal victim involvement suggests that the phenomenon of participation is far more widespread than has been indicated.

Incidents with a Moderate Degree of Victim Participation

As was noted when describing problem-solving homicides, involving the death of robbery victims, or elderly relatives, there could be instances in which the victim participated very directly in the interaction leading to death. This illustrates clearly the overlapping nature of the problem—victim precipitation occurs, as was said at the beginning, on a continuum, and no clear-cut divisions are possible. Nevertheless, in the "hot-house" family situation, so prevalent in urban industrial society, where members are constrained to live in close proximity, pressures may build up over a considerable period culminating in a homicide. Children who misbehave are sometimes the victims of severe aggression on the part of their parents, a pattern which may have persisted over a long period and which finally ends in a killing. It is arguable that a child who persists in behavior which his parents find intolerable can be said to contribute to their aggression, even if very young and unaware of the extent to which such behavior provokes the parents.

More evident is the part played by a victim who is killed by a spouse after a period of living together and involving a history of interpersonal violence; the parties to the homicide could almost be said to have interchangeable roles when it comes to the final act of aggression. Such acts of violence may have increased in frequency and/or intensity over time, with a corresponding increase in the severity of the injury, until, almost by accident, the attack is continued to the stage at which the victim dies. Here it is important to consider the intention of the offender at the outset of the attack; in many cases it is clear from the circumstances surrounding the case that the death of the victim was not intended, and chance plays a large part in the incidence of deaths such as these.

Homicides of the type just described usually occur in circumstances where the pressures result directly from emotional stresses within the family group, and where this results in death, it is usually confined to one person. Where the pressures originate outside the family the picture is different. Typically a husband may be overwhelmed by debt, by fears relating to the loss of his job, or by the continual struggle against poor housing, poor health, and lack of opportunities to escape from the cycle of deprivation. Consumed by despair he may resolve to eradicate his whole family, to take them out of society. Such an offender normally plans the deaths carefully, he kills his wife and children, the family pet—be it dog, cat or canary—and then immolates himself.[10] Rarely can it be said that family members contribute directly to their own deaths in such circumstances, but a closer study of the pattern of their family life not infrequently shows that insensitivity to the breadwinner's problems and a condemnatory attitude toward his handling of affairs have for long characterized and soured family relationships. Many such offenders have sought and received psychiatric help, often being diagnosed as schizophrenic, but there is some evidence to suggest that doctor and patient do not share the same definition of the problem,[11] and issues which have been considered as transitory or of little account by the psychiatrist are in fact the very ones which the offender sees as vital and insoluble.

As had been mentioned, homicides such as these occur relatively infrequently in the Scottish setting. Thus, in only 50 out of the 968 cases (5 percent) did the offender subsequently commit suicide, a proportion which may be contrasted with the English figure of 33 percent. It is difficult to account for this difference between the two national homicide statistics; Scotland shows a higher rate of unemployment, has a higher incidence of urban overcrowding and infant mortality, and Scotsmen have a lower life expectancy then Englishmen in corresponding occupations. However, the overall incidence of suicide in Scotland is lower than that in England and Wales,[12] and this fact, combined with the higher overall incidence of homicide provides an interesting confirmation of Henry and Short's hypothesis on the inverse relationship between the incidence of homicide and of suicide.[13]

In considering emotional relationships between offender and victim, the role of jealousy plays an important part. The response to rejection may be the use of great violence either at the time of rejection or later, when it seems clear that a new relationship between the rejecting partner and a third person is becoming significant. Both partners to the new relationship stand at risk. Much has been written about the delusional state of jealous murderers,[14] yet the relative imprecision with which doctors describe the nature of the delusional pressure and the reality of the existence of a bond of attachment suggests that many offenders who murder their loved ones do so not under any insane belief, but in a sane awareness of the extent of their loss. The contribution of the victim to this sense of loss, and the circumstances in which the offender discovers his loss, may well be key factors in determining the outcome. A lover who discovers his paramour *in flagrante delicto* is clearly more likely to respond with aggression than is one who has been weaned from the emotional involvement and for whom the affair is already diminishing in importance. It is clear that homicide in such circumstances occurs only when there remains a bond of affection in which the jealousy can root: as Morris and Blom-Cooper note,[15] Desdemona might have lived had she not been loved by Othello.

In studying homicides resulting from quarrels or disagreements a distinction must be made between long-standing disputes on the one hand and quarrels which flare up, escalate from verbal to physical aggression, and terminate in a fatal assault. The former group obviously include in all incidents clear evidence of victim participation, and a scrutiny of the Scottish cases indicates that the offender intended the death of his victim in a high proportion of the cases. However, simple quarrels are usually characterized by an absence of any intention to kill the victim, and in most cases the offender is later overcome by remorse. In the Scottish setting it was noted that both the offender and his victim had very often consumed large amounts of alcohol—certainly sufficient to impair their judgment—and without debt this contributed to the violence of the quarrel. Again a strong cultural component is involved, and it is interesting to observe that Verkko found that in Finland, Estonia, and Latvia high rates of both homicide and suicide resulted from a common cause—alcohol.[16] Wolfgang, too, found that alcohol was present in both victim and killer in 44 percent of his cases as compared with 9 percent for victims only and 11 percent for killers only.[17] Morris and Blom-Cooper discuss the role of alcohol in murder cases; they make no claim that the relationship between alcohol and the offense is a predominating one, or even a major contributive factor, but they do assert that there is often a casual link between homicide and the presence of alcohol in both the defendant and the victim and they suggest that it is frequently a precipitating factor in, for example, violent death resulting from brawls and street fights.

In the Scottish survey, more than half of the quarrels resulting in death were found to involve drunkenness in both offender and victim. In the cultural environment of the lower socio-economic groups in Scotland, particularly in cities, drunken arguments, which by nature of the circumstances cannot be resolved by verbal discussion alone, are expected to be solved, albeit temporarily, by a resort to physical aggression. Once the combatants come to blows, the expectation is that only one of them shall remain conscious and the fight continues on this basis. Often the one who is getting the worst of the fight resorts to the use of a weapon—ostensibly being carried for defensive purposes—and the risk of serious injury is obviously increased. A weapon is by no means always necessary, however, and not a few victims are killed by being kicked to death. In such incidents the role of the victims is evident; that this role is required of him by virtue of the sociocultural context in which he lives must also be understood.

As in the earlier discussion in relation to spouses, in the case of such drunken quarrels it is by no means always clear who the eventual victim will be. The roles are interchangeable until extraneous factors, such as superior physical strength or the availability of a weapon, determine the final outcome. This type of behavior must also be seen in its social context. Work by Henry and Short in America and by Verkko in Finland has drawn attention to the way in which people in low status groups tend to express their aggression in hostility toward others rather than toward themselves, and in conflict situations to communicate at the level of physical violence. Here, too, the concept of a subculture of violence is important, and will be referred to again.

The kinds of situations described above suggest that offender and victim are reasonably well known to each other, but it is possible to find examples of quarrels arising in circumstances in which the interaction between the two is extremely brief. For example, the offender may ask a brief acquaintance for a match, or a passer-by for a spanner with which to repair his car; if the victim is unable or unwilling to produce the desired article, he may be attacked and killed. Such incidents provide the basis of a quarrel, but not one of the victim's seeking, nor does he participate much in the interaction—he merely fails to provide the offender with what he wants. The analogy between such cases and incidents in which robbery was the prime motive is clear, but they are distinguishable insofar as the robber sets out with the intent of committing a particular crime—robbery—and the victim was always going to be robbed in the offender's intention. In the unlooked-for quarrel, the victim seems to have resented the verbal abuse, responded with further abuse and thus escalated the interaction into one of violence.[18]

Incidents With Much Victim Participation

Four types of incident can be subsumed under this category. Firstly, there are those in which police officers attempt to apprehend an offender or in which a private person attempts to detain a criminal or to intervene in an on-going fight. The victim in such cases clearly does not foresee that he is likely to be killed, but because of a sense of duty, or a wish to prevent further injury, he deliberately places himself at risk and sets out on a course of action which results in his death.

Analogous to this is a second group, where the victim colludes in a criminal act and disregards the possibility of a death arising. The most obvious examples concerns those females who allow illegal abortions to be performed on them. Here there is no intention on the part of the offender that the victim should die, but in the nature of things—lack of skill, unhygienic conditions, and so forth— the woman dies. There can hardly be a more clear example of victim participation in homicide.

The third group in this category is comprised of those victims killed from motives of revenge. Homicides arising in this context are not infrequently a temporal extension of the type of instantaneous quarrels referred to earlier. The two contestants leave the earlier scene of battle, the victim in the initial attack determines to wreak his revenge, plans his crime and becomes the offender. In the Scottish context, revenge killings seem to be very much a feature of the criminal subculture; criminal rivals seeking not a *modus vivendi* but rather a permanent solution to their mutual problem. That the offender and the victim could equally well change places is incontrovertible; chance and opportunity seem the determinants of who shall and shall not die.

Equally clearly involving victim participation is the fourth group of incidents, in which a gang, or a similar group, attack rival groups. While in the instant of the attack there may have been no victim involvement, membership of such groups clearly implies a recognition of future involvement in violence. Gang membership implies acceptance not only of the fact that one is likely to become a victim of another group's aggression, but further that, in certain circumstances, one may oneself be called upon to attack a member of another group. Such incidents arise in what has been described as the subculture of violence,[19] characteristic of Western urban lower-class society. The existence of such a subculture cannot be denied in the Scottish setting, and a recent account of a Glasgow gang speaks of the "cultural normality of *violence*" in that city.[20] Here, victim and offender share in the guilt of violence, for as Patrick observes, the victim is not selected casually. Attacks of this nature must be distinguished from those described earlier, in which a victim, unknown either personally or by affiliation to a gang, is attacked by a gang group.

The Innocent and the Guilty Victim

A study of the Scottish cases suggests that, apart from victims of problem-solving murder, who are killed in a deliberate and premeditated fashion, it is extremely difficult to find instances of wholly "innocent" and uninvolved victims. In about two out of three cases of homicide, the victim had participated in some measure in a way which encouraged the interaction with the offender in a progression to violence. Coupled with this is the finding that in many of these cases the offender did not, apparently, intend to cause the death of the victim, and, in not a few, was overcome by remorse at the realization of what he had done. This realization came later rather than sooner for many offenders, when the effect of alcohol had worn off. Indeed, in a substantial minority of cases the offender and victim had, until the last moment, almost interchangeable roles, and it seemed a matter of chance who lived and who died. Not uncommonly, victim and offender were taken to the same hospital, where one remained to be autopsied and the other transferred to a police station after treatment.

The Use of Discretion in the Administration of Justice

In the light of the foregoing, it is interesting to consider the response made by the police, the prosecution agencies and the courts to the different types of homicide. As was noted in the introduction, not every offender who could be charged with homicide is, in fact, so charged. Alternative criminal prosecutions have been found to arise from incidents in which a person was killed. The reckless discharge of firearms, assault, or possession of offensive weapons are lesser charges for which an offender may be prosecuted, even when the victim has succumbed to his injuries. Furthermore, it is by no means unknown for offenders not to be prosecuted at all, a matter to which further reference will be made below.

Already, then, one can discern a differential treatment of offenders at the stage of prosecution. It would be interesting to know to what extent decisions made at this point are determined by purely legal factors and to what extent they reflect public attitudes to different kinds of homicide. Certain types of killing, notably causing death by dangerous driving in infanticide, are generally viewed with considerable tolerance, and death resulting from drunken brawls or family quarrels receive relatively little attention. On the other hand sexual murders and the killing of young children other than by their parents excite a considerable degree of hostile reaction.

The discretion to prosecute in Scotland lies in the hands of the Crown, represented for this purpose by the Lord Advocate and aided in his work by Advocates-Deputy instructing staff at the Crown Office. Prosecutions are taken in the public interest, and the way such discretion is exercised is a difficult area to investigate, let alone to understand.

It is possible to identify some, if not all, of the categories of cases which will *not* be the subject of prosecution. Thus when a young unmarried girl is delivered of a child without medical assistance, and if she subsequently kills the child, usually no prosecution will follow on the grounds that she may well have been punished enough already. Again, when it is difficult to find truthful witnesses, or where witnesses are reluctant to give evidence, there may be cases which are not prosecuted in order to prevent the investigation of a costly and potentially unsuccessful court case, resulting in no more than the acquittal of the offender.

In cases where there is a decision to prosecute, but some doubt about the outcome, if the offender is willing to plead guilty to a lesser charge, this is frequently allowed on the grounds that expense and trouble are thereby saved. Again, if the facts of the case suggest that the victim is to some extent to blame, or that the offender acted by mistake or negligently, or had no intention to kill, a reduced charge may well be the only one proceeded with. Even if a charge of homicide—whether murder or culpable homicide—is pressed, it is open to the court, and in certain circumstances the jury, to convict only on a reduced charge. Thus it seems that decisions regarding prosecution are based upon both legal factors and public attitudes to different forms of homicide. But equally it seems that a third element is involved, one which may be of even greater significance, namely administrative convenience.

Turning to the question of disposal, in Scotland, as in England and Wales, there is a single penalty for murder—life imprisonment; for culpable homicide, the maximum penalty is also life imprisonment but the minimum can be as little as a discharge or an admonishment—an official court warning. Within the term "life imprisonment" there are also wide variations, ranging in recent times from eighteen months at one end of the scale to twenty-five years at the other, and some life prisoners have died in prison. Here then is further evidence of discretion in the judicial process, but it is by no means clear to what extent issues concerning the interaction or motive, intent, and victim participation are taken into account when considering the release on license of lifers.

Yet such considerations seem crucial, not only in relation to the future recidivism of the individual offender but equally in understanding the social circumstances which produced the climate in which homicidal attacks can take place. It will be important to consider the likelihood of an offender again faced with a set of circumstances sufficiently similar to those which brought about the violent behavior which earlier culminated in a homicidal attack. It is well recognized that in advising on suitability for release, psychiatrists pay particular attention to the mental state of offenders but it may be that their violent behavior is to some extent a response to constitutional or other physical disturbances engendered by the words or actions of the victims. Psychopathological factors are clearly of the utmost importance in the decision to release on license, but due consideration must also be given to the social circumstances and cultural background into which a man serving a life sentence is released. As was said at the beginning, homicide is a social relationship; to this should be added that it is a *human* relationship which takes place within a particular social and cultural context.

Notes

1.   See generally G.H. Gordon, *The Criminal Law of Scotland* (Edinburgh:

Green, 1967). For a discussion of criminal procedure see Renton and Brown, *Criminal Procedure according to the law of Scotland*, 4th edition by G.H. Gordon (1973).

2. D.J. West, *Murder followed by Suicide* (London: Heinemann, 1965).

3. B. Mendelsohn, "Victimology," in *Etudes Internationales de Psycho-Sociologie Criminelle* (1956), no. 1.

4. Salmond provides a neat distinction, dividing intention into "immediate" and "ulterior" intent. The former relates to the action, the latter to the reason for the action, and this latter he calls motive. See *Salmond on Jurisprudence*. (London: Sweet and Maxwell, 1957).

5. P. Bohannan (ed.), *African Homicide and Suicide* (Princeton, N.J.: Princeton University Press, 1960).

6. A similar distinction seems to have been drawn by Hoffman, when he describes (a) premeditated, felonious, intentional murder and (b) slaying in the heat of passion, or killing as a result of intent to do harm but without intent to kill. See W.F. Hoffman, *Pennsylvania Criminal Law and Criminal Procedure* 4th edition (1952), cited in M.E. Wolfgang and F. Ferracuti, "Subculture of Violence: An Interpretive Analysis of Homicide," *International Annals of Criminology* (1962). Wolfgang and Ferracuti suggest that "probably less than 5 percent of all known homicides are premeditated, planned intentional killings"; in the Scottish survey, more than one-third of the incidents could be classified in this category.

7. M.E. Wolfgang, *Patterns in Criminal Homicide* (Philadelphia: University of Pennsylvania Press, 1958), p. 245 *et seq.*

8. T.C.N. Gibbens and J. Prince, *Child Victims of Sex Offenders* (London: Institute for the Study and Treatment of Delinquency, 1963).

9. L. Burton *Vulnerable Children* (Routledge and Kegan Paul, 1968).

10. D.J. West, *Murder followed by Suicide.*

11. T.L. Dorpat, "Suicide in Murderers," *Psychiatry Digest* (1966), reports a short series of cases, characterized by psychotic or severely disturbed men killing their wives or lovers and then committing suicide. The relationships were marked by prolonged turmoil and he hypothesises that the murder-suicide was an acting-out of fantasies of re-union.

12. This has, however, been seen as a recording artifact. See B.M. Barraclough, "Are the Scottish and English Suicide rates really different?" *B.J. Psychiatry* (1972).

13. A.F. Henry and J.F. Short, *Suicide and Homicide* (Glencoe, Illinois: The Free Press, 1954).

14. R.R. Mowat, *Morbid Jealousy and Murder* (London: Tavistock Publications, 1966).

15. T.P. Morris and L. Blom-Cooper, *A Calendar of Murder* (London: Michael Joseph, 1964).

16. V. Verkko, *Homicides and Suicides in Finland and their Dependence on National Character* (Copenhagen: G.E.C. Gad, 1951).

17. M.E. Wolfgang, *Patterns in Criminal Homicide.*

18. Such sudden murders must be distinguished from the series described by J.W. Lamberti, N. Blackman, and J.M.A. Weiss, "The Sudden Murderer," *Journal of Social Therapy* (1958), where no profit or personal advantage was sought by the murderers, who were responding to provocation after a period of inability to conform to other's expectations.

19. M.E. Wolfgang and F. Ferracuti, *The Subculture of Violence* (London: Tavistock Publications, 1967).

20. Patrick J. (pseud.) *A Glasgow Gang Observed* (London: Eyren Methuen, 1973).

Part II
Mass Violence and Genocide

6 Mass Murder, Multicide, and Collective Crime: The Doers and the Victims

Bruno M. Cormier

This paper will deal with certain aspects of mass murder and multicide that may shed some light on collective crimes, but before proceeding it is necessary to define some terms.

Mass murder usually refers to a criminal episode in which a number of victims are killed within a short period of time, i.e., an hour, a day. Mass murders are generally committed by one person, though there are times when more than one person is involved.

Multicide is a term used to define a number of homicides committed by one person, but spread over a longer period of time, say, months or even years, and generally corresponds to an unfolding, deep-seated psychopathological process. The author usually selects a type of victim and repeats the murders periodically up to the time of arrest. Multicide is thus different from a homicide recidivist who kills twice in two unrelated situations, for example, in the course of a criminal career.

Collective crime also implies many victims, the difference being that the doers act collectively and group and individual psychopathology are closely interwoven. One could state that collective crimes are impossible without a prevailing group psychopathology which fosters the emergence of destructive drives which might otherwise remain in check. As genocide is the type of collective crime that will be mentioned here, some remarks on its definition within this context are also indicated.

We are accustomed to thinking of *genocide* as a crime committed by one group against another group.[1] The United Nations Convention on Genocide affirms that, "Genocide, whether committed in time of peace or in time of war, is a crime under international law . . . " and clearly states that it means "acts committed with the intent to destroy [a group] in whole or in part." Within this definition, killing one or a few persons because they are members of a "national, ethnical, racial or religious group as such" is as much a genocidal act as a massive attack on a group. One of the essences of genocidal acts is thus killing or causing bodily or moral harm to persons because they are what they are. Because the crime of genocide comes to our attention when many victims and perpetrators are involved, incidental genocidal crimes or acts of lesser magnitude have been neglected.

When referring to the perpetrators, the Convention refers to *persons* not to *groups*. It is thus theoretically and in fact possible that one person, acting alone and killing one or a few victims, can be guilty of the crime of genocide as defined

71

in the United Nations Convention. Up to now, crimes committed against
national, ethnical, racial or religious groups have been committed in states of
aggression and fanaticism and have involved many doers and victims. The
essence of such crimes being, in the last analysis, the killing of a person because
he is what he is, we can find in our penitentiaries criminals who have committed
crimes that are genocidal in quality. We will define a classification of crimes
against the person that permits us to isolate and study such offenders and from
there to see to what extent these authors of mass murder and multicide can
help us to understand the doers and the victims in collective crimes.

"Victimité" and "Monstruosité" in Collective Crime

Mendelsohn has coined the term "victimité," which we may translate as
"victimity." This is related ot the word, criminality, in the same way that
victimology is related to the word, criminology. "Victimity" stems from biolo-
gical, psychological, and social factors (and, one may add, cultural and psycho-
historical factors) which determine that individuals or groups are living in a
climate where they are prone, even forced, to become victims.[2,3]

We seriously doubt that the climate referred to as victimity, which produced
so many encounters between individual offenders guilty of crimes defined in
common law and their victims, is the same as the one that determines the
encounters between groups of doers and victims in collective crimes. Nevertheless, climate should be studied for both groups if we want to compare it.

It is my contention that the severe type of penitentiary inmates, the persistent offenders, the mass murderers, the homicidal offenders, do not have
much in common with the perpetrators of genocide or collective crimes committed in time of war, revolution or in the course of political liberation movements. This is not to say, however, that from the psychodynamics encountered
in penitentiary offenders we could not derive some knowledge to approach the
complex problem of participants in collective crimes. This paper will, in fact,
be such an attempt.

In the literature on genocide, much stress is laid on the atrocity of the acts
committed. In fact, Mendelsohn suggests that to designate the nature of these
acts, a new category of infraction (referred to as "monstruosité") should be
created in international law. We fully recognize the dreadful nature of acts
found in collective crimes, and they certainly take on a new dimension when
they are coldly and rationally planned. These admissions notwithstanding, we
must still recognize that the essence of genocide is not the brutal nature of the
crime, but the fact that its aim is to destroy a mass of victims. This is what is
really monstrous in collective crimes such as genocide.

As to the manner and style of techniques employed to inflict pain and
torture, we have to admit that a great deal of atrocity is sometimes found in

homicidal crimes. Certain types of homicidal offenders inflict the same type of excessive cruelty on their victims as have been described in collective crimes. We would refer the reader to Wilson's studies on murderers.[4,5,6]

Clinical Classification for the Study of Doers and Victims in Crimes of Homicide

In studying men found guilty of homicide, we need a frame of reference that would allow us to group together the criminological, psychological, and dynamic aspects, and one which would also encompass the total situation of the crime, that is, the doer, the deed, and the victim. We felt that this should allow for useful subgroups for research, diagnosis, prognosis, and treatment rather than lumping together murderers who have little in common otherwise. We defined three types of relationships in which homicidal acts occur, that is, specific, non-specific, and semi-specific.[7,8,9]

A homicide committed in a *specific* relationship is defined as one in which the relationship between the doer and the victim was such that the cause, the motivation, and the dynamics of the crime are to be found in the conflictual nature of the relationship. A specific relationship implies that the doer and victim know one another, but what is more important is the fact that the crime is understandable only within the conflicts between these persons. Marital murders and those committed within a family are classic examples of such homicides.

A homicide committed in a *non-specific* relationship is one occurring in a setting in which the doer either does not know the victim, or if he does happen to know him, the psychological relationship or other bonds that exist between them are not the determining factors. Homicide in this type of relationship often is not intended but may occur in the commission of another crime or be incidental, but the victims have no special psychological meaning for the doers, e.g. an armed robbery where killing is neither intended nor desired but the risk is tacitly accepted by the fact of carrying a lethal weapon.

Homicide committed in a *semi-specific* relationship is at one and the same time the most complex and the most difficult to define. In such homicides the doer kills because of motivation and psychodynamics that are to be found in his own psychopathology. He may or may not know the victim, usually the latter, and the meaning the victim has for the doer is found within his own pathology, which permits him to kill one or many victims, indiscriminately or because they happen to belong to a particular group with certain characteristics. A case of a sadistic killer of children who kills them for his own perverted gratification will be described later.

The most tragic crimes committed in semi-specific relationships are war crimes and genocide where victims are killed because of what they are rather than who they are. We will try to understand as many dynamics as we can of crimes that are committed in semi-specific relationships and which have a genocidal quality, and from there try to see to what extent we can understand the complex individual and collective psychopathology involved in the commission of genocide and other collective crimes.

As the definition of these terms indicates, they are based on the murderer-victim relationship, or how the murderer perceives the victim and how the victim is related to the murderer when such a relationship existed prior to the murder. Since the emphasis is on the psychological relationship, mutually shared or unilateral, between the doer and the victim, we must take into account that the quality of the relationship may change during the criminal process, i.e., from the pre-delictual to the delictual and post-delictual states. These changes of quality in the relationship while the criminal process is unfolding illustrate how personal conflicts can be aggressively acted out within a relationship where conflicts arise and from there displaced against the world at large.

Clinical Methodological Approach

From our encounters with penitentiary offenders during years of practice and research in clinical criminology, we selected some cases whose crimes were genocidal in quality. To speculate, as we will, whether, given a suitable climate, these offenders might or might not have participated in collective genocidal crime is truly an exercise in conjecture but one that may help to shed some light on those who participate in collective crimes.

A truer approach would have been possible if, at the time, interviews had been carried out with as many subjects as possible who were directly involved in the Nazi genocide. Unfortunately, this was not done and we are left with some extensive biographies and/or autobiographies, mainly on the leaders. No matter how interesting these may be, they have serious drawbacks for clinical studies and what is really lacking is knowledge on the rank and file. As to the many books written by survivors of the concentration camps, they have much to say about the perpetrators, but in the end, with a few exceptions, we are left with a faceless mass. As to collective or war crimes committed since, there seems to be no consistent initiative to delve deeply into the root cause of what we know to be man's inhumanity to man.

We will refer especially to the Nazi war crimes because they are well documented and have been the object of court trials. From the horror of these crimes, it was widely concluded that the leaders as well as the rank and file must have been criminal and insane. Now that many years have passed, we have to think that, clinically speaking, most of them were neither insane nor criminal in the sense in which we use these words in the practice of psychiatry and clinical criminology. If such is the reality for most, then a study of the perpetrators of of genocide may reveal itself to be far more difficult than the study of avowed criminals or persons who are mentally ill. The question might well be one that has been asked so many times: how could this really have happened if these people, both before and after the deed, were neither insane nor criminal?

The approach that we have taken here cannot throw any real light on these many perpetrators about whom we would like to know more. When, for the sake of this study, we assumed that criminals in a penitentiary who were guilty of crimes of genocidal quality would, given the opportunity, have been involved in collective genocidal crimes, we discovered that this assumption was incorrect. That is to say, the severe criminals selected as clinical examples showed more signs that they would not have been involved in such crimes. If our conjecture about these criminals leads us to believe what is really probable, that most participants in the Nazi genocide, and others that history has known before and since, were neither criminal nor insane, then we may have to acknowledge that genocide is a crime of many ordinary people who find themselves at a crossroads where psychosocial historical factors meet with complex individual and group social psychopathology.

It is in thinking of this crossroad that, despite the serious flaws in our methodological approach, we elected to pursue this study, if only because it might give us some clue on how men act individually and collectively at this stage of our civilization where survival is endangered more by rational, deliberate aggression than by uncontrolled, instinctual, even insane passions.[10]

Case Histories

The cases presented here, four known to us and two chosen from the literature, all have one thing in common. The offenses had genocidal qualities and were committed in a semi-specific relationship. We selected cases in which the subjects, apart from committing homicidal crimes in a semi-specific relationship, also committed such crimes in specific and non-specific relationships. This diversity will allow some speculation on the passage from individual to social pathology. Our major aim in this oversimplified clinical study of offenders found guilty of crimes of genocidal quality is to see whether an overt history of homicidal pathology would predispose these people to be involved in genocidal crimes in a climate favoring such crimes.

Case No. 1

In the years that have elapsed since we first knew the subject (1955) up to the time of his death (1972), a diagnosis of paranoia became evident to us, a diagnosis based on the same criteria as in the case of Wagner, to whom we will refer later.

The subject, a fifty-year-old multicide, was found guilty of the murder of four young boys. The genocidal quality of his crime arises from the fact that he killed these youngsters from motivations based on what children meant to him, no personal relationship existing between the victims and himself beyond the encounters necessary for the commission of the deed. These children were killed because they were children and the homicides were thus committed in a semi-specific relationship. The offenses occurred when he was in his forties, but he had previously been incarcerated for other offenses. During the last offenses, he had a powerful system of pathological defenses that allowed him to feel, soon afterward, as if no crime had been committed. Thus, the repetition of the sadistic killings up to the time he was apprehended.

This withdrawal of affect following an act of homicide is more serious in its potential consequences than the mechanism of denial, for it implies the full intellectual knowledge and recognition of the homicidal act without the painful affect, whereas denial (or part denial) implies that one wishes the deed had not taken place, without suppressing the painful affect.

In our view the absence of painful affect appropriate to the deed in the post-delictual homicidal state is related to an incapacity to be depressed, or a failure to engage oneself in a painful mourning process. We have commented in other papers on how depressive states, affect, and thinking are important etiological factors in the psychogenesis of criminal acts;[11],[12] but depression in all its manifestations also contains some limiting factors in criminal acting out. Self-depreciation and self-blame may lead to a degree of withdrawal into oneself where acting is minimal. Suicide is an extreme form of limiting factor.

In the severe psychopathology encountered in this subject, the inability to be depressed is replaced by paranoid mechanisms, ideation, and affect. In Kleinian terminology, this pathology is formulated somewhat differently, that is, a fixation in the schizoid-paranoid position prevents one from entering into the depressive position where one emerges ultimately with a capacity to be normally depressed. In the post-delictual state, the subject's comment regarding his crimes illustrates the paranoid world in which he was living, when he stated that "with these horrible hands I made four little angels." It is true that his hands were the instrument of the crimes, but beyond this reality he only holds part of himself responsible for the deeds and thus escapes the depression that would go with the acceptance that he, the whole person, was the author. His statement is partly pre- and partly post-delictual state. When he bade his victims pray and make their peace with God, the homicides were already pictured in his mind, along with the anticipated pleasure and he made full use of the ready-made religious belief that children who die go directly to heaven. In his paranoid omnipotence it was *he* who *decided to make the "four little angels."*

Multiple murders committed in a state of melancholia differ from those committed in a paranoid state with its grandiose and omnipotent features and lack of concern for the victims. The melancholic patient feels and expresses thoughts about his own inner unworthiness and his perception of the badness of the surroundings. When such patients express religious and mystical altruistic preoccupations regarding themselves and potential victims, and fantasies of reunification after death, the danger of mass murder is great, but different from the one just described. The melancholic thoughts of a mother who kills her children are well known. In crimes committed in a state of melancholia there is often deep concern, albeit pathological, for the world and the victims. The homicidal acts are usually committed in a specific relationship.

The psychopathology of the case described is so inwardly determined that at no time did it need any degree of group approval, nor could we legitimately claim that it would be more likely to happen in one political regime than another. In this particular case, to be part of a group venture in crime would have meant, to the subject, giving up the delusional belief in his own omnipotent strength, a delusion he can preserve only by remaining a lone operator.

Case No. 2

This man in his thirties had served two prison sentences for rape. The nature of the sexual offenses presents a choice of objects and mechanisms that have genocidal qualities, for example, the assault on a type of victim and the wish to impose by force a set of morals and values. For that reason we have included it in this series.

This subject was attracted by a type of full-breasted young woman whose style of dress emphasized these features. When he encountered such women, he would offer them a lift in his car, whether solicited or not, and it was in these circumstances that the two rapes occurred. Sometimes, instead of being sexually aroused, he felt quite enraged against such girls and became very religious and moralistic, blaming them for the evils they provoked, corruption of morals, seduction of men, and so on. In this state he became the prototype of the puritan who damns what his values prevent him from enjoying. He became a "preacher," warning hitchhiking girls of the impending dangers of being raped and assaulted. At times he felt these women should either be put in jail or forced to conform to certain moral standards. However, whether aggressively inclined, in a puritanical mood, or within his persecutory fantasies, he never really lost the intellectual insight that these affects and moods were in fact different facets of a basic problem. In the acting out of these impulses, or in his world of fantasy, clinically he showed overt signs of anguish and anxiety, fed by a keen awareness that he was either in danger of doing harm or had already done it.

This offender's reaction to his own aggression made us wonder how the perpetrators of genocide reacted to their aggressive deeds. Mention is made here and there in the literature that some did indeed develop symptoms, especially during the war when requests for transfer to other assignments were not granted.

Not enough is known on the reaction of presumably normal men in the process of adapting themselves to the role of official murderers.

In our view, when men are confronted with the type of duty that the S.S. were called on to perform in the concentration camps, and when unable to withdraw from such duty, it would at least be desirable that they develop a "reactive neurosis" that could have some similarity with the case we have just described, that is, fear of one's aggression. One can wonder if the "healthy" symptoms of a few or many could have prevented the group from going beyond certain limits. This thought appears, however, to be inspired by wishful thinking. In group psychopathology, especially when the affects and drives of a militant group are in full gear, the neurotic breakdown of some members would have little effect on group action. When the climate of destruction was well established and murderous acts were actually condoned as the order of the day, the fact that a few or many of the S.S. developed distressing symptoms did not result in restraining the group. Only the end of the war, with the attendant defeat, brought an end to the murderous group.

Case No. 3

A man in his mid-twenties committed two homicides within a month, with no apparent sexual motives, with ill-defined acquisitive aims, and in the presence of some delusional ideas. The post-delictual state of the first homicide was accompanied by intense anxiety and anguish; this latter was somewhat reduced, though still acute, in the pre-delictual state of the second homicide. The second homicide was partly committed as a means of "undoing" the first murder, and in doing so, "getting rid of" the anxiety and anguish. A chain reaction was put in motion, and clinically one could assume that a third murder would have been committed in order to get rid of the unbearable post-delictual state resulting from the second murder if arrest had not intervened.

One can speculate that the obsessive compulsive repetition partly responsible for the recidivism of homicide in this case may also play an important part in the group psychopathology of men involved in genocidal crimes. The mechanisms involved here are part of a broader psychopathology. The "getting rid of" and the "undoing" mechanisms were part of a self-defeating chain reaction insofar as it could never achieve its aim, i.e. getting rid of the anxiety and undoing the previous act. One can postulate that eventually a complete schizophrenic breakdown would have occurred in which total disorganization or suicide would have prevented the commission of further deeds. Also, to place this crime in its social context, external forces (here the arrest) were likely to intervene rapidly. This case was presented to illustrate two mechanisms found in the little explored field of recidivism in homicide, and not found in perpetrators of genocide, or, if present, in very few. Our provisional diagnosis in this case was schizophrenia simplex.

Case No. 4

This young man, now in his early thirties, was sentenced for a homicide committed when he was in his early twenties, when we first came to know him. He and his half-brother acted in partnership and homicide resulted from a crime that was initially acquisitive in nature. Intent on robbery, they attacked an old man, and in the process of committing the act, the acquisitive motivation was superseded by the retaliatory impulse to kill the old man, who in their view was an exploiter and a homosexual. Like the victim, the subject's half-brother was a homosexual.

Shortly after the crime, but prior to being arrested, the subject killed his half-brother as well. Killing him was not only a means of getting rid of a witness, but also a persecutory act against a homosexual, taking pleasure in doing so, in a way that resembles executions in the Nazi concentration camps, according to his own statement. (By way of clarification, it should be mentioned that when the subject was arrested, he was charged as an accomplice in the murder of the old man, and throughout his trial he maintained that it was the brother who had actually done the killing. The authorities continued to search for the brother who had, of course, disappeared.)

Born in the early 1940s, this young man had no actual experience of World War II, but one of his major fantasies was about being a member of the S.S., although he had no real knowledge of the part they played; for him they were strong people, a group who were killing or executing something bad. Prior to his S.S. fantasies, during adolescence one of his ideals was to become a policeman, this being occasioned by identification with the local chief of police who took a real interest in trying to help him when he was a delinquent child and adolescent.

In many of the interviews with him, the subject narrated with some pleasure the sadistic or perverted acts in which he had participated and it was at times difficult to separate fact from fancy. Soon after his incarceration a deep feeling of guilt manifested itself in a psychotic episode when, during a prolonged period of confinement in his cell, he hallucinated, hearing a voice repeatedly asking him, "Why did you do it?", the question referring to the killing of his brother. Ultimately, he confessed and disclosed the whereabouts of the brother's body.

This rather pathetic creature was able to inspire a degree of empathy as it was obvious throughout that even though he had inflicted a great deal of pain, he himself was suffering greatly. Having seen him in this psychotic state, we had no doubt that during the psychotic episode he genuinely suffered from an intolerable sense of guilt which could be dealt with only by confessing.

One may conjecture whether or not such a character would have found a ready-made outlet for the satisfaction of his sadistic impulses in the prevailing climate of the concentration camps. We cannot but note that he is practically a caricature of what one imagines a concentration camp executioner to be. The need of this man to confess out of deep-seated guilt in a psychotic phase, and when not psychotic, to narrate his deeds as a form of reenactment of the pleasure obtained at the time is certainly not the state of mind among the executioners after the war was over and the reality of the concentration camps was fully unfolded. There has been no urge to confess out of guilt; quite the contrary in fact.

One difference between this individual and the S.S. known through biographies, autobiographies, and case histories is the well-documented history of pathological character traits and actual antisocial acting out that we can trace back to childhood. In this case, the limiting process that put an end to his deeds was as pathological as the process that determined them in the first place. He drew a number of pictures of hangings where he was either the executioner or the one being executed. In these fantasies, the wish to be executed was dominant and to be the executioner a means of putting himself to death.

To kill in order to be put to death is a most tragic form of suicide. No matter what state he was in, in the last resort he was himself a bad object and in our view this is the important psychopathological nucleus of this case. This is not to say that there was not a good object somewhere, but it was always unreachable. He had always preserved a love for his mother, a mercenary prostitute who could not foster in him the growth of a good self that could somewhat counteract its opposite, the bad self.

We do not believe that this man, who depicted himself as a grotesque figure able to be involved in genocide and crimes against humanity, is in fact comparable to men who have been found guilty of such crimes. His deeds were explained by a lack of progress or an arrest at an early stage in his emotional development. We cannot say that he regressed to a primitive stage as he had never advanced very far in his development. Because of this primitive behavior, governed by the sadism and masochism found in the Kleinian schizoid-paranoid position, this man, like the first case described, could not receive group approval, nor would he seek it. It is our view that men like him do not involve themselves in militant groups although when such groups become a social force they may commit their crimes within the predominating social climate and ideology which has no meaning for them.

When we compare this case with what is known of some perpetrators of genocide, one of the great differences is that the latter had progressed to an advanced stage of development from which, in a given social climate and circumstances, they partly regressed, a regression which mobilized the potential of primitive impulses at the service of an ego in a defined psychosocial and historical conjunction. Such a regression takes place, however, in a determinant group psychopathology. This case suggests an important conclusion, that it is among ordinary people without gross psychopathology that we are most likely to find those capable of involving themselves in collective crimes.

Two Cases in the Literature

We have selected two cases among those written up in the literature: the Wagner case was extensively documented and observed over a period of a quarter of a century; the second case, Whitman, dates only a few years back (1966) and our knowledge of it comes from the journalistic rather than the scientific literature. In both of these cases, the mass murders unfolded in two phases. In the first phase, the victims were members of the family, and the crimes were thus committed in a specific relationship. In the second phase, the victims were selected and killed indiscriminately in a public place and were thus semi-specific.

The Wagner case was written up in America by Hilde Bruch,[13] based on the many articles by Professor Robert Gaupp, who knew the case from the time of the murders up to the death of the subject some twenty-five years later. Bruch states that between Wagner and Whitman "certain similarities can be recognized: seemingly well-functioning, intelligent, and ambitious men, leading exemplary middle-class lives, had quietly accumulated arsenals of weapons and had made many other arrangements for carefully planned mass murders." We will confine our summary of these two cases to selecting the material that can throw some light on the doer and his victims in mass murders with special reference to collective crimes.

The Wagner Case

Wagner was thirty-nine years old when, in 1913, he killed his wife and four children and afterwards, in a public place, killed eight men and one girl and severely injured twelve other persons. In the year preceding the crime, there was a gradual development of a mental illness ultimately diagnosed as paranoia. Wagner "felt persistently and excessively guilty about masturbation, in which he had indulged since the age of 18," which he considered a deep-seated crime. Through projective mechanisms he began to make "observations" and "hear" remarks pertaining to his "crime." After the mass murder, it became possible to reconstruct the content of his inner life, going back to 1904. "He felt himself continuously observed, mocked, and ridiculed, and lived in constant dread of arrest . . . and therefore he always carried a loaded pistol."

The pre-delictual state, apart from the marked paranoid delusions, presents a melancholic content found in mass murders committed in a melancholic state. "Gradually the conviction ripened that there was only one way out . . . He must kill himself and his children, *out of pity* to save them from a future of being the target of contempt and evil slander . . . Painful as it had been to kill his loved ones, he considered it an act of mercy. In his biography he spoke of himself as 'the angel of pity' . . ." In 1912 he felt he could find no refuge, "the people of Muehlhausen had made it impossible for him to lead a decent life . . . and to gain recognition as a literary figure and great dramatist."

Despite some appearance of similarity, Wagner in fact has little in common with the perpetrators of collective crimes. He saw the townspeople as his personal enemies. In collective crimes, the experience is not personalized, it is group against group. In the racial indoctrination which leads so easily to collective crimes, it is the group as a whole that is bad, not the individual. The bad group is depicted as the enemy of the people, the state, or humanity at large.

In his later years, he no longer felt that it was the townspeople who were plotting against him but that it was the Jews who were interfering with the dissemination of his extensive literary output. Indeed, in the psychiatric hospital to which he had been committed, he became a member of the Nazi party. His delusional anti-semitism had little in common with the widely accepted version that has prevailed for centuries and was on the upsurge in Germany.

The delusional beliefs (in the psychiatric sense) of one man are not a real cause for fear; it is in prejudices collectively shared that the real danger lies. In the latter years of his life, when his delusional system closely corresponded to the spirit of anti-semitism prevailing in Germany, one could nevertheless discern the difference between his delusional anti-semitism and the prevailing group prejudice shared by the population at large. As an individual, he might, with his grandiosity, have had traits in common with the demagogues, tyrants, or dictators, but a person like him, who feels persecuted by the crowd, is at the opposite end of the scale from the demagogue or dictator who is revered by the crowd.

In the Wagner case, we are thus far from the murderous impulses that are mobilized in many individuals at once in time of war, racial tension, or passionate hatreds that divide men into groups that fight each other. Genocides and war crimes can only be committed when group psychology and psychopathology prevail. Our feeling is that people like Wagner can hardly be involved in group psychology as long as they are lost in an overt personal psychopathology that determines and also circumscribes their acts.

The Whitman Case

In an excellent journalistic description of "The Many Faces of Murder,"

Bruce Porter[14] describes at some length the case of Charles Whitman, who, after having killed his mother and his wife, "barricaded himself on the observation deck of the University of Texas tower in Austin and began shooting everyone he could see through the telescopic sight on a high-powered Remington hunting rifle." The final toll was fourteen dead and 31 wounded. Porter reproduced letters and a poem, never before published, "that offer chilling insights into the workings of a mind that could remain lucid and analytical while planning and committing murder."

Not much is known about Whitman other than that he was an architectural student, former altar boy, youngest eagle scout in the history of the Boy Scouts of America, a crack shot in the Marine Corps, and the husband of a beauty queen. A curriculum vitae such as this would not lead one to believe that this upstanding young man would become a multicide and a mass murderer. For the moment, we will speculate on the dynamics based on abstracts from the letters he left which are reproduced in the article.

Prior to killing his mother and his wife, he wrote:

> I don't really understand myself these days. I am supposed to be an
> average, reasonable and intelligent young man. However, lately . . . I
> have been a victim of many unusual and irrational thoughts. These
> thoughts constantly recur . . .

The thoughts to which he referred were murderous impulses. He indicated that he had similar feelings in 1964. In the same letter, commenting about his wife prior to killing her, he wrote:

> It was after much thought that I decided to kill my wife tonight . . .
> I cannot rationally pinpoint any specific reason for doing this . . . the
> prominent reason in my mind is that I truly do not consider this world
> worth living in, and am prepared to die, and I do not want to leave her
> to suffer alone in it. I intend to kill her as painlessly as possible . . .

After he killed his mother, he wrote the following comments:

> I have just taken my mother's life. I am very upset over having done it.
> However, I feel that if there is a heaven she is definitely there now. And
> if there is no life after, I have relieved her of her suffering here on earth.
> The intense hatred I feel for my father is beyond description . . .

For the purpose of this paper, an exact diagnosis of Whitman is not relevant. At the moment, from what is available to us, we are more impressed with the depressive features than the paranoid ones, independently of a diagnosis. From these quotations, we can deduce that his mother and father appeared to him like the good and bad objects that the child has to struggle within the Kleinian schizoid-paranoid position, split objects that he had ultimately to reconcile in the depressive position.

Like a mentally disturbed individual and some criminals, Whitman is very conscious of this internal struggle leading to unbearable anxieties. One can say that in the end he came to feel that the world was bad, and he withdrew from it the objects that he loved, his wife and his mother. He left in the world the bad objects, represented by his father. Paradoxically enough, his desperate ascent to the tower to kill as many people as he could might possibly mean to liberate as many people as he could from the bad world where he himself could not live—symbolically, the world of his father. An opposite interpretation is also possible: that he killed in this world as many figures as he could who stood for his hatred of his father that, in his own words, went "beyond description." Indeed, both interpretations may have played back and forth in his tortured mind.

Whitman illustrates how important are the moods, affects, and drives in the psychopathology lived at the level of Klein's paranoid and depressive positions. The ego defenses are easily overwhelmed, and as to the superego, when one gets to that level one cannot speak of a true superego. The superego that exists in these stages of development is what has been referred to as the archaic superego, a struggle between split objects divided into two camps, good and bad, belonging at one and the same time to the inner world and projected to the outside. To live with an inoperative or barely operative ego and superego is to be at the mercy of one's moods, affects, and drives.

In this case, as in others we have studied, the wish to destroy the world or as many people in it as possible is obviously there. In certain cases, it may even be omnipotently wished for. The fact remains, however, that the psychopathology affects only one individual, although the victims could be numerous. Eventually such pathology is self-limiting as it is brought to an end from without, by intervention or arrest, or even more important, from within through mental collapse or suicide.

Comments

What we desperately need for clinical evaluation of the many thousands of guilty participants in genocide is probably irretrievably lost. They participated with varying degrees of guilt and awareness in the many functions attendant on the unfolding of the Nazi genocide. They came silently out of the ranks of the nation and returned to this anonymity when the deed was done. Now we must seriously question our spontaneous reaction when confronted with such enormity—"insane and criminal." Henry V. Dicks, who interviewed former S.S. troopers some twenty-five years after the event, is conclusive in that respect.[15] He expected to find in these men a criminal propensity that would still be identifiable, but he found the contrary. Neither prior to their involvement in the S.S., nor after the defeat of Germany put an end to this body, could he find in these men the murderous potential of their S.S. period. In only two of the eight cases could he postulate that they might have killed independently of the social climate that prevailed in Nazi Germany.

Dicks does not conclude that the eight men he studied are representative of the many thousands of "manual workers" involved in the concentration camps. However, when one looks at all available sources on the S.S., the evidence is strong that no matter what they became during the regime, a prior history of criminality or mental illness was not part of their background.

To say that prior to their S.S. involvement they were ordinary men and that when involvement ended they returned to their former status is not a facile explanation of their deeds. This statement renders considerably more complex the understanding of what men are capable of in certain psycho-social climates, i.e., mobilizing uncontrolled murderous drives under the cover of what they deem to be rational and reasonable ideology.

Most of the cases we have presented have a long history of behavioral and/or mental pathology. In the commission of their crimes, they were acting out their personal murderous impulses. It was not necessary for them to be involved in an organization that sanctioned such drives. When we state our belief that these men could not have been involved in true, systematic genocidal crimes, this is supported by the fact that their criminal acts were determined by their individual psychopathology, to the point that they stayed apart and lived on the margin of political and social preoccupations. These offenders were not basically interested in victims selected for them by the state, but in ones who fulfilled the needs of their own tragic and murderous psychopathology. None (save for one, in his fantasies) wished to be a member of an "elite" of executioners and murderers.

In studying collective crimes, one has to look at what an ordinary man is capable of rather than looking at the criminal and the insane, who may be better protected against the commission of collective crimes than the ordinary man who, presumably, is psychiatrically and socially healthier. This point is well illustrated in the case histories presented above where we could often elicit either self-limiting or self-defeating factors in their pathology, or fears and anguish over their aggressive impulses and acts (referred to in one of our cases as "healthy symptoms") that seem to be tragically absent in the "manual workers" of the concentration camps.

(We know that after the war started the S.S. supplemented their staff by common-law prisoners who became their trustees and were given a ground where they could enact their psychopathology, but they did not create this ground; they were, so to say, accessories after the fact. Their participation did not substantially change the fate of those the state had selected for extermination.)

We reached the same conclusions as Dicks, that in all likelihood, most of
the S.S. were neither criminal nor insane, he through studying former members
and we by looking at criminals with murderous acting out that could easily be
thought of as an ideal background for becoming mass executioners. The complexity of collective crimes resides in the fact that the group psychopathology
necessary for the commission of such crimes seems to come from the mass of
ordinary people and at the end confronts us with the feeling that it is among
ourselves that we could study this psychopathology rather than pretending
it exists in men who spend an important part of their life within the walls of
prisons or mental hospitals.

Conclusions

We said earlier that any reflection we could make on the recidivist homicides we have selected, even allowing for the genocidal quality of their crimes,
may well lead us to a cul-de-sac. We still feel very much at an impasse, although
not as great as we at first thought. In turning back to the main road, where life
goes on, we will try to reflect on the seemingly unbridgeable gap between
individual and group psychology and/or psychopathology.

In thinking about the suffering around him during the First World War,
Freud stated, "Think of the colossal brutality, cruelty, and mendacity which
is now allowed to spread itself over the civilized world. Do you really believe
that a handful of unprincipled place-hunters and corrupters of men would have
succeeded in letting loose all this latent evil, if the millions of their followers
were not also guilty?"[16]

A similar statement can be made about the brutality, cruelty, and mendacity
of World War II, and especially in reference to the crimes against humanity that
were part of it. Explaining the responsibility for collective crime by the psychopathology of a few leaders is sidestepping the real issue that such crimes would
not have been possible without the active approval of many and the tacit acceptance of many more. Thus, we are back to one of our original assumptions, that
the psychopathology of an individual cannot explain collective crimes. We are
also back to the question of what are the affects, drives, and actions of the groups
that commit such deeds.

It is accepted that the morality of a group is different from that of its individual members. It can be higher or lower, but it is neither the sum total nor an
average, it is a "constant" and "ever-changing" composite. Le Bon did not
elaborate about the quality of the links between members, and it was Freud, in
his study on group psychology and his earlier studies on the primitive hordes
who described the libidinal links that exist between the members of a group and
a leader.[17,18] These links are compared with those that exist between a hypnotist
and his subject, wherein the subject submerges an important part of his personality.

The leader of the group may be perceived as a beloved father who distributes his favors equally among his sons (followers). This group psychology that finds its roots in the libidinal links that leaders and groups share together has contributed an important psychodynamic concept. Nevertheless, we are still very much in the frame of reference of individual psychology and psychopathology. This contribution brought into group psychology and psychopathology libidinized links, affective components, and moods that remain unexplained in Le Bon's theories.[19]

In the analysis of individual criminal psychopathology, much emphasis is placed on the ego; in the final analysis it is the ego which acts. The concept of a collective ego is attractive but it does not lead to such useful concepts as the ego and the mechanism of defense in individual psychology. Like a person, a group has affects, moods, and drives, and it can act. Le Bon selected many examples of group behavior from the French Revolution. It would be a mistake, however, to believe that a group is always ready to follow its leaders blindly or to be drawn into the uncontrolled aggression of one or a few of its members. A group is able to moderate itself although we know little about the collective mechanism of defense. This knowledge may come later when we know more about group affects, moods, feelings, and impulses. For the moment we will limit ourselves to stating that it is our contention that groups are in dangerous pre-delictual states when paranoid and depressive affects prevail in their relationships. These moods, affects, and drives are influenced by the present problems (the here and now) located in the psycho-social historical dimension, the collective unconscious being one of these dimensions. Whereas we have techniques to reach the unconscious of an individual, no such techniques exist to measure the unconscious tempers of an ethnic or a national group.

Freud weighed the pros and cons of the inheritance of memory-traces of our forefathers and he said: "If we accept the continued existence of such memory-traces in our archaic inheritance then we have bridged the gap between individual and mass psychology, and can treat peoples as we do the individual neurotic."[20] The presence of a collective unconscious with its archaic and historical—near or distant—memory-traces is a fascinating concept. I have grave misgivings, however, at the thought of a super-therapist who would have a nation or the world as his patient; he would be as dangerous a figure as the worst dictator or tyrant.

It being our contention that dangerous pre-delictual states occur in the life of a group, as in the life of an individual, a first step would be to recognize such states as we do for individuals and develop techniques to make groups conscious of dangerous signs of impending collective crimes.

Many psychoanalysts hold that wishes, fantasies, and symptoms with death content are secondary formations dealing with vicissitudes encountered within the life instinct. We do not share this view but we recognize that it can be forcefully argued on the basis of the analysis of individual patients, highly different from those mentioned in this paper.

In reassessing all the avenues in group psychology and psychopathology, we find that the death instinct that seems to escape us easily in individual psychology is very much present, almost tangible, in group psychology. In group psychology we seem to be very near to circumscribing the death instinct and how it interplays with the life instinct. The presence of a death instinct might well be the final force behind collective crimes, regardless of who the victim is.

In describing the mental state prevailing during the commission of war crimes, genocide, terrorism in groups seeking their liberation (we have deliberately excluded war itself in order not to digress too far from the title of this paper), men think, feel, and act out collectively with a near absence of ego control. In such a collective state it is our belief that the mental content is similar to the one described in Klein's paranoid and depressive position.[21,22] The knowledge of and the insight into the prodromal signs of such collective regressive states in a group or a nation could, it is hoped, contribute to prevent the odious crimes always eminently possible in such dangerous collective pre-delictual states in which, at the end, we are all involved.

In a subsequent paper, we intend to study the clinical signs of such dangerous collective states. In the meantime, we would like to state now that the Hitlerian type of genocide and the acts of terrorists in the name of liberation of one's group, although both are considered as collective crimes, are determined by different psychopathology; in our view the first finds its roots in the paranoid position, the second in the depressive position.

Future studies on collective crimes must acquaint themselves far more than hitherto with the psycho-social historical forces transmitted from one generation to another but lived quite differently, consciously or unconsciously, by the different generations. Norman Cohn certainly had this historical factor in mind in his study entitled, *Warrant for Genocide.*[23] Lately, Vahakn Dadrian approaches the question of the Armenian genocide in a psycho-sociological historical dimension.[24] This type of study, as well as a return to some of Freud's earlier studies on civilization[25] and retaken lately by Marcuse[26] are new avenues to explore in an attempt to bridge the gap between individual and group psychopathology in the contemporary western world, the civilization with the worst record of collective crimes.

Recent studies pertaining to the subject of collective crime refer to Milgram's studies on obedience.[27,28,29] He was the first to our knowledge to study experimentally what has been referred to as the Eichmann syndrome, i.e., not guilty by reason of obeying orders. To have attempted to prove that such a statement had some foundation in ordinary men is to be considered as most courageous in a field where emotions can easily and understandably prevail. We can only urge the reader to acquaint himself with Milgram's work,[30,31] which Milton Erickson has referred to as a study into "the inhumanity of ordinary people." In our civilization, where so much stress has been laid on obedience, and where it has played an important role in individual and group life, Milgram rightly wonders if our culture provides adequate models for disobedience.

In the process of the socialization of children, we have learned a lot from their obedience to adults. Adults may now have to learn even more from their disobedience.

Notes

1. Bruno M. Cormier, "On the History of Men and Genocide," *Canadian Medical Association Journal* 94 (1966): 276-91; Idem., "De l'histoire des hommes et du génocide," *Annales internationales de criminologie* 8,2 (1969): 247-79.
2. B. Mendelsohn, "Le rapport entre la victimologie et le problème du génocide," *Extrait des Etudes de Psycho-Sociologie Criminelle,* Nos. 16 & 17, 1969.
3. B. Mendelsohn, "Les Infractions commises sous le régime Nazi sont-elles 'des crimes' au sens du droit commun?" *Revue de Droit International* (International Law Review), No. 4, 1965. Published by Antoine Sottile, Geneva.
4. Colin Wilson and Patricia Pitman, *Encyclopaedia of Murder* (London: Pan Books Ltd., 1964).
5. Colin Wilson, *A Casebook of Murder* (London: Mayflower Books, 1971).
6. Colin Wilson, *Order of Assassins – The Psychology of Murder* (London: Rupert Hart-Davis Ltd., 1972).
7. B.M. Cormier, C.C.J. Angliker, R. Boyer, G. Mersereau, and M. Kennedy, "The Psychodynamics of Homicide Committed in a Specific Relationship," *Canadian Journal of Criminology and Corrections* 13, 1, (January 1971).
8. B.M. Cormier, C.C.J. Angliker, R. Boyer, G. Mersereau, and M. Kennedy, "The Psychodynamics of Homicide Committed in a Semi-Specific Relationship," *Canadian Journal of Criminology and Corrections* 14, 4 (October 1972).
9. B.M. Cormier, et al., "The Psychodynamics of Homicide Committed in a Non-specific Relationship." (Unpublished paper).
10. B.M. Cormier, "Violence – Individual and Collective Aspects," *Criminology* 9, 1 (May 1971): 99-116.
11. Bruno M. Cormier, "Depression and Persistent Criminality," *Canadian Psychiatric Association Journal*, Special Supplement, Vol. 2, 1966, pp. S-208-220.
12. Bruno M. Cormier, "Passage aux actes délictueux et états dépressifs," *Acta Psychiatrica Belgica,* 1970, pp. 103-153.
13. Hilde Bruch, "Mass Murder: The Wagner Case," *American Journal of Psychiatry* 124, (1967): 693-98.
14. Bruce Porter, "The Many Faces of Murder," *Playboy,* October 1970.
15. Henry V. Dicks, *Licensed Mass Murder* (A Socio-Psychological Study of Some S.S. Killers) (New York: Basic Books, 1972).
16. Sigmund Freud, *General Introduction to Psychoanalysis* (New York: Garden City Publishing Co. Inc., 1920).

17. Sigmund Freud, *Group Psychology and the Analysis of the Ego*. The Inter-national Psycho-Analytical Library (Ed. Ernest Jones) Fifth Edition (London: The Hogarth Press and the Institute of Psycho-Analysis, 1949).

18. Sigmund Freud, *Totem and Taboo* (New York: Norton, 1952).

19. Gustave Le Bon, *Psychologie des Foules* (Paris: Presses Universitaires de France, 1895).

20. Sigmund Freud, *Moses and Monotheism,* The International Psycho-Analytical Library (Ed. Ernest Jones). No. 33, Third Edition (London: The Hogarth Press and The Institute of Psycho-Analysis, 1951).

21. Melanie Klein, *Contributions to Psycho-Analysis, 1921-1945,* The Inter-national Psycho-Analytical Library (Ed. Ernest Jones), No. 34 (London: The Hogarth Press, Ltd., 1950).

22. Melanie Klein, *Our Adult World* (New York: Basic Books, 1963).

23. Norman Cohn, *Warrant for Genocide* (New York: Harper & Row, Harper Torcl.-Books, 1969).

24. Vahakn Dadrian, "The Structural—Functional Component of Genocide: A Victimological Approach to the Armenian Case," paper presented at the second Interamerican Congress of the American Society of Criminology and the Interamerican Association of Criminology, Caracas, November 1972.

25. Sigmund Freud, *Civilization and Its Discontents,* The International Psycho-Analytical Library, No. 17 Fourth Edition. (London: The Hogarth Press, 1949).

26. Herbert Marcuse, *Eros and Civilization* (Boston: The Beacon Press, 1966).

27. Dicks, *Licensed Mass Murder.*

28. Jerome D. Frank, *Sanity & Survival—Psychological Aspects of War and Peace* (New York: Random House, Vintage Books, 1967).

29. Anthony Storr, *Human Destructiveness,* The Columbus Centre Series (Ed. Norman Cohn) (New York: Basic Books, Inc., 1972).

30. S. Milgram, "Behavioral Study of Obedience," *Journal of Abnormal and Social Psychology* 67, (1963): 371-78.

31. S. Milgram, "Conditions of Obedience and Disobedience to Authority, with Critical Evaluations," *International Journal of Psychiatry* 6, 4 (October 1968).

7

Condoned Mass Deviance and its Victims: A Preliminary Statement

Chanoch Jacobsen

The normative order in complex, industrialized societies, as well as their mechanisms of social control differ in a number of important respects from those that were prevalent in the more traditional, pre-industrial societies. In this paper, I shall not be concerned with the basic trends of institutional change—urbanization, industrialization, and secularization. These have been identified and analyzed by the great classic writers of modern sociology, Marx, Durkheim, Toennies, and Weber, and amply discussed by a number of distinguished contemporary scholars, so they need not detain us here. Instead, I wish to deal with certain specific aspects of the changes that have taken place in the institutionalized means of implementing the normative order and exercising social control, with some of the implications that these changes have for social interaction in modern societies, their functions and dysfunctions, and with the categories of people who may be expected to benefit or fall victim to these developments.

To summarize the gist of much of the social theory and research relevant to these issues, I would say that most of the mechanisms of informal social control implicit in the primary relationships of the extended family, the religious community, and the compact residential neighborhoods which were prevalent in the rural and small-town Gemeinschaft-type of society have been gradually replaced in the modern, secular, Gesellschaft-type of society by more formal mechanisms of social control. But the institutionalized agents of formal social control—schools, police, and other officials—seem to be, by and large, less efficient than might have been expected. This, I believe, is due in large part to the extreme functional differentiation that has taken place among the institutional life-areas, and the concomitant specialization of social control agents within closely circumscribed and formally defined categories of social interaction. A number of significant areas of social behavior, which were at one time controlled by family, religious community or neighbors, are in contemporary urbanized societies beyond the jurisdiction of the formal agents of social control. On the other hand, modern, urbanized man is also more anonymous, and therefore less easily surveilled and informally controlled even by his immediate role-partners. The net result is that man in contemporary mass-society is considerably freer in his day-to-day behavior than he was in earlier periods.

All of this is not new, and has been pointed out before. There is, however, one aspect of the normative order in mass society that has been recognized by only few, and, as far as I have been able to ascertain, analyzed in depth by none. I am referring to what Merton (1957, p. 318) calls the "institutionalized evasion of institutional rules." The phenomenon which Merton describes, citing examples from Williams (1954, pp. 347-66) and others, concerns the amount of leeway within which it is considered acceptable for people to deviate from the norms of their society. This leeway, according to Merton, is unavoidable and indeed necessary in complex social structures. It develops "when practical exigencies confronting the group or collectivity (or significantly large parts of them) require adaptive behavior which is at odds with long-standing norms, sentiments, and practices, or correlatively, when newly-imposed requirements for behavior are at odds with these deep-rooted norms, sentiments, and practices" (Merton 1957, pp. 347-66, and 1961, pp. 729-31).

Examples from our daily life readily come to mind. Take traffic offences, for instance. Road traffic, as Erving Goffman has recently pointed out, "has interesting features: relative uniformity of rules across regional and national boundaries . . . relative explicitness and exhaustiveness of rules accompanied by strict, formal social control; (and) *a widespread sense that it is all right to break a rule if you can get away with it . . .* " (Goffman 1971, p. 27, my emphasis). Institutionalized evasion, then, in this case as in many others, is an adaptive mechanism that enables the social system to maintain its normative order even while permitting widespread deviance from prescribed norms, thus picking up the lag between ever-changing situations calling for social control and the relative rigidity of the formal mechanisms that are meant to implement it.

So far, so good. However, lest we suppose that modern complex societies are moving, under the pressure of the need for functional adaptation, toward a blissful utopia of maximal mutual tolerance and unfettered expression of individual idiosyncrasies, I must point out some of the possible dysfunctions of such a development. These dynsfunctions, I submit, are to be expected at the societal, as well as the individual level of social interaction.

First, let us consider some of the latent implications of the value-orientations that serve to legitimize the pattern evasions. This legitimation, at least in the contemporary industrialized societies of the West, draws heavily on such highly institutionalized, one might almost say hallowed, concepts as tolerance, individual freedom, egalitarianism, and cultural pluralism. But apart from considerations of mutual tolerance and broadmindedness as causes for condoning deviant behavior, there are at least three other broad categories of possible reasons why the evasion of institutionalized rules may become patterned. First, society may be unable to react to the deviance. Second, the agent of social control or the victim of the deviant act may be afraid of possibly adverse consequence; and third, indifference. Nevertheless, whatever the reason for condonation may be in any particular case of deviance, the phenotypical overt behavior of the relevant role-partner is the same: there simply is no reaction. From the point of view of the deviant actor, therefore, it may be, and very frequently is

perceived and interpreted as deliberate tolerance, or at least permissiveness
by default.

Here I should point out what I consider to be a basic conceptual difference
between tolerance and permissiveness. Tolerance has to do with the stretching
and bending of the boundaries of the normative system, which, among other
things, allows for the mutual accommodation of heterogenous subgroups within
a society. As such, it implies a more or less conscious social act, by which
members of a society accord each other the privilege to deviate, within limits,
from the conventional standards of behavior. Permissiveness, on the other hand,
is the social climate that is generated by a widespread absence of reaction to
nonconforming behavior. Partly, to be sure, permissiveness reflects a liberal and
open-minded social attitude, which is positively valued in our prevalent value
system. But a very considerable part is due to either powerlessness, fear, or
indifference—all of which are generally seen as negative values.

There are many instances of deviant or nonconforming behavior in contemporary society in which the witness or even the victim himself lacks the means
to react in a manner that will be perceived by the deviant as a negative sanction.
A shopkeeper may brazenly overcharge us, but, if we need the purchase urgently
or there are no other shops around, we cannot take our business elsewhere. To
be sure, we may protest, but the shopkeeper, as likely as not, will reply: "take
it or leave it." In other words, our protest is not perceived as a negative sanction.
People know this, and therefore very often do not take the trouble to protest.
In another type of situation a person may feel capable of reacting quite effectively, say, by taking pot-shots at people who trespass on his private property,
but he is prevented from doing so by the formal normative system, which will
not permit him to take the law into his own hands. Again, in many cases, the
formal institutions of social control themselves are incapable of taking action.
Thus, when citizens of this country sometimes complain that so many motoring
offenders go unpunished, the police replies that it lacks the manpower and
equipment to patrol every road and intersection. Or, to take yet a different
example, a given law-enforcement agency, having apprehended an offender,
may find that it cannot proceed against him because, due to some circumstantial
formality, this particular case is beyond its jurisdiction. In short, the complexity
and formality of normative systems in modern societies tend to increase the
number of situations in which it is difficult or impracticable to react effectively,
that is, to negatively sanction the infringement of a norm. This, surely, is not
tolerance, but the effect is that of permissiveness.

The failure to react to deviant behavior because of fear of the consequences
is of course very common, and certainly not limited to contemporary society.
Recent, as well as ancient history abounds with examples of behavioral aberrations by the powerful, which were silently accepted by society, not because
people agreed with them, but because they knew only too well what would
happen to them if they protested. Clearly, at least some of the non-reaction to

deviance that is commonly ascribed to broad-mindedness is in fact little else
than plain fear.

A third possible reason, apart from tolerance, for non-reaction to deviant
behavior exists when the potential reactor is indifferent to either the deviant
person or the deviant act, or both. While indifference, too, is not confined to
modern societies, a number of characteristics of modern societies do tend to
encourage it. The general anonymity, and the secondary rather than primary
relationships prevalent in mass-society must result, on the average, in less
emotional involvement of the individual with any given deviant person or
deviant act. Under such circumstances there is less motivation to react, except
in cases where the potential reactor is himself the victim of the deviance. In
addition, there are the established values of egalitarianism and the right to
privacy, which a deviant may turn to his advantage by denying the legitimacy
of the reactor's interference in what he claims is his own business, thus putting
the victim in the position of being labeled a deviant himself. Finally, we should
mention the often monopolistic rights, wielded by formal agencies of social
control, to enforce compliance and punish deviance, rights which are zealously
guarded even when the formal agency itself is incapacitated by lack of resources
or bureaucratic red tape. All of these factors contribute, in some measure,
toward increasing the indifference of individuals in contemporary society to
deviance from the accepted normative pattern.

Although the annoyances and frustrations illustrated by these examples
may be considered too trivial to warrant the ponderous term of dysfunctions,
the frequency of their occurrence, relative to that of deliberate tolerance, broad-
mindedness, and respect for others' privacy, results in that the established
legitimacy of these values spills over, as it were, and sanctions a wide variety of
reasons for not reacting punitively to all kinds of nonconforming behavior.
Recalling now our earlier discussion of the functionality of widespread institutionalized evasion in complex societies, we arrive at the conclusion that what
we are witnessing is not merely an adaptive reaction to the complexities of
modern social systems, but also the gradual institutionalization of permissiveness, per se, as one of the dominant values in our value system.

What, it may be asked, is dysfunctional about that? At the macro-socio-
logical level, it raises the question of what will happen to the social order in
general, as more and more deviations from the normative pattern become
legitimized under the more dominant norm of permissiveness? We need not
go so far as to suppose that society will be overcome by a general state of
anomie. For one thing, some of the most central and basic mores will, presumably, remain and not be overruled by permissiveness. Besides, Goffman (1971)
as well as Garfinkel (1964) have both demonstrated very convincingly that we
regulate and mutually attune a great deal of our behavior quite unconsciously,
and thus maintain some of the public order in spite of our overt permissiveness,
Nevertheless, when the bulk of formal social controls, which are, after all, the

backbone and mainstay of complex social systems, become gradually over-shadowed and rendered ineffective by permissiveness, is it reasonable to expect anything else than social and economic malfunctioning and atrophy, in which none but the more rudimentary kinds of ordered social interaction remain intact?

There is, however, an alternative possibility. It may happen, and perhaps it is even likely, that the social metabolism will overreact before the permissive trend reaches such extremes, and attempt to maintain its coherence and adaptive viability by relinquishing some of the values that give permissiveness its legiti-mation. In plain terms, the possibility does seem to exist that values such as individual freedom, privacy, and mutual tolerance will be sacrificed to the imperatives of law and order.

The first potential victim of condoned mass deviance therefore, as I see it, is society itself. I do not think we have today reliable research evidence which can give us any clear indication of the contingencies under which a social system will either forgo some of its complexity and formality of organization, but maintain its cherished values at all costs—those costs including such things as technological development and economic growth—or, taking the alternative route, maintain its complex formal structure and economic viability while sacrificing some of its central values. Skinner, in a recent and much-debated book (1971), has ventured to come out clearly in favor of the second possibility. Having neither Skinner's temerity nor his academic standing, all I can suggest is that here is a problem which can and should be studied experimentally. For example, research settings such that used by Sherif and his associates in their Robbers Cave Study (Sherif et al. 1954), could, in my opinion, be adapted to put the issue to empirical test.

The second category of which I want to speak consists of not merely poten-tial victims to widespread institutionalized evasion, but of people who, in fact, are already victims now. These are persons who, for one reason or another, cannot exploit the laxity of social controls to their personal advantage. In the fiercely competitive climate of contemporary industrial society, which puts a premium on one-upmanship, such persons are victimized in the sense that the cards are institutionally stacked against them in the general scramble for achieve-ment and social position. They are victims without crimes.

Who are these people that cannot turn a permissive social climate to their advantage, and what could be the reason for their incapacity? Of course, the anxious, inhibited, timid, and socially insecure kind of person will always be less likely than the extroverted, daring, aggressive, and self-assured person to utilize a normative ambiguity and push permissiveness to its current limits. This, I take it, has always been so, and is not peculiar to modern complex societies. But, leaving matters of individual personality aside, I think we may assume that it is those social groups which would in any case tend to noncon-formity, that is, the conventionally defined deviants, that will find the growing permissiveness most rewarding. Replacing, as it does, the more stringent norms and vindictive attitudes that earlier periods displayed towards apprehended deviants, many of today's disadvantaged and marginal people should be in for a break.

But, if this is the case, then the reverse should also be true, namely, that the most conforming social groups will be also the most disadvantaged. Those groups, in other words, which have been socialized most effectively in their time, will be the victims in a society that is both competitive and permissive precisely because of their internalized adherence to the institutionalized normative pattern. In other words, the more successful our educators are today in shaping the personalities of the younger generation in the general mold of our institutionalized normative system, the more victims of permissiveness there are going to be in the future.

In sum, I have been arguing that modern complex societies are becoming, of necessity, progressively more permissive, and that permissiveness is being gradually institutionalized as a dominant value in its own right. This development, which I have interpreted as a basically functional adaptation to increasing structural complexity, carries with it certain latent dysfunctions for the society in general, and for certain categories of people within it. While the social system is going to be faced with the dilemma of having to choose between either losing some of its technological and economic viability or relinquishing some of its cherished values, the individual victims of the permissive society are going to be those who have most effectively internalized the institutionalized norms of their society.

Robert Merton, in an otherwise brilliant essay, asserted that social problems are of two generic kinds: deviant behavior and social disorganization (Merton 1961, p. 719). But what I have been describing here is neither deviant behavior nor social disorganization. Neither the individual nor the social system is malfunctioning: on the contrary, the social problem that I have outlined is a direct outcome of functional adaptation. It is, rather, a latent dysfunctional aspect of complex societies in general, which is gradually becoming manifest: a structural flaw inherent in a certain type of social system. As such, it clearly deserves further analysis and empirical study.

References

Garfinkel, Harold. "Studies in the routine grounds of everyday activities."
    Social Problems 42 (1964): 228-50.
Goffman, Erving. Relations in Public: Microstudies of the Public Order.
    Harmondsworth, Middlesex: Penguin Books, 1971.
Merton, Robert K. Social Theory and Social Structure. Glencoe: The
    Free Press, 1957.

Merton, Robert K. "Social problems and sociological theory." Chapter 15
    in R.K. Merton and R.A. Nisbet (eds.), *Contemporary Social Problems.*
    New York: Harcourt, Brace & World, 1961.
Sherif, Muzafer; O.J. Harvey; B.J. White; W.R. Hood; and C.W. Sherif.
    "Experimental study of positive and negative intergroup attitudes
    between experimentally produced groups: Robbers Cave Study."
    Norman: University of Oklahoma (multilithed), 1954.
Skinner, B.F. *Beyond Freedom and Dignity.* New York: Alfred Knopf, 1971.
Williams, Robin. *American Society.* New York: Alfred Knopf, 1954.

8 The Common Features of the Armenian and Jewish Cases of Genocide: A Comparative Victimological Perspective

Vahakn N. Dadrian

Introductory Note

At a time when the term genocide seems to be enjoying currency as a loosely applied label to stigmatize all kinds of official and unofficial measures initiated by or attributed to dominant groups vis-à-vis subject minorities, the need to define the area of genocide, to delimit its scope, to discern the problem-foci, to devise an appropriate methodology and to conceptualize it is becoming pronounced. Our century witnessed and endured two major holocausts without a significant number of social scientists, particularly sociologists, sensing an urgency to commit themselves to the task of studying it. This is an event which almost defies comprehension. Indeed, the paucity of social scientists engaged in such efforts is a cardinal fact of concern and renders the task both challenging and compelling.

In the aftermath of both holocausts, ample literature has been generated by survivors, participants, witnesses, decisionmakers, accessories as well an official documentary data. Yet, except for the area of survivor research, the bulk of that literature continues to remain unexplored. Eclectic and cursory utilization should not be confused with a systematic approach. In this respect Hilberg's *The Destruction of the European Jews* is a pioneering thrust into the field, even though it is basically descriptive and has a political science framework.

The present paper attempts to revolve around sociological categories. Its analytical bent is not intended to be consequential or exhaustive but rather suggestive by way of outlining the areas for further exploration. Its comparative scheme is meant to assist generalization through dissection and analysis, with the ideal types serving as instruments for that purpose. Finally, its victimological perspective is seen as adding a crucial but hitherto neglected dimension to the study of a problem the cumbersome and elusive nature of which is exceeded only by its macabre character.

I. Definition of Genocide[a]

Genocide is the successful attempt by a dominant group, vested with formal authority and/or with preponderant access to the overall resources of power, to reduce by coercion or lethal violence the number of a minority group whose

---

[a]For a definition of genocide by the UN Convention on Genocide, see Appendix I.

ultimate extermination is held desirable and useful and whose respective vulnerability is a major factor contributing to the decision of genocide.

Genocide therefore requires at least two polar elements, i.e., a perpetrator
and a victim whose conflicting but disparate power relations yield the vulnerability of the victim group in relation to the dominant group, and consequently
may also affect the pattern of genocidal victimization as a way of resolving the
conflict. The degree and kind of disparity in such power relations is therefore
viewed as a potential matrix within which different types of genocide may occur.

II. A Typology of Genocide

The following types are constructed from a victimological perspective in
that they involve submission relationships by subject victim groups vis-à-vis the
coercive power of perpetrator groups. The fact of submission issues from the
corollary fact of vulnerability. Hence genocidal consequences emerge here as a
function of the structural vulnerabilities and availability of the victim and the
response patterns to these by the perpetrator.

1. *Cultural*

Violence may be implied via threats to secure compliance with the wishes
of the dominant group. However, with actual compliance violence becomes
superfluous and thus the resulting behavior is in a Simmelian sense voluntary—
the option for non-compliance not having been exercised. In consequence,
non-violent genocide may ensue. Massive conversions in the religion of the
dominant group, systematic adoption of a large category of offsprings of the
victim group, discriminating practices to promote de-ethnicication, in brief,
the deliberate structuring of pre-emptive assimilation may be involved. Here,
the vulnerability of the subject is considerable as it is precluded from participation in the power structure—having been allowed only some form of
cultural or religious autonomy as a minority group. However two main considerations account for this pattern of victimization.

a.   The victim is not perceived as a source of acute and immediate threat to
     the dominant group, to justify resort to lethal violence.
b.   The victim is viewed as an asset in terms of its collective and individual
     properties and its compulsory assimilation is therefore regarded to be
     beneficial to the dominant group.

2. *Violent-Latent*

Whatever the scope and its intensity, genocide is here a by-product or
result of goals in the persuit of which unintended consequences develop. Military

operations, tactical or strategic in character, may engulf civilian populations. Peacetime relocations or wartime deportations of large segments of a minority group may exact heavy tolls and casualties, depleting the ranks of the affected group. When the dominant group persists in these violent efforts and refrains from obviating the adverse, unintended consequences, such behavior may be termed genocidal. Except for cases where the label "deportation" is misused to deflect from the actual goal of deliberate genocide, this type of genocide is subservient to the single objective of collective self-assertiveness in an emerging power confrontation which may attend an armed collision. Perpetrator and victim may not share the same social system and may in fact be part of different social systems in which they both may be dominant groups. Or, they may share the same social system as dominant and minority groups. In any case, the vulnerability of the victim group is operative in a dual sense. In order to prevail in the conflict, the perpetrator expends considerable effort on a secondary level of vulnerability by making the power base of the victim a target. Instead of or in addition to tackling the armed forces of the opponent or the secessionist or militant revolutionary parties of a minority, the perpetrator seeks to destroy or emasculate the manpower resources of these groups as a means of winning the contest. It is therefore important to differentiate between the primary vulnerability of the actual bearers of conflict and the secondary level of vulnerability of their bases of operation. In the same vein, it becomes necessary to differentiate between actual access to the resources of power in a social system or in a constellation of forces on the one hand, and potential access to such resources on the other.

3. Retributive

Genocide here is limited in scope insofar as the objective is confined to localized atrocities as a form of meting out punishment to a segment of the minority, challenging or threatening the dominant group. A concomitant function is to warn and/or intimidate potential challenges and deter the recurrence or spread of trouble. The scale of victimization is limited by the relatively low degree of vulnerability of the victim, which may have access to power in areas other than the target area, by the perception of a low degree of threat felt by the dominant group, and concomitantly, a low degree of mobilization of resources to carry out retribution, which under certain circumstances may be a covert form of utilitarian genocide. In fact local authorities on their own volition, or with the facit consent of central authorities, may initiate or allow pogroms. This type may also serve as an effort to test the kind of range of response on the part of the victim group and as a measure to extrapolate future schemes of more encompassing forms of genocide—in terms of contingencies.

4. *Utilitarian*

Genocide here is limited in scope because of such limited objectives as economic advantages, demographic considerations, military designs etc. It involves regional massacres en masse, segmental cross-country massacres, or limiting massacres to such categories as sex, age, religion, etc. The character of objectives is matched by the limited capabilities of the perpetrator vis-à-vis a resistant prone victim, whose vulnerability is further reduced by internal dissension besetting the perpetrator group. Predominantly exploitative designs of genocide imply a social system where calculative gains overshadow the penchant for atrocity and radial destructiveness. In such systems, a minority may or may not share significantly in the power structure, but it can count on effective sympatherizers and allies within the ranks of the perpetrator group. Mainly because of this, local authorities may also decide to resort to quick actions of atrocity, thus eliminating the need for consensus, persuasion, and legitimation.

5. *Optimal*

The destruction process here is massive, relatively indiscriminate in terms of victims' age, sex, and other categories, is sustained in duration, and aims at the total obliteration of the victim group. Consequently, the scale of casualties is maximum and victimization is optimal. This process is afforded by a unique combination of three conditions: (a) the highest degree of vulnerability of the victim, (b) the perpetrators' attendant perception of the victim as a source of acute, immediate, and perilous danger, and (c) maximum concentration of power in the hands of the perpetrator. Only unusual circumstances can render such a combination possible; they may involve national crises and/or international conflagrations. It is no accident, for example, that the two cases of optimal genocide of this century, the Armenian and Jewish, occurred during two global wars, i.e., World Wars I and II. In both instances, wartime emergency measures enabled monolithic political parties to consolidate and maximize their power at the same time emasculating their potential victims. Oligarchic leadership led to a totalitarian system in which the heightened vulnerability of any target group easily becomes a dependent variable of the maximized capabilities of the perpetrator group as an independent variable.

III. The Areas of Application of the Typology
     to the Two Cases at Hand

Among the many characteristics which the Armenians and the Jews share

as chronic victims of genocide is the fact of recurrence of various types of genocide in their respective histories. Indeed, before their experience of holocaust
during the two global wars of this century, both peoples historically were subjected to many of the types of genocide outlined in the preceding discussion.
In this sense, it may be argued that the optimal genocide they had to endure was
the culmination of an accumulative process of victimization.

Is there any relationship between these two sets of factors? In other words,
can the experience of successive massacres in the historical continuum enhance
the possibilities of recurrence and amplification of that experience? Such a
relationship may be afforded if there is no significant change in the overall
status of the surviving victim group and, concomitantly, if there is no accounting
and retribution as far as the perpetrator is concerned. In brief, yes, if the disparity
of power relations is sustained—to the continuing disadvantage of the victim
group—thus rendering the latters vulnerability a constant and a dependent variable
in the constellation of antagonistic forces which may be forming around subsequent intergroup conflicts.

Aside from the principle of sheer force ratios as a determinant of power
relations, however, there is an important social-psychological element calling
for depiction. When a minority is constantly persecuted and decimated under
given circumstances, certain images crystallize themselves around that minority
that have far-reaching consequences for the fate of that minority. For one thing,
dominant groups tend to view such a group as a convenient target for discharging
hostilities, for scapegoating, and for overall exploitation. In the process, the victim
becomes degraded and stereotyped.

A more important consequence refers to the development on the part of the
victim minority of self-conceptions which to a considerable extent tend to reflect
these stereotypes. The duality of this process of negative image formation is
highlighted by the fact that the two levels of imagery are attuned to each other.
At the extreme or ideal form of such duality, a potential perpetrator may be
tempted or emboldened to take a potential victim for granted, which in turn may
anticipate eventual perpetration as a matter of course. This coercion-submission
syndrome may, after a certain historical period, transcend the social-psychological
quality of its formation and may assume cultural dimensions. The victim group
particularly may develop traits and characteristics which render that syndrome
functional—in the absence of other alternatives. Thus, vulnerability acquires a
cultural as well as a power ratio quality. This is a victimological principle of
first magnitude. Its proper appraisal can shed much light upon the important
area of victim response patterns to past and future perpetration schemes. Such
patterns in turn tend to condition the shape and course of actual perpetration.

In the present case, the Armenian and Jewish responses to the coercion-
submission syndrome evince certain common features in need of singling out.
These features may be subsumed under the category of an ethos for cultural
distinction. Having been denied access to power and placed in a subordinate or

subservient position in their respective social systems, both peoples felt impelled to give vent to their collective urge of self-importance. This urge eventually became inveterate in the face of ongoing persecutions. They consequently stressed and cultivated a sense of historical antiquity and a corollary sense of religious distinction, the Armenians referring to the fact that they were the first nation to embrace Christianity as a state religion (about the turn of the fourth century), and the Jews to their special and unique relationship to God. The net result of this attitude was the historical crystallization of a minority ethnocentrism which adapted itself to the exigencies imposed by dominant groups but, given certain conditions of crisis in intergroup relations, almost always proved a suitable excuse for violent reactions on the part of dominant groups counterposed to them.

In terms of modern history, the Armenians brought this attitude to bear upon the Ottoman Turks, whom they felt they antedated in two respects: (a) historical birth, formation, and cultural heritage, and (b) territorial indignity—Turks being considered alien intruders, originating from the steppes of Central Asia, their historical birthplace. In the same vein, the Jews confronted various sets of dominant groups, with the only difference that the confrontation occurred in the Diaspora in which they were viewed as immigrants rather than part of the native population—as far as ethnicity was concerned. A chief by-product of such differential attitudes was, from the point of view of the victim, the eventual growth of resistance to total assimilation in the ranks of the dominant group and from the point of view of the perpetrator, the allied perpetuation of the heterogeneity of the social system. A standard response by the dominant group bent, among other things, on homogeneity, was the resort to the type of genocide termed cultural in this discussion.

Throughout history, Armenians and Jews have been inexorably subjected to this kind of attrition. Religion being a key issue, for four centuries (sixteenth to twentieth) periodic massive conversions to Islam within the Ottoman Empire significantly depleted the ranks of the Armenian people; they often involved the wholesale absorption of villages of the various regions of Anatolia and Eastern Armenia.

As to the Jews, the two areas where such compulsory assimilations were notable, are indicative of the trend of converting a heterogeneous society into a homogeneous one on the part of dominant groups involved. The Spanish Inquisition represents one such episode; it extended from Manila to Lima and to Sicily, covering the entire Spanish Empire and spanning 300 years of Spanish history. On March 31, 1492 Ferdinand and Isabella decreed the expulsion of all Jews from Spain. Already in the thirteenth century, there were forced mass conversions of the Jews in Spain. One principal reason was the desirability of keeping them in the mainstream of society, as the Jews, unlike other minorities, were considered by the dominant group to be an integral part of Spanish culture and history (as the Armenians were regarded by most Ottoman Turks). Thus, compelled to accept baptism, *conversos* came into existence on a large scale and the Inquisition, established by papal decree in 1478, was to probe the genuineness of such conversions. The manner of the probe resulted in an even greater number of conversions attended by hidden ethnocentrism that was fostered by separate ghetto life.[1]

The Jewish experience of assimilation in Russia was also preceded by occasional pogroms and mass exodus but was less compulsory or institutionalized, compared to the episode of Spanish Inquisition. Long before the advent of the Soviet regime in Russia, Lenin in a sense epitomized the attitude of the Russian dominant group, when he reacted to Jewish efforts of organizing themselves in a *Bund* in order to deal with rampant anti-Semitism in Tzarist Russia and parts of Eastern Europe. These involved Jewish workers from Lithuania, Poland, and Russia, whose response patterns were branded by Lenin as "infantile," "foolish and comical rage" etc. He finally blasted these ethocentric efforts with an exhortation: "the Jewish problem amounts to: assimilation or isolation," only to continue: they must "cease to be alien and blend with the general mass of the population. That is the only possible solution of the Jewish problem."[2] It is revealing to note that when advancing more or less identical arguments in a rather thorough analysis of the nationality question in 1913, A.C. Miassnigian, "The Lenin of the Caucasus," a close associate of Lenin and an Armenian, capable of sensing the ordeals of persecution, displayed compassion for the plight of the Jews and tried to make allowances for their ethnic endeavor.[b]

The second type of genocide termed violent-latent, has practically no application to either Armenian or the Jewish case. The sustained vulnerability and availability of both subject groups throughout history helped make them ideal targets for the other types, thus rendering latency superfluous and non-violence unnecessary in their treatment by dominant groups. As to the types numbered 3 and 4, i.e., retributive and utilitarian, both are seen as having ample application for both groups. They operated interchangeably, became precursors of optimal genocide, and occasionally retributive genocide was enacted to deflect from the hidden end of utilitarian genocide. Most anti-Jewish pogroms in Russia, and the massacres of 1895-96 by Sultan Hamid and that of 1909 in Adana, Turkey, are illustrative of retributive types as being central, and utilitarian types as being incidental to the motivation of perpetrators. Addressing this problem, a student of the Spanish Inquisition goes so far to claim that punitive measures were acquisitive motives in disguise. "Facts prove beyond a doubt, that the

---

[b]" . . . the Jews represent among us an element suffering from legal disabilities and inequities. They are for a long time bearing the painful yoke of persecution. There is no corner on earth where one can not hear their cries; there is no fist which might not be directed to their face. The persecutions of the Jews constitute an endless martyrdom, an eloquent and tortuous martyrdom. I wonder if any other race could survive all the obstacles and agonies to which the generation of Israel has been subjected and still is being subjected."[3]

extirpation of Judaism was not the real cause, but the mere pretext, for the establishment of the Inquisition by Ferdinand. The true motive was to carry on a vigorous system of confiscation against the Jews, and so to bring their riches into the hands of the government."[4]

The burden of this discussion on the applicability of the typology is to indicate a historical pattern of victimization in which vulnerability plays a key role. That role becomes even more pronounced when a succession of genocidal acts are seen remaining unchallenged before, during or after the enactments, thus allowing the principle of vulnerability to compound itself historically and in a sense paving the ground for the near ultimate form of genocide, namely, the optimal.

IV. A Sketch of the Outstanding Common Features of the Armenian and Jewish Cases

This sketch is suggestive in terms of specific areas which constitute problem-foci and which may lend themselves to the task of conseptualization. In this respect, the following areas are discerned for further concentration.

1.   Primary Importance Common Features.

    a.   Both acts of genocide were designed and executed during the exigencies of so-called global wars, or world wars.

    b.   In both instances, the principal instruments for the conception, design, and execution of the holocausts were political parties (Young Turks and Nazis) who invested themselves with monolithic power and literally took over the functions of their respective states.

2.   Secondary Importance Common Features.

    a.   The war ministries, and the selected organs and outfits of the affiliated military structures, were subverted and utilized for the manifold purposes of genocide.

    b.   Economic considerations involving official as well as some personal designs of enrichment at the expense of the relatively better off members of the victim group, played a key role.

    c.   In both instances, the victims groups were minorities whose overall vulnerability was matched by the degree of ease with which the dominant groups implemented their schemes of extermination.

3.   Tertiary Importance Common Features.

    a.   Cultural and religious, and in a sense racial, differences separated the

victim groups from the perpetrator groups—notwithstanding the incidence of certain patterns of assimilation and even amalgamation
through which multitudes from both groups were, and felt, identified
with one another. Indeed, many Ottoman Armenians and German
Jews felt politically and socially, if not culturally, identified with
the respective dominant groups.

b. The crucial role of bureaucratic machinery in the administration and
supervision of genocidal violence.

c. Sanctions, both negative and positive, were the operationally controlling factor in both cases through which military and civilian personnel,
from the highest to the lowest echelons of the administrative set-up,
were demoted or promoted, punished or rewarded, threatened or
cajoled on the basis of their attitudes and performances vis-à-vis the
processes of genocide.

V. The Structural Determinants in Both Cases of Genocide

A central element of this paper discussed so far is the notion of power, the
unequal distribution of which within a heterogeneous social system allows for
domination and for its by-product, i.e., a superordinate group in that system on
the one hand, and one or more subordinate groups on the other.

The relationships between these two principal categories of groups are reflec-
tive of their statuses in the configuration of power. With status persistence, the
relationships remain established and patterned. The patterning develops from the
rise of mutual expectations, which in turn affect mutual responses. In brief,
there is an element of attunement of behavior in the interaction of the respective
groups which flows from the fact of mutual expectations. To the extent that such
expectations are widespread and stable in the attendant relationships, to that
extent the social system may be regarded as structured. To the extent that these
expectations are taken for granted by the respective groups, the structure may
be viewed as functional. In terms of its relevance to a study of genocide, the
above postulate suggests that a given social structure in a sense facilitates and,
under certain circumstances, preempts the mutually attuned roles of perpetrator
and victim.

These roles are best highlighted in the coercion-submission dichotomy. In
pursuing victimology, this structural problem warrants major consideration.
Indeed, when closely examined, the handling of power by a dominant group
reveals structural dimensions which further illuminate the underlying processes
of genocide and, as far as the ultimate form of a given social system is concerned,
the functional character of genocide.

It is understood that power has a twofold utility. When it is confined to latency, its usefulness is exercised in terms of threats and threats of sanctions. This may result in coercion on the part of a dominant group, and may set the pattern of a compliance relationship on the part of a subject group placed in a submissive position vis-à-vis the dominant group. By grasping the structural properties of heterogeneous system, one may locate the origin and flow of power and its purposive handling by a potential perpetrator group. As Bierstedt pointed out, the sources of power involve (a) numbers of people, (b) resources, and (c) social organization.[5]

In this constellation, the manner of social organization is of overriding import. The resources can be rendered subservient to the projected and specified goals of that organization. Etzioni's typology with reference to coercive organizations harboring a corresponding bureaucracy illustrates the point.[6] The fact is that such organizations imposed by dominant groups end up institutionalizing the goals of the dominant group, thereby also converting power into legitimate authority. Legitimacy in this sense is perhaps the most important structural element that bears upon the submissive response patterns of a subject minority; it may serve to convert such subject groups into potential victims.

In the comparative perspective of the Armenian and Jewish cases of genocide, the most salient feature seems to be this coercive aspect of institutionalized power exerting itself in the form of compelling and arbitrary authority. The rationale in the conception and design of both genocides seems to be anchored in the sense of legitimacy flowing from such authority. The values underlying this sense of legitimacy are intimately linked with the intoxicating spell of power that has a distinct organizational quality and is therefore structural in character. The norms that regulate the handling or the manipulation of that power are likewise organizational in their arrangement and enforcement. In the phase of implementation of the genocidal designs, the organizing principle extends to the task of mobilizing available and improvised resources required. One may even argue that the task of enabling the participants in atrocities to rationalize and justify "guilt-free massacres" involves organization of a particular kind. The dominant group can ill afford to neglect, for example, the necessity of properly and securely motivating its members, at least those actively involved in the tasks of extermination, for the various aspects of the enactment of genocide.

In the Armenian case, the structural disabilities were preempted by the Ottoman Turks the moment they conquered Constantinople in 1452 and became the undisputed and sustained dominant group in their extensive and heterogeneous empire. Status deficiencies were effected by two correlative principles: (1) The theocratic values of Islam and (2) The oriental norms of conquest which tended to divide a society into the two absolute categories of victor and vanquished.[7] For centuries, legal rights, interracial social intercourse, partipation in the mainstream of national and political life, and culture contacts were all dismissed with contempt—as far as the non-Muslim minorities were concerned. The resulting segregation, the principle of unpredictable toleration, with all attendant practices of discrimination, prejudice, disdain, economic exploitation, involving mainly excessive and at times unbearable taxations, and confiscations, combined to emasculate the Armenians as a minority and helped usher in a latent ethnicity which was further reinforced by the denial of structural opportunities to assimilate or to amalgamate with the dominant group. The emerging patterns of social organization created an enormous and durable cleavage in power postures, at the same time producing dangerous zones of friction of intergroup conflict. Thus the vulnerability of a minority became institutionalized within the social structure of Ottoman society.

In the case of the Jews, the fact of vulnerability has manifold aspects which antedate the Nazi regime, transcend the boundaries of Germany and Europe, and embrace the excesses of Christianity and Islam. The fact of status deficiency is a legacy which is as diffuse in space as it is recurrent in time.

Speaking of Nazi Germany, it is difficult to disregard episodes and attitudes which form a historical body of tradition favoring anti-Semitism in Germany, including the verbal onslaughts of Luther. Yet, in spite of pockets of ghettos which came into being and in a sense became a necessity for multitudes of Jews, the absence of continuous and categorical policies of exclusion from the mainstream of German national life entailed a process of conditional assimilation through which a considerable portion of German Jewry throughout modern history became entwined with German nationhood. The retorts of assimilationist as well as Zionist publications in Germany during the turbulences of 1933, are eloquent confirmations in this regard. *The Central-Verein Zeitung,* for example, proclaimed the Jewish pathos for Germany in an editorial by repeating Goethe's famous line: "If I love you, what business is it of yours?" To which the Zionist *Yüdische Rundschau* replied: "If I love you, then it *is* your business," adding, "The German people should know: a historical alliance, hundreds of years old, cannot be severed so simply."[8]

To further confirm this point, Hilberg, the noted author of *The Destruction of the European Jews,* contends that: "In 1933, the Jews were almost completely integrated into the German community."[9]

The systematic demise of the Jews coincided with the restructuring of that German community through National Socialism. Whereas the Young Turks had merely to rearrange the Ottoman social system to achieve their goals, the Nazi had to institute radical new schemes for the same purpose. The inception of these schemes may be traced to the initial NSDAP party program of February 24, 1920 in which a racist doctrine proclaimed that: "No Jew may therefore be a member of the [German] community." This act of exclusion was institutionalized in a dramatic way when, on April 7, 1933, a decree provided that Jewish ("non-Aryan") officials were to be retired, and in September 1941 a decree compelled the Jews to wear a yellow star. In between, boycotts, anti-Jewish propaganda, and violent outbursts culminating in the massive riots of November

1938, helped prepare the ground for the holocaust. The institutionalization of power involved the purposive reorganization of the civil service branch of bureaucracy, the armed forces, industry, and the party, resulting in stages of emasculating the Jews. The coercive apparatus, initiated through the Enabling Act on March 20, 1933, proclaimed first supreme values, with norms to regulate their incorporation in German institutional life, only to proceed later with the economic-utilitarian phase—as a prelude to isolation and ultimate victimization of the target victim.

In analyzing the adverse reactions of the top Nazi leaders to the sporadic hostile outbursts against the Jews, one discerns a common thread of aversion against unorganized elementary forms of collective behavior. As Hilberg relates, except for Propaganda Minister Goebbels, nearly all of them were opposed to the idea. Instead, they wanted a systematic approach to the problem through which division of labor, legitimacy, legality, task orientedness, and above all efficiency could be mustered.[10] The institution of concentration camps and the related destructive process were the culmination of this approach, which helped to isolate, intimidate, impair, and eventually incapacitate the victim group. Maximum organization of power and auxiliary resources coincided with the effected maximum vulnerability of that group yielding optimum destructive results.

The status of vulnerability and the correlative roles played by the Armenians and Jews throughout their histories entailed consequences for them which need to be stressed once more. Over a period of time the social-psychological character of such submissive role playing became so regularized that it acquired a quality of constancy. Both peoples came to take such role playing eventually for granted—as their way of adapting to and surviving conflicts. Hence, submissiveness crystallized itself as a cultural pattern for both peoples.

In the Armenian case, this trait immensely facilitated the swift execution of genocide. Notwithstanding the rise and operation of a few revolutionary parties bent on contesting the dominant Ottoman Turks, the overwhelming majority of the Armenians in the Empire, led by their clerical and business leaders, favored accommodating and placating their potential executioners in the hope that such a course of action may reduce the rate of casualties—should worse come to worse.

In the Jewish case, a similar, if not identical, pattern obtains. As Hilberg consistently argues: "Preventive attack, armed resistance and revenge are almost completely absent in 2000 years of Jewish ghetto history. Instances of violent opposition . . . are atypical and episodic. The critical period of the 1930's and 1940's is marked by that same absence of physical opposition."[11] He concludes, stating that "The reaction pattern of the Jews is characterized by almost complete lack of resistance."[12]

The understanding of the optimal character of the two holocausts, and the degree of their successes, requires key consideration for the argument stated above, which touches the very core of victimology as a tool of analyzing genocide.

VI. The Symbolic Interactionist Perspective

Historic evidence, involving the two cases of genocide under discussion, highlights the incidence of social-psychological processes by virtue of which a host of interpretations, "definitions of the situation,"[13] and "dynamic assessments"[14] are indulged in before judgments are reached and corresponding actions are constructed, by *both perpetrators and victims.* The generating and attaching of meanings to the selected features of given situations on the conflict, the mental assumption of the roles of the other group, the consideration of alternatives, the weighing of suitability, risk, and consequence, etc., are all part of a deliberate process which precedes and attends the enactment of genocide. In practical terms, this condition means attribution to the victim by the perpetrator of dangerous, hostile intentions; the designation of the victim, for example, as a serious national threat and/or as a "vermin"; a determination of the need for a drastic punishment; the detailing of procedures to be followed for the enactment; and the official defense of the act, or its concealment, or its deflection. For the victim, involved are the anticipation of worse punishments, a desire to avoid them, reckoning with possibilities of mercy or relenting from the antagonist, realization of powerlessness, and consequent surrender to the course of events preempted by the perpetrator, etc.

In brief, the opposing groups invest and guide their interactional patterns with certain symbols, with a measure of significance in terms of chances of outcome, intent, and consequences. The resort to mass violence on the one hand and the overall response to it on the other are by-products of deliberations and judgments which attend the evolving processes of hostile interaction. Both the perception of the conflict and the singling out of the alternatives to resolve it, are a distinct category of behavior involving evaluations and, hence, the generating and assignment of symbols to the act and the conditions surrounding the act which is being contemplated. This is the general sense of symbolic interaction used here.

In a more specific sense, however, symbolic interactionism places a high premium on meanings as a central element, a nexus so to speak, which interconnects the actions and responses of actors involved in interaction, and which provides for the attunement, the fitting together, of the actions and responses in question. Its key value stems from its emergent, rather than stable and fixed, quality.

When applied to the relationships between a dominant group and a subject minority, the truism needs to be repeated that such relationships, like most other relationships, involve an ongoing process. Even in most structured social systems there is a flow of activity which becomes shaped as it evolves and as such possesses a certain degree of autonomy, a sort of self-regulatory mechanism, which tends to overshadow such structural determinants as social position, status, role, authority, power, etc., in the final product of social behavior. The patterns of interaction

are endowed with elements of a dynamism that transcends in import institutionalized social arrangements, cultural values, and norms. The same argument
may be advanced with respect to psychological categories such as feelings,
memories, needs, impulses, perceptions, motives, and overall attitudes. All
these suggest that meaning-oriented behavior is dictated or mainly conditioned
by the automatic release or application of these psychic urges, the independently preexistent character of which is presumed or is taken for granted.

As Blumer cogently pointed out, however, the meaning which other
people (be they friends or foes), institutions, ideals, expectations of others,
and situations have for a given actor "grows out of the ways in which other
persons act toward the person" with regard to the categories mentioned above
in connection with describing meaning.[16] Thus meanings are evolving social
products which condition and are conditioned by an attendant process of interaction, and determined by a defining activity that accompanies the interaction.
In other words, the generating of meanings as the basis of action and response
patterns involves an interpretative process in which, for example, a perpetrator,
a victim, the act of perpetration, the conditions of victimization, and the overall circumstances surrounding the enactment of genocide configure.

In this complex and somewhat elusive process, both perpetrator and
victim discern elements of the configuration to which they are gravitated as
calling for meaning-assignment. This gravitation is a form of self-sensitizing.
The actor indicates to himself that, for which he has to assign a meaning. In
this stage of self-interaction, the actor holds a dialogue with himself by commun-
icating internally with himself. In doing so, he enters the most crucial stage of
symbolic interaction through which he indulges in manipulatory proneness.
With polarized attention, "The actor selects, suspends, regroups and transforms
the meanings in the light of the situation in which he is placed and the direction
of his action."[17]

The significance of this fact is that perpetrator and victim do not mechan-
ically adopt and apply the meanings they discern in interaction. Rather, they
"handle" these meanings in a manner which is geared to the most suitable course
of action in an evolving interactional engagement; in the process, the meanings
are manipulated in terms of their situational utility and always in terms of taking
the other party of interaction into account. For instance, before making a final
judgment, conducive to decision-making, a perpetrator may try to imagine
the possible response patterns of a potential victim.

The particular relevance of this aspect of theory to the two cases of genocide
is embedded in two mechanisms of meaning handling in the interactive processes
of the perpetrators and victims involved: (1) The defining of the potential victim
as an acute source of peril, arising out of a sense of threat, and (2) The decision-
making regarding the perpetration of genocide.

Earlier, the factor of victim vulnerability was singled out as an arch determinant. But, one should realize that throughout history heterogeneous social

systems existed in which a dominant group faced a host of highly vulnerable minorities with whom conflicts were dealt with by means other than genocide. Likewise, in a given heterogeneous system in which genocide became instrumental, often there were several minorities with various degrees of vulnerabilities. The Third Reich and the Ottoman Empire fall under this category. The question which poses itself here is: why and how is a particular minority selected for victimization?

It is suggested that the selection and targeting of a particular victim requires more than a condition of vulnerability. Its logical and empirical corollary is the defining of the victim as a source of threat—a definition which has its roots primarily in the evolving interactions with the victim group. Historical precedents, cultural traditions, and structural potentialities are seen here merely as auxiliary factors. In the Armenian and Jewish cases, a unique combination of *vulnerability* and *definability* is seen as a factor which helped induce the respective perpetrators to consider radical measures as a response pattern. The awareness of historical antecedents of victimization of both peoples served to reinforce the criteria of selection and targeting.

VII. Some Aspects of Application of the Symbolic Interactionist Perspective

In the definitional exercises of the young Turks, the Armenians were labeled first and foremost as traitors of the Empire. Not only were they associated with secessionist designs, but they were also branded as saboteurs of the Turkish war effort. The meanings allied with such interpretations were not the result of abstract considerations but emerged in the course of the Turks' dealings with Armenian political leaders. The "handling" of such meanings was linked with their experience of an Armenian reform movement seeking to redress centuries–old abuses inflicted upon them, and to achieve a limited autonomy within the confines of the Empire. The interventions of European powers, the latter's record of assisting other Christian subject groups seeking emancipation from Ottoman yoke, Turkish internal upheavals, and military setbacks in two Balkan wars preceding World War I were all events that sensitized the dominant group toward particular channels of definition.

In the process, the manifold contributions of the Armenians to the Empire, the large number of Armenian casualties, and instances of intrepidity on their part in the Balkan wars and even in the rudimentary phases of World War I, were disregarded. Above all, the sustained and massive suffering of the large part of Armenian community (essentially agricultural) in the provinces at the hands of marauding Kurds, cruel administrators, and religious fanatics was ignored with remarkable selectivity in interpretation and manipulations of meanings. It seems that when a powerful group becomes frustrated for a variety of reasons, the awareness of such power vis-à-vis a vulnerable group, which may be only indirectly and tenuously associated with such frustrations, serves to charge the interaction with such a group with special meaning.

Images are called forth which lock attention on certain points and bar sensitivity to others. To be sure the awareness of the vulnerability of the subject group plays a key role in the type of images being called forth. Not the principle of relevance but that of suitability, not objectivity but subjective expediency govern the formation of such images. *But throughout this process, the targeted victim remains a conditioner of the end product of the actions and responses of the perpetrator—in terms of its interactive involvement.*

The exigencies of World War I, during which few Armenians were caught in acts of espionage, desertion, and sabotage, and the role of Armenian volunteer corps serving against the Turks as advance units in the Russian army, heightened the ire of the dominant group suffering major military setbacks and acute economic hardships. The central meaning that emerged in the mind of the perpetrator group related to a symbol of threat, amplified by wartime crisis, and attended by an urge for drastic measures, for purposes both of impulsive punishment and functional eradication. The assurances, conjurations of loyalty, supplications, and large-scale actual sacrifices for the Turks and Turkey at the outset of World War I marshalled by the leaders of the Armenian community was their anticipatory response to Turkish designs for radical measures. As such, they constituted elements of interaction, which were then interpreted by the Turkish authorities in terms of their significance for a felt resolution of the problem. That pattern of interpretation sensed and locked in the probable compliance rather than resistance posture of the Armenians. Implied in this statement is the hypothesis that had the Armenians organized themselves against such an eventuality and in concerted actions defied and dared the authorities, the Turkish definitional and interpretative patterns might have followed a different course—possibly one of caution and circumspection.

As far as the Jews were concerned, their vulnerability too invited and facilitated suitable definitions conducive to radical measures of extermination. Even though gypsies and Poles were also target victims of genocide by the Nazis, the selection of the Jews as a major target stands out. In arguing that this choice was not "accidental," Hilberg maintains that: "No other group could fill this role so well. None was so vulnerable."[18] But, the multifarious phases of Nazi versus Jewish interactions applied the actual dynamism of hostility. Its rudimentary stages may be traced to Jewish reactions of the 1920 Nazi party program, which was attacked by the "Jewish press" against which the party had "fought back."

In this exchange, "many a harsh word" had been said against the Jews, but according to Göring, the Jews had produced the greater volume of invective.[19] The resulting sequence of interaction encompasses a web of events covering pogroms, boycotts, hostile press, and diplomatic exchanges within and without Germany through which anti-semitism and anti-Germanism crystallized themselves as two polar channels of intergroup conflict. In *Mein Kampf* Hitler produces autobiographical data revealing the impact of youthful deprivations and other adverse experiences in relation to the Jews in Austria as a source of his anti-semitism.[20] His extreme sensitivity towards ridicule and hostility is further evinced in his September 30, 1942 Reichstag speech in which he recalled how the Jews of Germany "laughed about my prophecies. I do not know whether they are still laughing or whether they have already lost all desire to laugh. But right now I can only repeat: they will stop laughing everywhere, and I shall be right also in that prophecy."[21] The definitional climax of these altercations and excesses was reached on September 1, 1939 when Hitler, in a major speech in the Reichstag accounting for the outbreak of the war, attributed to the Jews the desire "to exterminate the Aryan peoples of Europe . . ."[22] Coincidental with the former decision of genocide, Himmler is reported to have remarked in the summer of 1941 that if the decision "is not carried out now, then the Jews will later on destroy the German people."[23] After the destruction was set in motion and at a time when it was in full gear, i.e., in October 1943, Himmler reiterated this view: "We had the moral right vis-à-vis *our* people to annihilate *this* people which wanted to annihilate us."[24]

The symbolic interactionism endemic to *decision-making processes* revolves more or less around similar patterns of defining, interpreting, meaning distillation, and manipulation. Alone, there are two additional elements to be considered. One refers to the ultimate in symbolism, namely, when meaning handling is accomplished, a judgment is made which then serves as the basis of appropriate actions and responses. Until such judgments, all interpretations have a deliberative quality of assessment, for which reason action is suspended, or deferred. The other element points to the vast array of opportunities which a global war for a potential perpetrator affords.

In his diaries, Goebbels contended, "If we did not fight the Jews, they would destroy us. It's a life-and-death struggle between the Aryan race and the Jewish bacillus . . . Fortunately a whole series of possibilities presents itself for us in wartime that would be denied us in peacetime. We shalle have to profit by this."[25] Hilsberg concurs with this latter point maintaining that because of the war, "the uniqueness of the opportunity became compelling."[26]

The opportunities involve not only the mobilization of resources, but above all the incidence of a major catalyst—for conflict ridden, crisis saturated, and frustration torn dominant groups. There is ample evidence in both instances of genocide to corroborate this point. With respect to the Armenian case, Toynbee forcefully argued and belabored the point by concluding during the war that "the war was merely an opportunity and not a cause"[27] and reiterated this point more than half a century later when he declared that "[this] genocide was carried out under the cloak of legality by cold-blooded governmental action."[28]

American Ambassador Morgenthau narrated conversations with wartime

Turkish leaders in charge of the genocidal enactment also bearing on this point. For instance, on June 17, 1915, in a telegram to his foreign minister in Berlin, Wangenheim, German ambassador to Turkey, reported the assertion of Taleat, the Turkish Minister of Internal Affairs, made to Dr. Mordtmann, a staff member of the German Embassy, that the Ottoman government "is intent on taking advantage of World War I in order to finally get rid of internal enemies, meaning the indigenous Christians" (Den Weltkrieg dazu benutzen wollte, um mit ihren inneren Feinden, den einheimischen Christen gründlich aufzuräumen).[29] In a similar statement, Taleat is quoted boasting to Prince Hohenlohe-Langenburg, the deputy German ambassador in Constantinople on August 31, 1915, when the genocide had run its optimum course: "La Question armenienne n'existe plus" (The Armenian question no longer exists).[30]

Enver, the Turkish Minister of War and a co-equal to Taleat in wielding power, is reported to have made a similar admission to Dr. Lepsius, the German protestant minister and author who rather desperately tried to intercede on behalf of the Armenians. According to Ambassador Morgenthau, Enver bragged that the Turks "at last had an opportunity to rid themselves of the Armenians and that they proposed to use it." The same ambassador contends that in a personal exchange during August 1915 with him, Taleat emphatically stated, "We have got to finish with them."[31] Göring and Himmler in their turn admitted to the war offering a precious opportunity for a "final solution" of the Jewish problem.[32]

The victimological significance of this aspect of the problem is that from the condition of mere strain, to that of crisis, to a precipitate crisis, and eventually to the cataclysm of war, the negative imagery of a victim undergoes intensification: it is revived, vilified, accentuated, and brought into sharp focus for meaning attribution and meaning handling as preliminary for the ultimate judgment, which then becomes tantamount to a decision-making for extermination. The assessment of cost and consequence, the anticipation of probable or improbable deterrence from the outside, resistance and/or compliance by the victim, and the maximizing of the vulnerability of the victim are all ingredients of a definitional process which is critically influenced by the overall climate and temper of the war.

Appendix I
The U.S. Convention on Genocide

On December 11, 1946 the General Assembly of the U.N. passed by unanimous vote a resolution affirming that genocide is a crime under international law and for the perpetration of which principals and accomplices are punishable. Subsequently, the Assembly called for the institution of a "Convention on genocide which would define the offense more precisely and provide enforcement procedures for its deterrence and retribution." After two years, the draft of the *Convention on Genocide* was presented to the General Assembly, which adopted it. The Convention came into force January 12, 1951, after it had been ratified by the requisite twenty nations.

This Convention defines genocide as follows:

Genocide means any of the following acts committed with intent
to destroy, in whole, or in part, a national, ethical, racial or religious
group as such:

(a) killing members of the group;

(b) causing serious bodily or mental harm to members of the group;

(c) deliberately inflicting on the group conditions of life calculated
    to bring about its physical destruction in whole or in part;

(d) imposing measures intended to prevent births within the group;

(e) forcibly transferring children of the group.

The convention also stipulates that any contracting party may call upon the U.N. to initiate action, under its Charter, for the "prevention and suppression" of acts of genocide. Also, any such contracting party may bring charges before the International Court of Justice.

Appendix II
A Cursory Review of the History of Genocide
and Quasi-Genocidal Acts

The Bible records numerous instances in which conflict between a weak and a strong nation was resolved by the strong trying to exterminate the weak. In the third chapter of Deuteronomy, for instance, the Hebrews, bent on gaining a foothold in Palestine, are depicted as sanguinary destroyers. (See also 2 Kings 15:16 for a similar account.) The Assyrians, Babylonians, and Egyptians were also noted for their savagery in this respect.[33] The conquests of the Huns, Mongols, and Tatars, the story of the Crusaders and the sequel of religious wars in Europe are equally illuminating. Speaking of modern times, however, Toynbee makes a point of the genocidal disposition of the British when he correlates it with the "English method of overseas settlement."[34]

Touching on this point, and describing it as a "chapter in the history of the triumph of 'civilization' over savagery," American social anthropologist George Murdock narrates the treatment by the colonists of the Tasmanians as "wild beasts to be ruthlessly exterminated."[35] Another colonial people, the Dutch, are described as bent on exterminating the native blacks in the interior of the Cape of Good Hope, because, as a rule, European stock farmers in South Africa viewed the natives as an inferior race unworthy of any human rights.[36] Another form of a quasi-genocidal act is attributed to the Portuguese in Brazil, who were eager to kill off the native Indians resisting their acts of settlement; a widespread practice in this respect is reported to be the introduction in Indian villages of clothing taken from victims of the smallpox.[37]

Speaking of North America, another student reports of the tactic of exploiting rifts in the victim's camp by pitting one faction against another, one tribe against another tribe, and thus promoting fratricide as a convenient practice of genocide. As early as 1717, a South Carolinian gives poignant testimony of this policy, which was a characteristic one throughout the United States.[38] Most American colonies indulged in the practice of paying rewards (bounties) for Indian scalps; as a policy, this practice was first adopted by the Dutch in New Amsterdam, emulating their compatriots in the East Indies who discovered the low cost of employing individuals on a commission basis in the task of extermination.[39]

Notes

1. Henry Kamen, *The Spanish Inquisition* (London: Weidenfeld and Nicolson, 1965) J.A. Llorente, *A Critical History of the Inquisition of Spain* (Williamstown: John Lilburre Co., 1967); Cecil Roth, *The Spanish Inquisition* (New York: Norton, 1964); "Marranos and Racial Anti-Semitism . . . A Study in Parallels," *Jewish Soc. Studies* 2 (1940): 234-48.
2. Lenin, *Works*, Vol. 7 (Moscow: International Publishing Co.), pp. 92-104. Also in Vol. 6, see "Does the Jewish Proletariat Need an Independent Political Party?" pp. 330-85.
3. A.C. Miasshigian, *Undeer Yerker* (Selected Works), (Yerevan: State Printing House, 1957), p. 98.
4. Llorente, *A Critical History,* Preface, p. XVII.
5. Robert Bierstedt, "An Analysis of Social Power," *American Sociological Review* 15 (1950): 736.
6. Amitai Etzioni, *A Comparative Analysis of Complex Organizations* (New York: Free Press, 1961).
7. Werner Cahnman, "Religion and Nationality," in *Sociology and History* (Glencoe, Ill.: Free Press, 1964), p. 275.
8. Appeared in the April 13, 1933 issue of *Judische Rundschau* with *Central-Verein Zeitung* editorial, in Raul Hilberg, *The Destruction of the European Jews* (Chicago: Quadrangle Books, 1961), p. 30.
9. Hillberg, *Destruction of European Jews,* p. 32.
10. Ibid., pp. 23-29
11. Ibid., p. 10.
12. Ibid., p. 662.
13. W.I. Thomas, *The Unadjusted Girl* (New York: HarperTorchbooks, Harper and Row, 1967), p. 42.
14. R.MacIver, *Social Causation* (Boston, Mass: Ginn & Co., 1942), p. 292.

15. For a full discussion of the concept see Herbert Blumer, "Society as Symbolic Interaction," in A.M. Rose, *Human Behavior and Social Processes* (Boston: Houghton & Mifflin 1962), pp. 179-92; Idem., *Symbolic Interactionism, Perspective and Method* (Englewood Cliffs, N.J.: Prentice-Hall, 1969), particularly Chapter I, pp. 1-60; and T. Shibutani (ed.), *Human Nature and Collective Behavior* (Papers in honor of Herbert Blumer) (Englewood Cliffs, N.J.: Prentice-Hall, 1970), particularly Chapters 1, 3, and 4.

16. Blumer, *Symbolic Interactionism,* p.4

17. Ibid., p. 5.

18. Hilberg, *Destruction of European Jews,* p. 641.

19. *Trial of the Major War Criminals,* Vol. IX., p. 273 (Testimony by Herman Göring.) Nuremberg 1947-49, 42 volumes in German, quoted in Hilberg, ibid., p. 18.

20. Adolf Hitler, *Mein Kampf* (Transl. Ralph Manheim) Boston: Houghton Mifflin, 1943), pp. 52 ff.

21. Hilberg, *Destruction of European Jews,* p. 266.

22. Ibid., p. 266.

23. Ibid., p. 564.

24. Ibid., p. 647. (In a speech made by Himmler at Cruppenfuhrer at Foznan, October 4, 1943.)

25. Louis Lochner, *The Goebbels Diaries 1942-43* (Garden City, N.Y.: Doubleday, 1948), p. 148.

26. Hilberg, *Destruction of European Jews,* p. 639.

27. Y. Bryce, *The Treatment of the Armenians in the Ottoman Empire 1915-1916* (Compiled by Toynbee) (London: His Majesty's Stationery Office, Sir Joseph Causton & Sons, Ltd., 1916) p. 633.

28. A. Toynbee, *Experiences* (New York: Oxford, 1969), p. 341.

29. Johannes Lepsius, *Deutschland und Armenien, 1914-1918,* (Potsdam: Tempelverlag, 1919), p. 84.

30. Ibid., p. XXVI.

31. H. Morgenthau, *Ambassador Morgenthau's Story* (Garden City, N.Y.: Doubleday, 1918), pp. 298-338.

32. Hilberg, *Destruction of European Jews,* p. 266.

33. H.N. Brailsford, "Massacre," *Encyclopedia of the Social Sciences,* Vol. 10 (New York: Macmillan, 1937). Cf. "War," in Hastings (ed.), *The Dictionary of the Bible* (New York: Scribner, 1963), pp. 964-65.

34. A. Toynbee, *The Study of History,* Vol. I (London: Oxford University Press, 1934), p. 465.

35. G.P. Murdock, *Our Primitive Contemporaries* (New York: Macmillan, 1943), pp. 16-18.

36. I.D. MacCrone, *Race Attitudes in South Africa* (London: Oxford University Press, 1937), pp. 89-136.

37. Donald Pierson, *Negroes in Brazil* (Chicago: University of Chicago Press, 1942), p. 6.

38. D.D. Wallace, *History of South Carolina,* Vol. I (New York: American Historical Society, 1934), p. 213.

39. B. Shrieke, *Alien Americans* (New York: Viking Press, 1936), p. 5.
On the Subject of Scalping, cf. A. Locke and B.J. Stern, *When Peoples Meet: A Study in Race and Culture Contacts* (New York: Progressive Association, 1942), pp. 165-70. See also, Clark Wissler, *Indians of the United States* (New York: Doubleday Doran and Co., 1940), pp. 302-303.

9

Organizations as Victims in American Mass Racial Disturbances: A Reexamination

E.L. Quarantelli and Russell R. Dynes

Several years ago we suggested looking at the notion of organizations as victims and illustrated it in the massive racial civil disturbances in the United States from 1964 through 1969 (Dynes and Quarantelli 1970). This paper updates and extends that earlier preliminary version in a number of ways. We include a wider range of data, pay more attention to the differences among the various disturbances as well as the range of the illegal activity undertaken in them, and generally attempt a more systematic theoretical examination of organizatonal victimology on a mass scale.

Our overall position is that selectivity of organizations as victims in disturbances is to be accounted for by certain kinds of collective definitions of the situation held by participants. These definitions are partly created in the context of a disturbance, and partly draw upon pre-disturbance definitions. The definitions, while not dependent upon the intrinsic characteristics of organizations, are related to such social organizational variables as class, status, and power.

The Literature

As Reckless points out, while there are crimes without victim, "most crimes have something to do with an object outside the perpetrator" (1973, p. 91). The object can be persons or physical items of some kind. Criminology as such is primarily concerned with the study of such behavior on the part of perpetrators.

However, by far the largest concern in the field, as manifest in research and writings, is with the behavior of perpetrators or doers against other individuals or their personal property. The evidence on this activity is that, at least in the United States, there is victim differentiation. Thus, the yearly reports of the United States Uniform Crime Statistics and the National Opinion Research Center survey for the President's Commission on Law Enforcement and the Administration of Justice clearly show that income, race, age, and sex are factors influencing the probability of being a personal victim (Ennis 1967).

The research in this paper was supported in part by PHS Grant 5 R 01 MH-15399-04 from the Center for Studies of Mental Health and Social Problems, Applied Research Branch, National Institutes of Mental Health.

121

Various explanations have been advanced to account for such differentiation and selectivity. One minor but persistent theme in the literature on criminology is the importance of the relationship between the offender and the
victim. In fact, von Hentig states that: "In a sense, the victim shapes and molds
the criminal . . . it is not a totally unilateral form of relationship. They work
upon each other profoundly and continuously, even before the moment of
disaster. To know one we must be acquainted with the complementary partner"
(1948, pp. 384-85). This particular theme has been most notably advanced in
attempts to account for certain types of personalized crimes, such as criminal
homicide, forcible rape, and aggravated assault. Thus, Quinney notes that
"because of the presence of interaction between persons in a situation of violence, the *victim* is a crucial agent in the action that is taken. Victims, in other
words, tend to precipitate their own victimization" (1970, p. 250). As many as
a fourth of all homicides (Wolfgang 1958), three-quarters of the aggravated
assaults (Pittman and Handy 1964), and a majority of rapes (Amir 1967) have
in some studies of American crime been labeled as being victim precipitated,
with the victim making a direct, immediate, and positive contribution to a criminal act of which he or she is the object.

In the literature there is much less attention paid to situations where organizations rather than persons as such are victims of crime. Even the frequency
and amount of such non-personal illegal activity in America is largely unknown.
As a report of the President's Commission on Law Enforcement and Administration of Justice states: "It is very difficult to discover the exact extent to which
businesses and organizations are the victims of crime. . . . Few attempts are made
to keep systematic records or report such crimes to any central place" (1967,
pp. 41-43). There is little evidence but some speculation that "some businesses,
like some people, are more likely than others to be victimized by crime" (1967,
p. 83). Thus, it is supposed that there is considerable crime against organizations
and it is guessed that there is differentiation in organizational victimology, but
little is actually known.

In view of what has just been said, it is not surprising that an interactional
view and an attempt to focus on the victim has only infrequently been applied
when an organization rather than a person has been the victim. Most work using
this kind of framework, such as by Schafer (1968), focuses exclusively on personal crimes. Very few studies have attempted to take specific aspects of organizations into account in trying to understand the victim-offender relationship.

However, there are some exceptions in the literature. For instance, Cameron
(1964), in her study of shoplifting, alludes to certain crime-facilitating characteristics of organizations, such as the spread of self-service. In a more systematic
study, Camp (1967) suggests that both banks and bank robbers define their
confrontation situations as ones in which each, for different reasons, believes
they have nothing to lose by committing a bank robbery or being its victim.
The banks expect formal agencies of social control to assume prime responsibility

in preventing robberies, while bank robbers perceive such control groups as
quite directly ineffectual, and thus banks become likely and easy victims.
Smigel (1955), using a somewhat different approach, examined the relationship of the size of the organization as related to public attitudes toward
stealing. He found, using an all-white sample, that lower class persons were
less disapproving of stealing than were higher status individuals, and that the
size of the organization appeared to make a difference in these attitudes. In
general, there was more approval of stealing from large than from small businesses. Attitudes towards pilfering and thievery from different size governmental units was somewhat mitigated by conceptions of loyalty and patriotism.
Horning (1973), in a study of factory workers, found that they made a three-
fold classification of property: personal, corporate, and property of uncertain
ownership. Pilfering was condoned only for those items in the last category
which were inexpensive, small in size, plentiful, and intended for personal
and not commercial use by the factory worker thief.

In a recent compendium and partial review of the literature, Smigel and
Ross examine crimes against bureaucracies, that is, large, impersonal, and
formal rule-structured corporate or governmental organizations that "are the
popular victims of many contemporary property crimes" (1970, p. 4). They
attribute the vulnerability of such groups to their unpopularity and to the
opportunities provided by bureaucratic procedures. Unpopularity is seen as
stemming from the downplaying of personal relationships by bureaucracies,
the conflict of interests between bureaucrats and their clients, and the ineffi-
ciency that results from stressing organizational means rather than ends. Opportunities are seen as related to the fact that most crimes against bureaucracies are
unobtrusive or have low visibility. This latter matter, combined with unpopularity of victims, results in very low public stigmatization of the perpetrators
of such crime. This in turn is not unrelated to the fact that most persons who
steal from bureaucracies lack criminal records and criminal self-conceptions
and "are able to regard their conduct as not inappropriate given their conception of the nature of the victim" (Smigel and Ross 1970, p. 10).

As random, unsystematic, and based on weak empirical data as the above
statements are, they constitute the core of theoretical discussions about organizational victimology in the literature. Our own research is aimed at contributing
to this currently scanty body of knowledge. We have looked at a major category
of events, i.e., the recent massive racial disturbances in the United States, and
asked if the same patterns and explanations advanced about victims in the literature also held in these situations.[a] Our three major questions were: who were

---

[a]Unless otherwise documented, all examples used are drawn from and all figures cited
are computed from unpublished data in the files of the Disaster Research Center at The
Ohio State University.

the victims, were they differently attacked, and if so, could an explanation be found in the offender-victim social relationship?

The Nature of the Mass Civil Disturbances

The number of separate massive civil disturbances that can be said to have occurred in American urban ghettos from 1964 through 1969 depends upon the definition used for identification. We used two major criteria. First, we limited our analysis only to disturbances that involved mass activities by black people in the streets and excluded events confined within buildings, such as is typical of many school and college disorders. This limitation was used so as to exclude situations less likely to have community-wide ramifications and those which would be less likely to potentially involve a wide range of illegal acts. The other major identifying criterion was the deployment of extra police forces in the community. As in other extreme stress situations such as natural disasters (see Quarantelli and Dynes 1970), this kind of action is usually a clear indicator that the event is beyond the normal range of everyday emergencies.

A total of 325 events met our two criteria and involved around 300 different communities.[b] Vandalism, looting, arson, and sniping occurred in most of these disturbances. At a minimum, 227 of these events were marked by arson. Vandalism took place in 212 of these situations, and looting in around 150 of them. Sniping was less frequent, with only 51 communities reporting it in the context of a mass disturbance. The order of frequency here is not inconsistent with that found by the Lemberg Center for the Study of Violence using much broader criteria than we did in identifying black racial disturbances from 1967 through 1969 (Baskin et al. 1971), but our data do not agree with Fogelson's assertion that arson was less widespread than looting (1970, p. 150),[c] or that "looting happened in just about all the riots" (1970, p. 147).

Overall total costs and specific losses to particular communities were not insignificant although perspective requires noting that the American racial disturbance casualty figures pale considerably when compared with the nearly 800 deaths occurring in Northern Ireland over a shorter time span, or the annual

---

[b]That the criteria used to identify disturbances are crucial is suggested by the following observation. The Lemberg Center for the Study of Violence lists 1,816 disturbances from 1967 through 1969 (Baskin et al. 1971), whereas the U.S. Senate committee dealing with disturbances lists only 173 for 1965 through the first seven months of 1968. Even using the criteria of the presence of arson, firebombing, looting, and/or sniping, the Lemberg Center lists 701 disturbances for the same three year time period.

[c]Although Fogelson uses Newark as an example of a disturbance without arson (1950, p. 150), an official study of the disturbance indicates that while many of the more than 250 fire alarms were false, at least 13 cases of very serious blazes occurred (Report for Action 1968).

number of those who die in Indian riots (e.g., in only one week-long 1969 disorder in Ahmedabad, over 1,000 persons were reported killed). In the events we examined, more than 185 persons were killed and at least 8,500 injured. Apart from substantial indirect losses in commercial trade, tourist business, and delayed production of goods, the dollar costs in direct property damage alone was in the millions. One partial study for the years 1965-1967 alone estimated $210 million in property damage and $504 million in economic losses (Downes 1971, p. 507). This is probably a very conservative figure, for the McCone report stated that the damage to 997 stores in Watts alone amounted to around $40 million (1965).

While these figures are impressive insofar as the American scene is concerned, it is not this that interests us. Neither is it the fact that according to American legal codes, arson, vandalism, looting, and sniping are all criminal offenses. Other impressive figures (say for the widespread student disturbances that surfaced in the later 1960s) could be cited. In just one single disorder on the Ohio State University campus, for instance, more than 260 police officers sustained some injuries, more than 150 persons were treated in hospitals for gunshot wounds or tear gas effects, over 900 people were eventually arrested, and costs to the police department alone amounted to over one quarter of a million dollars (Dynes, Quarantelli, and Ross 1972). Likewise, arson, vandalism, looting, and sniping did not surface for the first time in American society; similar illegal acts pocket the history of labor-management relations in the United States. One historical survey notes hundreds of such incidents in recounting more than 160 interventions of state and federal troops in labor disputes that resulted in more than 700 dead and several thousand seriously injured (Taft and Ross 1969, p. 380).

What is of major interest to us is that the conflict that started to surface in American cities in the early 1960s was different in many ways from racial disorders of the past. It is for this reason we have deliberately spoken of civil disturbances rather than riots. We specifically use this terminology to distinguish the recent conflicts from the earlier, one might almost say classic, prototype riot confrontations between collectivities of white and blacks, as in East St. Louis in 1917 (Rudwick 1964), in Chicago in 1919 (Chicago Commission 1922), or Detroit in 1943 (Lee and Humphrey 1943). In these situations, groups of whites fought groups of blacks, with the initiative usually being undertaken by the whites. What started to happen in the early 1960s was the emergence of a different form of civil disturbance.

A forerunner of what was to come was provided in the disturbances in Harlem and Bedford-Stuyvesant in New York City and Rochester and Philadelphia in 1964. For several days, large numbers of blacks, generally avoiding attacking whites, looted and burned more than 800 stores and assaulted the police, at a total cost of nearly 500 injured and over 1,000 arrested as the result of the mobilization of massive police forces and the National Guard. But it was the outbreak in 1965 in Watts, Los Angeles, with its 34 dead, over a thousand injured, nearly 4,000 arrested, and the activation of 13,900 National Guardsmen that marked a clear turning point and a movement away from the traditional racial riots of the past. Watts initiated a pattern that escalated and then dwindled over a five-year period. Manifest most clearly in Cleveland and San Francisco in 1966, in Detroit and Newark in 1967, and in Chicago, Pittsburgh, and Washington in 1968, the pattern took the form of massive police and military activity in the face of widespread arson, vandalism, looting, and sometimes sniping by blacks. Very seldom was there any actual confrontation of groups of blacks and whites, except as it was evident in police action. What occurred in this kind of conflict was not a direct clash between two groups, but the attack of one group against the symbols or representatives of the larger society.[d]

Not all the disturbances took the same form. What happened in Watts and Detroit, for instance, was not identical to what occurred in Akron (see Lively 1969) or Milwaukee (see Flaming 1968), insofar as type of precipitating incidents was concerned, duration of the event, degree of leadership, explicitness of demands, involvement of counterrioters, and/or a number of other factors that could be mentioned. Thus, on the basis of such differences, various writers (e.g., Janowitz 1968; Goldberg 1971; and Mattick 1968) have developed a typology of disturbances. Nevertheless, when all is said and done, despite these differences, all the events we are considering did involve collectivities of blacks engaging in acts of arson, vandalism, looting, and sniping directed not at other people, but primarily at certain property and certain representatives of the larger American society. Heterogeneity in leadership patterns or incident differences in initiators of actions and the like do not preclude roughly common and similar lines of disturbance behavior or social consequences of them.

Of course in these disturbances, there was a considerable range in the scope of involvement of participants. That is, different numbers of ghetto inhabitants participated in the various criminal acts. Clearly sniping involved by far the fewest people, seemingly undertaken in all instances by only a literal handful of men. Arson and particularly vandalism were undertaken by far more persons, mostly young men and male adolescents. Looting was clearly the most inclusive behavior, engaging both men and women, and as films of some of the events showed, practically the whole age range possible from pre-teenagers to senior citizens. Differential participation in the disturbances seems an undeniable fact.

Nevertheless, the events we are talking about were *mass* civil disturbances insofar as magnitude was concerned. This is true in counting, whether one uses absolute or relative figures, or whether one uses measures of only very active

---

[d]In the disturbances there were occasional attacks by blacks against whites, especially passing motorists and inquisitive reporters. But such attacks stand out because of their rarity, did not occur in most disturbances, and never involved clashes between groups made up of different racial categories.

participants or totals of everyone present including those who were but street spectators at scenes of disorder. The disturbances were not the handiwork of a few isolated individuals or a small adolescent gang or two. The analyses by Fogelson and Hill indicate that in what were the major disturbances as much as a fifth of the total ghetto population probably actively participated in the various illegal behaviors (1968, pp. 217-44). This means that even in the smallest cities where disturbances occurred hundreds of people were involved, and in the larger cities such as Los Angeles the figure during the Watts disturbance may have reached 50,000 (Fogelson 1971, p. 184), and in Washington, 20,000 (Gilbert 1968, p. 224). Without question, the numbers of the involved varied from one event to another and the proportions of the participants engaged in different illegal acts almost certainly ranged considerably from one disturbance to another, but overall, each incident we are considering was the action of a mass aggregate of persons if not massive collectivities.

Furthermore, the more active elements in the disturbances had the indirect support of many more. Caplan recently reviewed ten major survey studies on attitudes expressed by blacks regarding disturbances and found that "about one third to one half of the ghetto residents surveyed express support for riots" (1970, p. 60). While attitudinal expressions are not always translated into overt behaviors, such studies do indicate that a significant portion of black communities did not perceive disturbance activities as aberrant behavior on the part of a few deviants.

For most purposes, therefore, it seems useful to think of the disturbances as massive assaults. The property and symbolic objects that were the victims of attack were directly attacked by many, who had the indirect support of far more persons. Differential participation in the disturbances can be granted while still insisting that what occurred represented a mass and collective attack. And what was directly victimized was not other people—neither black nor white—but selected kinds of property and certain symbolic objects. All of the widespread offenses common to the disturbances had an organization as victim. This is most obvious in the three offenses involving property—vandalism, looting, and arson, but we will additionally try to show that it was also true of sniping, since in most instances the victim was "chosen" because he somehow represented an organization.

Objects of Differential Attack

Not only were organizations rather than persons the prime object of attack, but there was even further selectivity in terms of what types of organizations were attacked. To understand this degree of selectivity of victims, it is necessary to clarify two widespread but mistaken views about the disturbances which are relatively common among the "lay" public, but also prevail in some academic circles, although in the latter case they are usually disguised in more sophisticated language. These misconceptions have to be cleared up here, for otherwise they would imply that a consideration of the "victim" is irrelevant to understanding such behavior. That is, acceptance of these views would suggest that the criminal behavior is almost independent of the perceived characteristics of the object attacked.

First, there is much emphasis in the discussion of criminal activities during such disturbances on the fact that the offenses occur in a context in which social control mechanisms are weak or inoperative. Much is made of the supposed difficulties in deploying enough police and extra-community law enforcement agencies including the National Guard. The assumption seems to be that given temporary difficulties in traditional social control agencies, certain kinds of criminal offenses are predictable, if not expectable. Thus, the report of one task force of the National Commission on the Causes and Prevention of Violence states that in disturbances the police are unable to mobilize quickly and "pending the arrival of sufficient forces, the inadequate number of policemen available cannot stop the rioting and arrest looters and others who are violating the law" (Campbell, Sahid, and Stang 1970, p. 311). In brief, illegal behavior will occur if police organizations cannot operate in their usual manner.

These notions are linked to a second view that the baser tendencies of human beings will surface when external social control is absent or weak. In the context of mass disturbances, it is supposed that the thin veneer of human qualities is ripped off, and man is revealed as a rapacious animal. Assertions are made that this same kind of antisocial behavior will manifest itself in other extreme social situations such as natural disaster emergencies (see Banfield 1968; Mattick 1968, p. 28; and Oberschall 1968). In short, not too deep down, human beings are predatory and aggressive creatures, with Mr. Hydes replacing Dr. Jekylls when the opportunities present themselves.

Given such assumptions about man's inherent criminality and the necessity of external social control, the illegal behavior seen in mass disturbances can easily be viewed as random in expression and irrational in form. Thus, Mattick, in discussing one type of disturbance,[e] talks of "the 'irrational' riot of an 'irresponsible' group" who have "no real causes" but "false motives" and "is irrational because it has no real, or no legitimate objectives" (1968, p. 26-27). Such views are particularly likely to be confirmed by the destruction of property through vandalism or arson. Crimes involving direct and personal gain are to many people somewhat understandable, but not sheer destruction. However, even looting seems meaningless to many persons for it is assumed to be undertaken with little discrimination as to object of attack, a belief reinforced in the American racial disturbances by the tendency of mass media reports and pictures

---

[e]It would be incorrect to imply Mattick generally views all disturbances as irrational. He does not, but the type cited is one that he does use in his analysis.

to depict the unusual if not the bizarre (thus, accounts and views of looters taking dozens of clothing hangers or setting fire to garbage cans). Sporadic, isolated, and random sniping appears even more bewildering.

If the two viewpoints just discussed were valid, they would make consideration of the organization as victim irrelevant. However, neither view has much validity. The absence or weakness of the police in a given situation does not directly or even often lead to illegal or criminal behavior. Fogelson summarizes the existing evidence very well when he noted: "according to the extensive historical and sociological literature on European and American disorders, neither looting nor arson, and not even assault, is an automatic consequence of the breakdown of public order. There are . . . many instances of rioting without lotting, arson, and assault" (1970, p. 142). Similarly, there is little evidence that the socialization process merely gilds a fragile and easily discarded human facade upon a brute beast (Stone and Farberman 1970), and even less support for the notion that in other kinds of extreme stress situations, such as natural disasters, plundering or other antisocial behaviors come to the fore (see Quarantelli and Dynes 1972).

Perhaps of even greater importance is that it can be shown that not only were organizations the victim of attack in the disturbances being discussed, but that there was additional discrimination in what kinds of organizations were victimized. There was a selective pattern operative. There was discrimination in selection of objects for attack, whether this was by way of vandalism, looting, arson or sniping.

The pattern of damage in the mass disturbances clearly centered on small retail business establishments. Industry-wide insurance figures for the Newark outbreak show, for example, that over two-thirds of the damage reports (with over 100 reports each) were for liquor stores and bars, clothing and small department shops, groceries, multiple-occupant commercial buildings, cleaners, and furniture stores. In contrast, dwellings—either apartment or family houses—made up only about 2.5 percent of all buildings damaged or destroyed in some way. Institutional and public properties, such as schools and churches, constituted less than one-fourth of one percent of the full total. In Detroit, the same type of retail stores made up more than 55 percent of the damaged property; dwellings of all kinds less than 10 percent, and there is evidence that most of these were affected indirectly as a result of attacks upon commercial properties. Not even one-half of one percent of all buildings damaged were public or institutional in nature. Of the 600 buildings burned in Watts over 95 percent were retail outlets. Another study of the five most heavily hit precincts during disorders in Boston, Washington, and Chicago found that "only 14 of the 111 businesses damaged or looted during the civil disorders were not retail or service businesses" (Aldrich and Reiss 1970, p. 191). This pattern was consistent even in smaller scale disturbances. Thus, it was almost exclusively retail or service stores that were looted out of 85 in Kansas City, 46 in Trenton, and 50 in

Richmond (Professional Standards Division 1968, p. 3.19). Elsewhere the pattern was the same.

Participants in disturbances did not burn their own homes or those of their neighbors. They generally also did not set fire to any kind of residential dwellings. The one major exception in all disturbances where a number of homes burned was in Detroit where the fire department (quite contrary to the desires of their officers in the field, and only under explicit order from higher authorities) had to, under protest, withdraw their equipment, permitting fires set in commercial buildings to engulf nearby residences housing 274 families. Arsonists, as well as looters, vandals, and snipers were not indiscriminate in their attacks: some categories of objects were clearly more often victims than others.

Furthermore, with the exception of police and fire departments (which we shall discuss shortly), almost all other local public agencies seemed immune to attack. Public buildings or facilities are notably absent in damage statistics or reports. Part of this could be explained by their relative absence with ghetto areas, but schools, welfare offices, health clinics, post offices, antipoverty headquarters, and so on do exist, but did not become victims. One elementary school was burned during a disturbance in Cambridge, Maryland, but the source of the arson is unknown and neighborhood blacks helped man the fire lines and provided armed guards for fire fighters in the situation.

This last example, a not totally atypical one, does highlight the mixed response fire department personnel, equipment, and facilities drew from participants in disturbances. In many instances, fire departments were objects of direct attention. Thus, from 1966 to 1967 harassment of firemen occurred in 67 out of 101 major disturbances. It is our impression that in the vast majority of these cases, the harassments tended to be primarily verbal in nature or a failure of spectators to stay or remove themselves out of the way of firemen doing their tasks, as is the norm under usual circumstances. In other instances, the attacks were more serious, and went beyond pelting firemen and equipment with stones, bricks, and bottles. During the Newark disturbance, 33 separate incidents of sniper shootings at fire stations or apparatus were recorded. That even this may have been more harassment than attack is indicated by observations made in the Cleveland disturbance where some black groups made a determined effort to discourage fire fighters from extinguishing some of the 531 fires. A report on this incident notes, however, "They used rifle fire, barricades and cut hose lines with machetes to intimidate rather than harm" (O'Hagan 1968, p. 24). Nevertheless, one review on fire fighting during civil disturbances written in 1968 observes that: "deaths and injuries of fire fighters during these incidents exceed those experienced by the police" (O'Hagan 1968, p. 34).[f] On the other hand, there are many instances of ghetto inhabitants going out of their way to assist firemen, to help them at their tasks, sometimes providing them armed protection, and often warning or alerting them to fires that had just been or were going to be set.

---

[f]In the Watts disturbance, for example, 136 firemen were injured compared with 90 policemen.

In contrast to this mixed pattern of attack and support of firemen, the police were clearly more often the victim of direct attack. They were most often the objects of assault ranging from being showered with missiles, bricks, stones, and Molotov cocktails to having their equipment (and in a few cases their police stations) or persons bodily attacked. The nature and frequency of this activity is well captured in most accounts and films by newsmen and needs little additional documentation, although it perhaps should be noted that 38 percent of all injuries in 164 pre-1968 disorders studied by the Kerner Commission, were sustained by law officers (Kerner 1967, p. 164). For example, 44 police officers were injured in Milwaukee (Flaming 1968). The police were also the prime focus of the most serious, but also by far the most infrequent criminal offense, sniping. Some reports of sniping were, of course, simply descriptions of random shooting by uneasy security forces in the disturbance areas. In some cases, at least, "snipers" have turned out to be policemen shooting at one another (a kind of event which recently reoccurred in a New Orleans motel shootout when for hours after the sole sniper had been killed, police exchanged shots and wounded one another). Furthermore, in instances where sniping did occur, it is not clear whether it was not more often directed towards organizational equipment rather than personnel. Police cars often appear to have been the usual targets, but of course personnel will frequently be near this kind of equipment.

This is not to imply that public officers have never been targets. Four firemen suffered gunshot wounds during the Watts disturbance, although all survived. Both a policeman and a fireman were killed in Newark with their deaths attributed to snipers. Of the 38 people that died from gunshot wounds in Detroit, five were thought to have been victims of snipers, including one fireman. However, what is important about the very low loss of life from snipers in the American ghetto disturbances is that it suggests that such shootings as did occur were probably symbolic rather than instrumental in intent. This is supported by the observation that there were only two casualties from 152 different sniping incidents, many involving more than one shot, in Newark (Report for Action 1968, p. 136). The almost insignificant casualty rates can hardly be attributed to poor marksmanship as Boskin (1969) and others have noted.

Overall, the picture is clear insofar as victimization in the disturbances we studied was concerned. Organizations rather than persons as such were the victims.[g] But there was a selective factor as to which type of organizations

---

[g]While a substantial number of the injured in the disturbances were white persons, practically all those killed were black ghetto residents. For example, only two of the 26 persons that died in Newark were white. In Watts, but three of the 34 dead were white. Thirty-three out of the 43 killed in Detroit were black. Three out of four that died in Milwaukee were black. This loss of life among participants in disturbances rather than by personnel of social control agencies has been well demonstrated to be the usual historical pattern in most societies (Rude 1971).

were victimized. Certain kinds of businesses and certain kinds of public agencies were singled out far beyond random chance.

Explanations of Differential Attacks

To the extent that a selective pattern of victimization has been noted in the disturbances, explanations for it have not been lacking in accounts provided by scholars and researchers, not to mention the popular press, ghetto residents, the police, and those arrested in the events. The academic analyses have generally tended to give different explanations for the looting as over against how they try to account for other kinds of illegal acts. For example, looting is often linked to some kind of economic exploitation; whereas arson, assault, and sniping, treated almost always separately from looting, are frequently related to some form of psychological oppression. Most analyses too tend to combine "objective" factors as seen by the researcher with "subjective" factors as reported by participants. Thus, in what in many ways is by far one of the better analyses available, Berk and Aldrich (1972) examine selection of targets on the basis of five possibilities: as objects of retaliation, familiarity with the store, the attractiveness of merchandise, proximity to the disorder sites, and as symbols of white society. In addition, there is a strong tendency to attempt to correlate pre-disturbance attributes of individuals, especially attitudes, to activities during the disorders. Most of the empirical studies, as McPhail (1971) has noted, assume it is possible to go from certain pre-disturbance states of individuals to behavioral outcomes in disturbances, without having to take into account the processes by which behaviors are built and developed.

Obviously implied in our remarks is a questioning of the full validity of the explanations advanced to the extent that they do not explicitly treat attacks upon victims as a generic class of phenomena, fail to use consistently the participant's point of view of perceptions, and do not in some way address themselves to the fact that mass civil disturbances and actions within them are, if a priority of sociological classification has to be applied, instances of *collective* behavior. We suggest a better analysis might develop by relating the generic phenomena of attacks to social organizational dimensions as these are perceived by participants interacting during the development or careers of disturbances. Before detailing this, some further remarks need to be made about other current explanations.

Many of the attempts to account for looting and its selectivity have the underlying theme of direct retaliation for economic exploitation or the notion that "the poor pay more" (Caplovitz 1963). For instance, it is frequently asserted that supermarket chains charge higher prices in ghetto located outlets. Certain commercial enterprises, it is said, demand exorbitant rates for credit or do not grant it at all to inner city residents. The objective fact of white ownership of ghetto stores has also been frequently singled out as a major factor in the selective attacks during disturbances. More rarely, attempts have been made to make a case in terms of impersonal economic exploitation by gigantic corporate structures.[h]

All these explanations might seem to explain particular cases of assault, but there is considerable evidence which contradicts each as a general explanation for the selectivity. Some studies have not found any differential pricing in chain supermarkets or even neighborhood stores in ghetto areas (Marion et al 1969). Certain types of business depending very heavily on credit operations, such as used car dealers, were almost never attacked in the disturbances. Despite "soul brother" signs in some cases, enough black owners and managers were victimized to raise questions about the importance of white ownership as a major general variable in the selective attacks (e.g., 38 percent of 555 business establishments that sustained damage or loss in Washington, D.C., had black managers and were managed by persons different from owners). Many industrial concerns, branch plants, and facilities of large corporations were available for assault in many disturbance areas, but were left completely untouched.

A few attempts have been made to account for looting in almost "economic man" terms. Thus, Oberschall states that looting "needs no complex explanation beyond the simple desire to obtain" consumer goods on the part of those lacking them "when the opportunity to do so involves a low risk of apprehension by the police" (1973, p. 330). Apart from the point noted before that the historical evidence clearly indicates that the absence of social control agencies does not automatically generate illegal acts, such an explanation fails to square with easily made field observations. For example, one of the authors observed during the Watts disturbance that a very large discount outlet of a national chain, with huge and unprotected glass windows, stood untouched across the street from a number of iron-barricaded, small shops (some locally owned) that had all been attacked en masse, looted, and burned. In a situation of equivalent opportunity for attack, less accessible and less lucrative targets were struck, an observation other researchers have made elsewhere also.

The rarer attempts to account for attacks on the police have almost taken it for a self-evident fact that they should be victims in the disturbances. In some ways the arguments implicitly advanced roughly parallel the themes of economic exploitation discussed earlier except the emphasis in this connection is on political oppression. It is frequently said that the police and other formal social control agencies are the prejudiced representatives of the politically dominant white sectors of American society and are resented as such. It is claimed that policemen abuse their power in routine ghetto patrolling and mistreat black citizens in far worse ways than they do their white counterparts. Verified cases of unnecessary

---

[h]For a discussion of many of the views noted in this paragraph, see the Kerner Report (1968).

use of force in ordinary incidents in the ghetto also have been cited as a major factor in the initiation of disturbances leading to attacks upon the police (thus, the Kerner report states that "some 40 percent of the prior incidents involved allegedly abusive or discriminatory police action" (1968, p. 120)). In more radical statements, it is asserted that the police are an "army of occupation" backed up by other social control agencies ruthlessly maintaining power in colonial enclaves or the black ghettos, or as Blauner puts it, "the police are the most crucial institution maintaining the colonized status of Black Americans" and "protecting the interests of outside exploitation and maintaining domination over the ghetto by the central metropolitan power structure" (1969, p. 399).[i]

Some of these explanations may be relevant to particular incidents, but again they do not seem to provide a general explanation for the selectivity involved. While it is true that most American blacks are negative to current police practices and behaviors, they do not reject the notion of policing as such (Fogelson 1971, p. 53) and in fact want more and better police presence in their neighborhoods. There is some evidence that when social class factors are taken into account, blacks are no more mistreated than white citizens in contacts with law enforcement agencies (Reiss 1971). Incidents of police behavior quite similar to those taken as "precipitating events" for the disturbances have occurred often enough without generating disorders so as to lead to considerable suspicion that the actions as such are primarily responsible for attacks upon the police. Taking the disturbances as a whole, the police more often than not were ignored rather than assaulted. Also, while firemen sometimes came under attack, more obvious authority figures, National Guardsmen, were only very rarely victimized. In the two disturbances in which federal troops were used, they were almost totally ignored.

There are a number of attempts to account for assault against the police in almost pure frustration-aggression terms. It is a viewpoint derived from participants. That is, participants in most of the urban racial disturbances in recent years have indicated that they were responding to police brutality. More generally assumed is that ghetto blacks have almost total, barely contained, and unqualified hostility towards the police and any other governmental or political authority figures of white society. But in this approach little attention is directed to explaining why such attitudes should lead to direct assaults, and exactly what there is about disturbances that should change what is normally latent hostility into open attack. In terms of opportunities in disturbances, there was a rather high degree of selectivity as to when, where, and what policemen were victimized plus the fact already alluded to that in a number of cases, black counterrioters did try to help the police in clearing areas and

---

[i]A number of the views alluded to in this paragraph are discussed in Skolnick (1969).

calming the population (Anderson, Dynes, and Quarantelli, in press). As discussed earlier, police and police equipment were without doubt the victims of attack and more than any other category of potential objects of attention; but ideological rhetoric to the contrary, there was not an across-the-board, constant, continuous, and indiscriminate assault upon the social control agencies involved; if anything avoidance of them was a far more characteristic pattern of the bulk of the black participants in the distrubances.

Class, Status, and Power Aspects

It seems rather clear that the selection of organizations as victim cannot be easily understood by assuming that simple "objective" characteristics are the basis for discrimination. Other factors are more influential than whether the victims do or do not actually have certain "objectionable" features. Far more important is how organizations, especially classes of them, are perceived and come to be perceived in the course of a disturbance. In essence, what is involved is that certain social organizational dimensions get involved during a disturbance in what is perhaps best described as a collective definitional process.

Max Weber (1946), a long time ago, pointed out the importance of class, status, and power in social relationships and as part of the social structure of most social situations. He indicated (and subsequent research has supported him) that these variables are seldom perfectly correlated in given situations. We would suggest that within the American ghetto community, these dimensions are perhaps more closely correlated than is usually the case. Ghetto residents, while far better off than their ancestors in the past and substantially more wealthy than their current counterparts in African, Asian, and Latin American communities, are clearly low in the possession of economic goods relative to other Americans. Their social prestige and their political power is equally minimal, relatively speaking. Thus, in sociological terms, there is low status consistency.

One occasional reaction to this low status consistency is what is sometimes manifested in mass disturbances. However, while low status consistency may be a fact of life of most ghetto dwellers, in itself it is neither an explanation of disturbances nor of the selective attacks on victims within them. If it were an explanation, the black areas should be in constant turmoil and all possible targets signifying low status should be victims of attack, but obviously this is not the case. What is important rather are the dimensions involved, as they come to be collectively defined before as well as during disturbances. What is crucial is not the "objective" situation, but how the dimensions of class, status, and power are perceived or defined. We suggest that it is variations in such definitions that account for the selectivity of attacks on organizational victims in disturbances.

In another context, we said that looting in civil disturbances could best be understood as temporary collective redefinition of property rights within the ghetto areas (Quarantelli and Dynes 1968). The problem can be approached this way if property is conceived of as normative definitions of the right to use community resources, rather than as material objects. Widespread looting in mass disturbances is a manifestation of an extensive albeit temporary socially supported reversal of traditional definitions of property. Established procedures are rejected, including the usual mechanisms of distribution and pricing.

Such a process of collective definitions and redefinitions is not operative solely at times of disturbances. It is always going on, particularly among dissatisfied groups such as those found in American ghetto areas. Ghetto blacks particularly come to perceive their low economic status in the course of their contacts with certain types of retail stores. Such stores are for most ghetto inhabitants where economic realities become apparent. It is there that the limits of the weekly pay check and its inelasticity becomes obvious. Such stores likewise highlight the range of goods potentially available within the larger society which could be obtained only if property rights were differently defined. Certainly, as surveys show, whatever the actual facts might be, many blacks *believe* they are overcharged or given inferior or spoiled goods in neighborhood ghetto stores (Campbell and Schuman 1968). Thus, because of this definitional process retail stores are especially vulnerable to being negatively defined.

A similar analysis could but will not be made of how the police also come to be negatively viewed in terms of their everyday operations in the ghetto. The development of a collective definition, for example, of "police brutality" can be buttressed by experience. However, such experiences are neither necessary nor essential. As many surveys show, most blacks *believe* they are mistreated by policemen. Thus, police-black interactions are seen as symbolizing the low political standing of blacks.

Retail stores and the police, of course, are in many ways the key points of contact between the ghetto and larger white society. For a number of ghetto blacks, in fact, the two types of organizations involved are not only where they have the most direct interaction with dominant white society but, more important, they are social situations which many of the blacks perceive as illustrating their low status consistency. Furthermore, the three dimensions of income, status, and power can combine and recombine in a number of ways. Retail stores symbolize not only lack of economic resources but a despised style of life. Perceived police activity not only reflects absence of political power but also a lowly way of life. Fire departments, especially since they tend to have almost exclusively white personnel, also symbolize to a degree black inability to exercise power and to have access to higher income positions.

Nevertheless, all this would still not explain why the major organizational victims in disturbances are retail stores and the local police, with minor attention being paid to firemen. Such pre-disturbance definitions as discussed merely raise the probability that such kinds of targets would become victimized in the emergent situation that characterizes a disturbance. As Berk (1972, pp. 113-18) has noted, it is a major research error in much collective behavior analysis to assume a direct link between antecedent conditions and consequences without closely examining the behavioral processes in between.

A disturbance is a collective behavior situation with constantly emergent norms and relationships (see Weller and Quarantelli 1973). That is, there is the continuous surfacing of new definitions and social relationships in the situation. Since new definitions are rooted in old social structures, it is not surprising that with a pre-disturbance perception of retail stores and the police as symbols of low status consistency, participants in disturbances are likely to attack those symbols. Turner, in talking of the development of collective behavior in general, notes that "the rumor process serves to bring symbols into selective salience and to reconstitute their meanings in relation to shared requirements for action" (1964, p. 407). We are essentially saying the same thing with respect to what leads up to certain objects becoming the focus of attack in the disturbances we are considering. In the course of interacting with others in the disturbances, the participants, partly falling back on old definitions of symbolic indicators of low status, see as salient certain types of organizations, which considerably raises the probability they will be attacked.

Thus, reaction to the lowly economic position is partly revealed in looting, which, in one sense at least, is seen as temporarily redistributing wealth. The perceived low prestige in the ghetto style of life can partially be seen as being reacted to in the smoke of the arsonist. The ghetto style of life has such low values in this connection that there can be little loss. Perceived political powerlessness is responded to by attacks on the symbols of power which are around the ghetto area, such as police and fire personnel. There is an old saying that possession is nine-tenths of the law, but ghetto residents as a whole have neither possession nor the law. The disturbances reflect this, and retail stores and the police are the victims, less because of actual discriminatory or repressive behavior on their parts, but more because ghetto residents see them as symbolizing their low status consistency.

Of course, which particular stores and what specific police are attacked (a problem we are not addressing in this paper) are determined by many other factors. McPhail (1971) generally discussing collective behavior in disturbances, suggests that the line of action that is likely to develop in any given situation is dependent on such circumstances as availability of people and objects of interaction, the course of the mobilization of any new emergent group, and the specific interactional patterns that will occur. If this is so in a disturbance some "innocent" victims might be selected. Given a strong negative definition of a grocery chain and its reinforcement during the interaction in a disturbance, many outlets of such a company may be attacked. But conversely, certain stores might be "saved" from destruction by a positive general definition. Something of this kind could explain the fact that in the 1968 disturbances in Washington, for instance, many outlets of one supermarket chain were attacked while practically none of the stores of another company in the same neighborhood were touched.

The kinds of fluid social situations and the selective foci involved in the disturbances we have been discussing certainly seem best explained in terms of a collective definitional process. If there is one thing that mass disturbances were, it is that they were the acts of collectivities rather than individuals. These acts, furthermore, were for the most part public rather than private; it was notorious that looting, for instance, was not done secretly and furtively, but openly and in public view. Finally, instead of the criminal acts being disapproved of as they would normally be, the illegal actions of participants generally had substantial social support of other local ghetto residents.

However, collective definitions and redefinitions may change quickly. This is especially likely to occur when other, higher values come into the picture. This can be seen in the two following examples known to the authors. In one, firemen were attempting to put out fires in a cluster of small stores. They were being harassed by what is often described as an "angry" crowd, when a wall of a building collapsed, burying two firemen. Immediately members of that crowd started to help the firemen rescue their co-workers. What moments before had been objects of attack now became human beings needing "our" help.

In another disturbance, units of a fire department battling a major store conflagration were being subjected to verbal abuse and threats by the nearby ghetto dwellers. Wind conditions changed suddenly, raising the possibility that the fire would spread into the next block, which consisted primarily of private homes. While the fire officials on the scene wanted to continue their activities, police officers forced them to withdraw from the area. The residents of the threatened homes pleaded with the firemen to stay and offered armed protection to any units that would remain.

Such rapid transformations from harassers and hecklers to helpers and protectors shows the volatility of the definitions that develop. Thus, a redefinition of property, for instance, setting the stage for vandalism or looting can come about very rapidly in a collective context. In the same fashion, there can be very quick redefinitions sometimes back to earlier conceptions, whether about people or things. Any static kind of analyses trying to relate pre-disturbance attributes or conditions to behavior in disturbances can not handle well such drastic shifts in behavior. Any assumptions of a generalized belief (a la Smelser 1963) or fixed common motives (a la Gurr 1970) shared by all or most participants seem equally inadequate in an explanatory scheme. A situational rather than a dispositional kind of analysis would seem to be far more appropriate.

Conclusion

We have examined who the victims were in the American urban racial disturbances of the 1960s, what different types of victims were attacked, and if the offender-victim social relationship could account for the behavior. The literature on victims is relatively scanty but did offer the clue that certain aspects of organizations might raise the probability of their being attacked. An analysis of our own data and studies conducted by others indicate that organizations were overwhelmingly the victims in the disturbances, but that certain types of organizations were very disproportionately singled out for attack. Various explanations advanced to account for such selectivity seem to be inadequate to account for the phenomena generally. We suggested that a starting point for a general explanation might be the social organizational variables of class, status, and power. Ghetto blacks see themselves as ranking low on all three dimensions and perceive their interactions with certain kinds of organizations as symbolizing this fact. These perceptions of certain organizations rest not on any intrinsic characteristics of the organizations but how such entities are defined in predisturbance times, and if such definitions are reinforced during periods of disorders. During the latter kinds of situations, there is the emergence of collective behavior which is particularly manifested in a public and socially supported definitional process which can shift very quickly. Selectivity of organizational victims in disturbances therefore is to be accounted for by variations in the definitions, which are partly dependent on perceived patterns of exchanges between blacks and organizations operating in the ghetto. Our analysis here does not, and was not intended to, account for the disturbances or why specific objects were attacked, but it does give some meaning to the available data on the selection of certain types of organizations as victims in mass disturbances.[j]

References

Aldrich, Howard and Albert J. Reiss. "The Effect of Civil Disorders on Small Business in the Inner City." *Journal of Social Issues* 26 (1970): 187-206.

Amir, Menachem. "Patterns of Forcible Rape." In Marshall Clinard and Richard Quinney, *Criminal Behavior Systems: A Typology*. New York: Holt, Rinehart and Winston, 1967, pp. 60-75.

Anderson, William, Russell Dynes and E.L. Quarantelli. "Counterrioters in Urban Disturbances." *Society* (in press).

Banfield, Edward. "Rioting Mainly for Fun and Profit." In James Q. Wilson (ed.), *The Metropolitan Enigma: Inquiries into the Nature and Dimensions of America's Urban Crisis*. Cambridge, Mass.: Harvard University Press, 1968, pp. 289-308.

----

[j]For organizations as actors in disturbances see the *American Behavioral Scientist* issue on "Urban Civil Disturbances: Organizational Change and Group Emergence," edited by Dynes and Quarantelli (1973).

Baskin, Jane et al. *Race Related Civil Disorders 1967-69*. Waltham, Mass.: Lemberg Center for the Study of Violence, 1971.

Berk, Richard. "The Controversy Surrounding Analyses of Collective Violence: Some Methodological Notes." In James Short and Marvin Wolfgang (eds.), *Collective Violence*. Chicago: Aldine Atherton, 1972, pp. 112-18.

Berk, Richard and Howard Aldrich. "Patterns of Vandalism During Civil Disorders as an Indicator of Selection of Targets." *American Sociological Review* 37 (1972): 533-47.

Blauner, Robert. "Internal Colonialism and Ghetto Revolt." *Social Problems* 16 (1969): 393-408.

Boskin, Joseph. "The Revolt of the Urban Ghettos, 1964-1967." *Annals American Academy of Political and Social Science* 382 (1969): 2-14.

Cameron, Mary O. *The Booster and the Snitch*. New York: Free Press, 1964.

Camp, George M. *Nothing to Lose: A Study of Bank Robbery in America*. Ph.D. dissertation, Yale University, 1967.

Campbell, Angus and Howard Schuman. "Racial Attitudes in Fifteen American Cities." Supplemental Studies for the National Advisory Commission on Civil Disorders. Washington, D.C.: U.S. Government Printing Office, 1968, 1-207.

Campbell, James; Joseph Sahid; and David Stang. *Law and Order Reconsidered*. New York: Bantam, 1970.

Caplan, Nathan. "The New Ghetto Man: A Review of Recent Empirical Studies." *Journal of Social Issues* 26 (1970): 59-75.

Caplovitz, David. *The Poor Pay More*. New York: Free Press, 1963.

Chicago Commission on Race Relations. *The Negro in Chicago*. Chicago: University of Chicago Press, 1922.

Downes, Bryan T. "Social and Political Characteristics of Riot Cities: A Comparative Study." In James A. Geschwender (ed.), *The Black Revolt*. Englewood Cliffs, New Jersey: Prentice-Hall, 1971, pp. 332-49.

Dynes, Russell and E.L. Quarantelli. "Organization as Victim in Mass Civil Disturbances." *Issues in Criminology* 5 (1970): 181-93.

Dynes, Russell R. and E.L. Quarantelli (eds.). "Urban Civil Disturbances." *American Behavioral Scientist* 16 (1973).

Dynes, Russell R.; E.L. Quarantelli; and James L. Ross. *Police Perspectives and Behavior in a Campus Disturbance*. Washington: Law Enforcement Assistance Administration, 1972.

Ennis, Philip H. *Criminal Victimization in the United States: A Report of a National Survey*. Washington, D.C.: U.S. Government Printing Office, 1967.

Flaming, Karl. *Who "Riots" and Why? Black and White Perspectives in Milwaukee*. Milwaukee: Milwaukee Urban League, 1968.

Fogelson, Robert M. "Violence and Grievances: Reflections on the 1960s Riots." *Journal of Social Issues* 26 (1970): 141-64.

Fogelson, Robert M. *Violence as Protest: A Study of Riots and Ghettos*. Garden City, New York: Anchor, 1971.

Fogelson, Robert M. and Robert B. Hill. "Who Riots? A Study of Participation in the 1967 Riots." Supplemental Studies for the National Advisory Commission on Civil Disorders. Washington, D.C.: U.S. Government Printing Office, 1968, pp. 217-48.

Gilbert, Ben W. *Ten Blocks from the White House: Anatomy of the Washington Riots of 1968.* New York: Praeger, 1968.

Goldberg, Louis C. "Ghetto Riots and Others: The Faces of Civil Disorders in 1967." In James A. Geschwender (ed.), *The Black Revolt.* Englewood Cliffs, New Jersey: Prentice Hall, 1971, pp. 414-31.

Gurr, Ted R. *Why Men Rebel.* Princeton, New Jersey: Princeton University Press, 1970.

Horning, Donald. *Blue Collar Crime.* New Haven, Conn.: College and University Press, 1973.

Janowitz, Morris. *Social Control of Escalated Riots.* Chicago: University of Chicago Center for Policy Study, 1968.

Kerner, Otto et al. *Report of the National Advisory Commission on Civil Disorders.* New York: Bantam, 1968.

Lee, Alfred and Norman Humphrey. *Race Riot.* New York: Dryden, 1943.

Lively, Edward. "Report of the Akron Commission on Civil Disorders," 1969 (unpublished).

McCone, J.A. et al. *Violence in the City: An End or a Beginning?* Los Angeles: Governor's Commission on the Los Angeles Riots, 1965.

McPhail, Clark. "Civil Disorder Participation: A Critical Examination of Recent Research." *American Sociological Review* 36 (1971): 1058-73.

Marion, B.W. et al. *Food Marketing in Low Income Areas: A Review of Past Findings and a Case Analysis in Columbus, Ohio.* Columbus, Ohio: Cooperative Extension Service, The Ohio State University, 1969.

Mattick, Hans W. "The Form and Content of Recent Riots." *Midway* 9 (1968): 3-32.

Oberschall, Anthony, "The Los Angeles Riot." *Social Problems* 15 (1968): 335-38.

Oberschall, Anthony. *Social Conflict and Social Movements.* Englewood Cliffs, New Jersey: Prentice Hall, 1973.

O'Hagan, John T. *Fire Fighting During Civil Disorders.* New York: International Association of Fire Chiefs, 1968.

Pittman, David and William Handy. "Patterns in Criminal Aggravated Assault." *Journal of Criminal Law, Criminology and Police Science* 55 (1964): 462-70.

President's Commission on Law Enforcement and Administration of Justice. *The Challenge of Crime in a Free Society.* Washington, D.C.: U.S. Government Printing Office, 1967.

Professional Standards Division. *Civil Disorders After-Action Reports.* Washington, D.C.: International Association of Chiefs of Police, 1968.

Quarantelli, E.L. and Russell R. Dynes. "What Looting in Civil Disturbances Really Means." *Trans-Action* 5 (1968): 9-14.

Quarantelli, E.L. and Russell R. Dynes (eds.). "Organizational and Group
    Behavior in Disasters." *American Behavioral Scientist* 13 (1970).
Quarantelli, E.L. and Russell R. Dynes. "When Disaster Strikes (It Isn't Much
    Like What You've Heard and Read About)." *Psychology Today* 5 (1972):
    66-70.
Quinney, Richard. *The Social Reality of Crime.* Boston: Little Brown, 1970.
Reckless, Walter. *The Crime Problem.* 5th edition. New York: Appleton-
    Century-Crofts, 1973.
Reiss, Albert J. *The Police and the Public.* New Haven, Conn.: Yale University
    Press, 1971.
Report for Action. Trenton, New Jersey: Governor's Select Commission on
    Civil Disorder, State of New Jersey, 1968.
Rude, George. *Paris and London in the Eighteenth Century: Studies in Popular
    Protest.* New York: Viking Press, 1971.
Rudwick, Elliott M. *Race Riot at East St. Louis, July 2, 1917.* Carbondale, Ill.:
    Southern Illinois University Press, 1964.
Schafer, Stephen. *The Victim and His Criminal: A Study of Functional
    Responsibility.* New York: Random House, 1968.
Skolnick, Jerome H. *The Politics of Protest.* New York: Ballantine Books, 1969.
Smelser, Neil. *Theory of Collective Behavior.* Glencoe, Ill.: Free Press, 1963.
Smigel, Erwin O. "Public Attitudes Toward Stealing as Related to the Size of
    the Victim Organization." *American Sociological Review* 21 (1955):
    320-27.
Smigel, Erwin O. and H. Laurence Ross. *Crimes Against Bureaucracy.* Prince-
    ton, New Jersey: Van Nostrand Reinhold, 1970.
Stone, Gregory and Harvey Farberman (eds.). *Social Psychology Through
    Symbolic Interaction.* Waltham, Mass.: Ginn-Blaisdell, 1970.
Taft, Philip and Philip Ross. "American Labor Violence: Its Causes, Character
    and Outcome." In Hugh Graham and Ted Gurr (eds.), *Violence in America.*
    New York: Bantam, 1969.
Turner, Ralph. "Collective Behavior." In Robert Faris (ed.), *Handbook of
    Modern Sociology.* Chicago: Rand McNally, 1964.
Von Hentig, Hans. *The Criminal and His Victim.* New Haven, Conn.: Yale
    University Press, 1948.
Weber, Max. *Essays in Sociology.* New York: Oxford, 1946.
Weller, Jack M. and E.L. Quarantelli. "Neglected Characteristics of Collective
    Behavior." *American Journal of Sociology* 79 (1973): 665-685.
Wolfgang, Marvin E. *Patterns in Criminal Homicide.* Philadelphia: University
    of Pennsylvania Press, 1958.

**Part III
Children's Victimization**

10

The Battered Child: A Review of Studies and Research in the Area of Child Abuse

Emilio C. Viano

A Grim Picture

A recent poll by the Institute for Social Science in Bonn showed that 77 percent of Germans consider beating an animal the worst of twelve major crimes. Child beating was fifth. There are half a million members of the German Humane Society for Animals and a mere 20,000 in its counterpart for children.

Figures can, and often are, wrongly used. But the fact remains, there is an upward trend in West Germany—among other countries—in the number of cases of child abuse.

An article in the weekly news magazine *Der Spiegel* carried the title: "The Germans Detest Children." It described the staggering rate of child abuse, woefully inadequate legal machinery to prosecute guilty parents, and formidable evidence of widespread hostility to children. "In no other industrial nation are so many children mistreated as in West Germany," claimed Friedrich Lejeune, president of the German Association for the Protection of Children. The Munich psychologist Heinz Rolf Luckert put it another way: "We beat our children dumb in this nation." It's a grim picture.

Children have been considered to be the property of parents for centuries and, consequently, adults have had a free hand to do with their offspring what they pleased. Only recently has our society begun to seriously question where the rights to health and, in some cases, life, begins. It was not until 1875 that our society was forced to recognize the existence of what is now referred to as "the battered child syndrome." At that time, the New York Society for the Prevention of Cruelty to Animals was presented with the case of a little girl, Mary Ellen. She was discovered chained to her bed and suffered from severe malnutrition, as her daily diet consisted of bread and water. After that case was taken to court, the Society for the Prevention of Cruelty to Children was founded. It was formed to " . . . rescue children from vicious and immoral surroundings and to prosecute offenders to prevent the cruel neglect, beating or other abuse of children . . . and for the enforcement of all laws for the protection of minors from abuse."[1]

In 1946, J. Caffey first reported that subdural hematoma in infants was frequently accompanied by injuries to the long bones.[2] Then, in 1953, Silverman described multiple bone injuries as the "disease of infancy."[3] Finally, in 1962, Kempe and his associates coined the term "battered baby syndrome" to " . . . categorize clinical conditions in young children who have received serious physical abuse, generally from a parent or foster parent."[4] It becomes readily apparent that the recognition of child abuse is a relatively new phenomena in our society.

In the past five to seven years, there has been an increased awareness and reporting of child abuse, but it still remains difficult to acquire statistics on the problem. Estimations have been made which place the rate of abuse at 250,000 cases a year, with 37,500 of those cases resulting in death or serious, permanent damage.[5] In addition, Dr. Ray E. Helfer has stated more children under the age of five die from "parentally or guardian inflicted injuries than from tuberculosis, whooping cough, polio, measles, diabetes, rheumatic fever and appendicitis, combined."[6]

In Germany, the incidence of child abuse is high by European standards. One thousand children die annually because of beatings and other forms of sadistic torture.

The book "Kinder in Deutschland" reports that 95 percent of child abuse cases never reach the court. The author claims that there are actually 30,000 to 80,000 cases of child abuse each year and there is an upward trend. In West Germany, the fatality rate is 38 percent, compared with 25 percent in Britain, 19 percent in France, and 12 percent in Italy.[7]

The difficulty in the assessment of the problem stems first of all from the various definitions of abuse; then, the abuse may not come to the attention of the medical authorities; it may not be diagnosed as abuse; or it simply might not be reported. Neglect and abuse range from deprivations of food, clothing, shelter, and parental love, to death. The problem has been termed "battered child syndrome," "unrecognized trauma," and "maltreatment syndrome in children." The Massachusetts Society for the Prevention of Cruelty to Children defines physical abuse as " . . . any situation in which a child is physically mistreated by an adult to the point that care or protection by a source outside the family is needed."[8] Neglect is viewed in both a legal and social framework by the M.S.P.C.C. It is referred to in terms of parental rights and corresponding duties. Adelson believes abuse is more than just an act of commission, but includes acts of omission, also. He states, " . . . deprivations of adequate nutrition are equally dangerous to the child's welfare."[9] Elizabeth Elmer has defined abuse as merely a physical assault by an adult against a child. Neglect, she says, is chronic failure of the adult to protect the child from obvious physical danger.[10]

With regard to the fact that abuse may not come to the attention of medical authorities and it is not diagnosed as such, several authors have explained this phenomena psychologically. It is felt that doctors are disinclined to believe parents could actually beat or neglect their children. The examining physician, as a result of the hesitancy, gives the parent the benefit of the doubt. According to Raffalli: "Physicians have great difficulty both in believing that parents could have attacked their children [and] in undertaking the essential questioning of parents on this subject."[11]

The physician, who might also be a parent, may perceive the parental role to be threatened (doctor's children get bruises also). Consequently, much mixed feeling is evidenced on the part of the physician.[12] It has also been suggested that some physicians fear court procedures, adverse publicity, or simply do not know the correct method to follow. In many cases, physicians are unfamiliar with the "battered child syndrome" due to a lack of appropriate training in medical school. A study done in the Washington, D.C., area revealed a large percentage of physicians who lacked awareness of the battered child syndrome, or necessary community procedures to follow. It was concluded from this study," . . . the lines of communication between the medical profession and the government and community agencies have not been effective in familiarizing physicians in the area with the syndrome."[13] In addition, private physicians lack laboratory facilities necessary for an adequate investigation and are hesitant to defy the traditional "doctor-patient relationship." They often ask, "Can I ask a patient to pay for X-rays which may be used against him in court?" But then another question must also be asked. Who is the patient—the battered and abused child or the parent who pays the bill?

Finally, a parent who batters his or her child is likely to take the child to a different hospital every time hospitalization is required. This tactic is an evasive measure used to detract attention, as no record of previous injuries are on file at the particular hospital.

It will be the purpose of this paper to review some of the more important studies done in the area of child abuse. We will attempt to highlight who the parents are who use their children as ash trays, drown them in scalding water, burn them, throw them downstairs, bang their heads against walls and radiators, suffocate and starve them. Who are these children and how are they protected? How might these atrocious crimes be prevented? What are the legal aspects of the problem and how is the syndrome diagnosed? In each study cited only that portion relevant to the topic under discussion will be considered.

Who Are the Parents?

The first comprehensive study in the area was conducted by Dr. C.H. Kempe in Colorado. He took a national survey of hospitals to elucidate the incidence of the "battered child syndrome" during a one-year period. Seventy-one hospitals reported a total of 302 cases, of which 33 died and 85 sustained permanent brain damage. In one-third of these cases, proper diagnosis was followed by some form of legal action. Kempe states the type and degree of abuse varies from the extreme of murder, where psychosis is generally apparent in the parent, to the other extreme, where no overt harm is done. In these latter cases, parents (usually the mother) go to a psychiatrist with feelings of guilt and anxiety related to fantasies of harming their children. Such fantasies may extend to slapping behavior. These parents are usually treatable. In all battering parents, Kempe concludes, there is a defect in the personality which allows their aggressive impulses free expression. In addition, there appears to be a prevailing philosophy of "do unto others as you were done unto."[14] Experts at a symposium on child abuse held in November 1972 in Gaithersburg, Maryland, agreed that children who are physically abused by their parents tend to batter their own children after they themselves grow up and become parents. Studies show that a majority of teenage murderers were battered children.

This finding has been substantiated—for example—by studies such as the longitudinal one conducted in the District of Columbia by Silver, Dublin, and Lourie. This study revealed a definite pattern of violence breeding violence and used as an example Sirhan Sirhan, a battered child, and the convicted assassin of Robert F. Kennedy.[15] Kempe states that the parental-child rearing behavior is generally passed on from one generation to the next. There appears to be an identification by the child with the abusing parent. It is a personality defect, and a previous history of abuse, rather than a psychopathic personality or a low socioeconomic status that battering parents have in common. Kempe also found the battered child to be illegitimate, premaritally conceived, or born at some other inconvenient time.[16]

Another study, conducted by J.C. Holter and S.B. Friedman, was designed to assess the usefulness of early case findings in the prevention of further child abuse. In this project, two surveys were conducted. The first was done by a team of investigators and the second, a follow-up, was administered by nurses at the homes of the parents. The sample included all children who entered the emergency room of the University of Rochester Medical Center with injuries. The sample consisted of nineteen children from eighteen families. Forty percent of the children were classified "accident group," 38 percent were in the "repeated accident group," 11 percent were in the "suspected abuse group," and 11 percent made up the "accident with neglect group." The child, the family, and the environmental factors associated with the accident were examined. Twelve of the parents were white, while six were non-white. There were ten Protestant, seven Catholic, and one Jewish units. Fourteen of the families were complete family units, while four were broken. It was discovered that all groups experienced "stressful lives" at the time of the "accident." There was an acute family illness at the time, marital discord was evidenced, difficulty in rearing children was expressed, as well as financial strain, social isolation, and lack of support from family, friends, and professionals. The families expressed similar problems, but the abusive parents, it was concluded, handled their problems in a different manner—i.e., they beat their children.[17] The abusive families were usually new to the community and there appeared to be "marked psychopathology or mental retardation"[18] in fourteen of the eighteen families. The battering parents were seen to be immature, dependent, impulsive, rigid, self-centered, rejecting, angry, and had themselves been abused as children. The majority of these parents were self-supporting, but their income was insufficient to meet the daily needs of the family. In addition, these parents volunteered little, if any, information about the "accident," were evasive, and made contradictory statements with regard to the injury. They exhibited hostility toward the child because he sustained an injury and appeared uninterested in the diagnosis, prognosis or treatment given the child. Finally, these parents displayed little or no guilt and remorse.[19]

A third report was made by L. Adelson on the investigation conducted by the Cuyahoga County Coroner's Office. The deaths of five infants caused by starvation were studied. It was found that the histories of terminal illness, given by the mothers, were similar in all five cases. The information offered, however, refuted clinical evidence. The common remark given was: "He was fine up until about a day or so ago." Investigations of the home environments revealed long periods of willfull neglect and an unwillingness and failure to seek available medical attention for the child. Three of the five infants were found in deplorable conditions. One of the more grotesque cases follows: "He was found dead in his crib by a family friend who had stopped in at the home. A bottle of sour milk was in his crib and maggots were crawling around in his soiled diapers."[20] Three of the five were born out of wedlock, as were their eight siblings.[21]

In an epidemiological study conducted in New York during a one-year-period, 313 children from 293 families were reviewed. One-half of these families were on welfare rolls. The mother more frequently abused the child of her own sex than did the father. Ninety percent of the mothers were over twenty years of age and two-thirds of the sample were married, but 35 percent were either divorced or separated. In 17 percent of the cases at least one parent had undergone some form of institutionalization—penal, mental, etc.—while 50 percent suffered from present psychological difficulties.[22]

J.D. Delsordo reviewed a study conducted by the Pennsylvania Society for the Prevention of Cruelty to Children. The eighty cases of abused children were classified according to type and method of disposition. In this section of the paper, only the type of parent will be mentioned. The first type, the mentally ill parent, comprised four of the eighty cases. The second type of parent was one who abused the child as a result of an overflow of parental frustration, irresponsibility or lack of belief in oneself. The parental frustrations were taken out on the children in the form of physical abuse. These parents made up thirteen of the eighty cases. The third category was "nonspecific parental disturbance" which resulted in severe abuse to the child. In these cases (eight of the eighty cases), there was no evidence of psychosis in the parents, there was parental dependency, and the child was seen as a burden and as a source of competition. Fourthly, there were twelve parents who battered their children as a result of harshness in discipline. These abusers were rigid and unfeeling. They beat the child (usually an adolescent) because of a failure to comply with parental expectations or participation in a forbidden act. Finally, there were those parents with misplaced conflicts who abused their children. The conflicts were projected onto the child and the family unit or marital unit was in some degree of conflict. The child was either illegitimate, premaritally conceived or was brain damaged. The abused child was perceived as a defeatable adversary, a pawn in the family conflict.[23]

David Gil, in a study where he found 6,000 cases of child abuse reported in 1967, classified parents into two categories. The first group consisted of patent psychotics with pervasive anger, depression, and passive-aggressive personalities. They were also cold disciplinarians. The second group was impulsive, but adequate, and experienced either marital conflict or an identity crisis. Gil found more cases of child abuse among socioeconomically disadvantaged homes, especially those with large or broken families. In addition, these cases were more representative of the second type mentioned.[24]

Elizabeth Elmer, who has done a great deal of research in the area of battered children, points to the fact that there have been radical changes in child rearing in the past 100 to 150 years. Prior to that period, aggression toward children prevailed. In the eighteenth and nineteenty centuries, children were seen to be results of carnal sin and possessed by the devil which had to be beaten out of them. She suggests the possibility that abusive parents have been, in some way, insulated from the acculturation process.[25] In her study of a Pittsburgh hospital, she and her associates found a large incidence of neurotic and psychotic behavior, impulsive behavior in areas other than child rearing, little guilt or anxiety, marital instability, early emotional deprivation, physical or mental illness, environmental pressure, such as poverty or substandard housing, lack of preparation for pregnancy or birth, and finally, a belief that the child was unhealthy and troublesome.[26]

The Massachusetts Society for the Prevention of Cruelty to Children conducted a study on child abuse in an effort to determine the extent of the problem and its basic characteristics. Their method of study consisted of a seminar series for the committee members involved, and questionnaires sent out to various agencies at two different stages. The first questionnaire dealt with the type of abuse encountered and the people involved. The second questionnaire requested more detailed information on each case. After the data were gathered, they were analyzed by the seminar. It was found that the families involved had lived in the same place for many years, but were not integrated into the community. They were self-supporting, but had serious social problems such as marital conflicts, financial problems, etc. In addition, more than 50 percent of the children were premaritally conceived and the parents were young at marriage and time of abuse. Their personalities were characteristically hostile and aggressive. They were not only rigid and compulsive, but lacked warmth and rejected their children. These parents were more concerned with their own pleasures and perceived the abused child responsible for their troubles. These battering parents were observed to be passive and dependent and a paternal physical disability was often evidenced. The home atmosphere was angry, rigid, and strictly disciplined.[27]

After a careful review of several studies conducted in the area of child abuse, one is left with the distinct impression that a great many contradictions and inconsistent findings have been reported. Some investigators have commented on the absence of psychopathology in the abusing parent, while others insist it is prevalent. Kempe found no correlation between abusive parents and low socioeconomic status. Gil's findings are to the contrary, however. Parents were found to be young at the time of marriage and at the time of abuse. This fact was also refuted in another report. Some researchers found the families to be new to the community, while others insist the parents are oldtimers. The only consistent findings were with regard to previous abuse, social conflicts, and instability. Social problems which result in abusive, violent behavior in parents occur anywhere—in the slums, in middle-class America, as well as in the upper echelons of society. It matters not whether one is rich, poor, old, young, intelligent or ignorant. What matters instead is the fact that the interplay of mental, physical, and environmental stresses which result in family instability and violence against defenseless children occurs anywhere in our society. No one is immune. It is everyone's concern.

Who is the Battered Child?

Most of the previously cited studies give descriptions of the children who were victimized at the hands of their parents or guardians. The most essential feature one gathers from the data available is the fact that the child who is abused is usually too young to give an account of the incident or is too frightened to do so.

According to Edith Lee, supervising probation officer of the San Francisco Juvenile Court, the type of parental abuse depends on the type of child. If the child is illegitimate, which is often the case, and the woman later marries the father of the child, this child will usually receive the fury of the mother. Many times, the child is an unwanted economic burden; the mother and father do not have the money or time to do the things they want. This child, too, will receive the brunt of parental frustration. In addition, the child may resemble an unliked spouse, or be a pawn between two conflicting adults. Usually the parent's conflict is below the surface, whereby the parent hates the child but does not know the reason why.[28]

In the study of physical abuse conducted by the Massachusetts Society for the Prevention of Cruelty to Children, it was discovered that one-half of the patients in their sample were under seven years of age and three-fourths of the children were under thirteen years. These children were not unusual in terms of mental ability, but all had seriously impaired parental relations. They tended to overreact to hostility, depression, hyperactivity, and destructiveness. Although they could not relate to their parents, these children were able to form successful interpersonal relations with other relatives, peers, and teachers. They were perceived to be innocent victims of something more than their behavior.[29]

Elizabeth Elmer and Grace Gregg, in a review of a Pittsburgh hospital, described the developmental characteristics of fifty abused children. In this particular study, medical charts were examined, as well as medical histories from other sources. Social service reports were studied and a series of two interviews with the mothers of the abused children were conducted. Responses to two standard questionnaires were also reviewed. The results of the study revealed most of the battered children lived in or near urban Pittsburgh, were from a low socioeconomic level, and Protestant. Thirteen of the children were white, seven black, ten males, and ten females. The children were subsequently divided into two groups. The first group consisted of eleven children who functioned normally with no previous medical history. The second group of nine was comprised of those children with significant past medical histories. As might be expected, the parents of the children in the first group said the child sustained the injury just recently. The parents from the second group insisted their children suffered from long-standing organic diseases. Also noted from this study was: "... prolonged neglect more frequently accompanies the abuse of Caucasian children than Negro children."[30] Severe physical abuse was also found to be predictive of unusual differences in development. Growth failure, which is reversible, was also noticed in this sample of abused children.[31]

According to Milowe and Lourie, there are various defects in the abused child which may be seen as precipitating factors which lead to a lack of responsiveness on the part of the child (retardation, blindness, etc.) The end result of this lack of child responsiveness is parental frustration and aggression. These investigators also feel the battered child demonstrates a developmental lag. It is difficult to assess whether the lag was evident from the time of birth or whether it resulted from an emotional deprivation and physical abuse.[32]

In an epidemiological study conducted in New York in 1964, Simons et al. discovered more than two-thirds of the 313 abused children observed were less than five years old. More than twice as many nonwhite children were abused when compared to the incidence of white abuse. At least 10 percent of the battered children had previous severe disabilities, such as brain damage, eye or orthopedic impairments. In addition, 32 percent were illegitimate.[33]

Richard Galdston made intensive observations of those children admitted to the Children's Hospital-Medical Center in Boston. These patients ranged from three months to three and a half years, with the largest group between the ages of six and eighteen months. They did not possess the verbal or motor skills necessary to provoke the abuse. The behavior exhibited by these children while in the hospital was significant. They all displayed extreme fright upon contact, whimpered, hid under the sheets, were apathetic and withdrew from tactile stimuli. There appeared to be a blunting of all external manifestations of inner life, as they sat motionless. After the stay at the hospital, the children gradually moved from this lethargic state of passivity to increasingly active behavior manifestations.[34]

C.H. Kempe, in his pioneer study, found clinical manifestations of child abuse to range from mild ("failure to thrive") to severe (injury to soft tissue and skeleton). The children in his sample were generally under three years of age, their general health was below par, poor skin hygiene was obvious, as well as injury to the soft tissue, and malnutrition.[35]

Finally, Morris, Gould, and Matthews made observations based on several studies conducted in hospitals. They dealt, generally, with the implications for early identification of neglectful or abusive parents, for the prevention of further abuse and neglect. The authors studied the case records and follow-up studies of thirty-three severely neglected or battered children from twenty-nine families, and twenty-three children brought to the hospital for "failure to thrive." It was concluded from their research that neglected and battered children cry hopelessly during the hospital examination and treatment, but otherwise cried little in general. These children did not look to their parents for reassurance, nor did they exhibit any expectation of comfort. They were wary of physical contact, apprehensive when other children cried or when adults approached the crying children. They were less frightened of the ward and adjusted rather quickly to their new life style. They were always on the alert for danger and in constant search for something—food, favors, services, etc.[36]

Our feelings after reading the material available on battered children are not completely solidified. On the one hand, several studies show that the abused child is often afflicted with some abnormality which results in parental frustration. But often the child is a relatively normal, healthy specimen. He or she evidently "cries a lot," "wets or soils his pants," "disobeys" or "is impudent and stubborn." This form of behavior is characteristic of many unbattered children as well. The literature on the subject also points to the fact that the abused child is usually the only battered child in the family, that in fact, the other children are generally treated with much affection. The battered child is a specific, defenseless object of frustration to the parent. He or she does nothing, objectively speaking, to provoke or promote the abuse, but is rather a convenient scapegoat for the parent who is a victim of social, psychological and environmental stress. Society's "hands-off" policy in this respect is illustrated, for example, by the fact that a Society for the Prevention of Cruelty to Animals was established prior to the establishment of one for the protection of children. In addition, today we still speak of honoring the "doctor-patient" privilege. The patient, in the case of a battered child, is believed to be the parent. In other words, the child has no respectability and lacks moral worth. Instead, the child is the property of the parent. The results of the various studies inclined us to believe that battered children exist everywhere, in all shapes and sizes. With few exceptions it does not seem that a specific *type* of child provokes it own abuse: rather the environment is the guilty and provocative agent.

The Diagnosis

The diagnosis of a battered child is often very difficult to accomplish for several reasons. Some of these reasons have already been mentioned in the first section of the paper with regard to the physician. The doctor is so abhorred by the notion of child abuse, he may fail to consider it as a possibility. This refusal, or denial to recognize the existence of the syndrome, unfortunately results in a poor prognosis for the child, as abuse is characteristically repetitive. There is frequently a differential diagnosis of syphilis, tuberculosis, blood dyscrasia, scurvy, rickets or neoplasm made. These ailments, however, are usually discarded after the appropriate clinical, laboratory or X-ray examinations are administered.[37] If a doctor waits for the obvious signs of child abuse, it is frequently too late. In one particular case study, it was found that 10 percent of the children died, while 30 percent suffered severe brain damage.[38]

The diagnosis of an abused child will usually begin if the physician's suspicion is aroused by a story given to explain the injuries which is at variance with the clinical facts. The age of the child is also indicative, as is the nature of the particular injury. Generally, the appendicular skeleton is the recipient of the trauma caused by adult traction or torsion.[39] The more severely abused child reveals external evidence of trauma, such as bruises, cuts, burns, and soft tissue swelling. The child is frequently unable to move certain extremities.[40] However, the physical manifestations vary from skin abrasions and bruises to ruptured organs in the head, thorax, abdomen or pelvis. Failure to thrive, vitamin deficiency, and death are also seen. Subdural hematoma, with or without a fracture, is very frequent.

Parents often take their children to different hospitals for each incidence of abuse in an effort to eliminate any suspicion. A self-professed innocence pervades, as the parent explains, "He fell out of bed," or "I don't know how it happened. I just can't keep an eye on him everyday." If a doctor's suspicion is, nevertheless, aroused, he should order complete X-rays of the child. The X-rays reveal different injuries sustained by the child at the various stages of healing, with no clinical disease to account for them. If a bone has been previously broken there will be a thickening of the bones outer covering where the break occurred. Multiple fractures in various stages of healing or a separation of the bone from the joint and membrane can also be seen from the X-ray.[41] In other words, an X-ray gives the incidence of prior abuse. As Kempe et al. state, "To the informed physician, the bones tell a story the child is too young or too frightened to tell."[42]

The X-ray is an imperfect tool when used to define a social problem. This examination can depict only the condition of the bones. It cannot spell out the succession of events which resulted in the abuse, nor can it identify the abuser. In the words of one author, "They are a firm starting point for an exploration of social factors."[43] X-rays do provide a permanent record of injuries to the child and they release physicians from a dependence on hearsay evidence. Radiologic findings serve as an initial tool for case finding and are also a subsequent guide for management of the case. Following the diagnosis of a case, subsequent action must be taken to insure the safety of the abused child. Before a discussion of prevention and protection, a review of the existing laws concerning the matter is essential.

The Law

The battered child is not generally brought to the attention of the appropriate authorities, and these agencies are therefore limited in their resources for amelioration of the situation. In addition, it is difficult for society and the law to distinguish where the line should be drawn between severe punishment (which is allowed) and physical abuse. It is in this light that the law, for the most part, addresses itself to the protection of the children, rather than the punishment of the parents.

The U.S. Children's Bureau of the Department of Health, Education and Welfare, in an effort to focus attention on the problem, alert medical professionals to the extensiveness and seriousness of the battered child syndrome, and set in motion community action to provide better services for both the child (protective) and the parent (rehabilitative), drew up a model law in 1963 which required all physicians and institutions to report all suspected cases of child abuse. According to this model law, the report from the physician would include the names and addresses of the child and the parents or caretakers; the child's age, if known; the nature and extent of the injuries (including any evidence of previous injuries); and finally, ". . . other information that the physician believes might be helpful in establishing the cause of the injuries and the identity of the perpetrator."[44] Immunity from liability was granted to the reporting physician. In addition, the law established that neither the physician-patient privilege, nor the husband-wife privilege were grounds for excluding evidence. Any physician who does not report a suspected case of

child abuse would be guilty of a misdemeanor. All the subsequent state
statutes were based on this model law.[45]

As of 1965, every state in the union has enacted a law which provides
for the intervention by society when parental care is perceived to be dangerously faulty or insufficient. In every state the statutory provisions give juvenile courts power over "neglected children." These neglect provisions vary
from state to state. Some focus on the caretaker's behavior, others stress
the place of abode, while still others emphasize the child. The juvenile court,
also, has the power to keep the child in his home and still provide adequate
protection. Protective services aim at the effectuation of constructive changes
within the family where there is evidence of child abuse. The Children's
Bureau, in addition, recommends that in communities where public welfare
agencies offer protective services, they be the agencies which receive medical
reports, not the police department, as previously suggested.[46]

J. B. Reinhart and E. Elmer have written an article in which they comment
on the legislation proposed by the Children's Bureau. They feel the model law
offers the establishment of clear procedures to be followed if abuse is suspected;
it eliminates the prejudices in the management of these children; and should
facilitate the detection of dangerous situations. The child is removed from the
family while the situation is evaluated and a beginning base is provided for an
accurate estimate of the incidence of child abuse. However, on the other hand,
the law concentrates its efforts on the child seen by a physician with no regard
to the possible danger of siblings. Mandatory reporting might also increase the
hazards for the child—the parent will be disinclined to take the injured child to
a physician. A hardship is also caused the adult caretaker. A premature criminal aura is caste of him, even if he is innocent. Finally, Reinhart and Elmer
feel the term "battered child" implies a criminal willingness and leads to a
cut and dried impression of a child beater. According to the authors, in reality,
only a small percentage of abusive parents are seen to be willfully cruel or
criminal.[47]

Thus, in some states legislation has been proposed that would decrease
criminal penalties for child abuse. It is contended that the penalty has not
been effective and that it has been a detriment to the reporting of incidents.
Consequently it is felt that such a move would encourage persons to report
suspected cases to the authorities. For example, in Maryland, the proposed
bill would reduce the maximum penalty for child abuse from fifteen years
imprisonment to six months and a $1,000 fine. It would also place the
offense in the misdemeanor category. It is now a felony. Conversely, the
proposal would create penalties—up to thirty days in jail and a $100 fine—for
"professionals," such as teachers, doctors, and social workers, who fail to
report suspected cases.

It also seems possible that early signs of familial deterioration can be
seen by others than a physician. Those persons who have normal access to

families and children, such as day care center officials, nurses, child welfare workers, etc., should have the same obligations now thrust on physicians, in an effort to protect children and prevent further abuse. In addition, since more and more cases of abuse are recognized, school officials should be less ready to sit back and do nothing about the problem. Is it the duty of the principal, the guidance counselor, the social worker or the teacher to report a suspected case of abuse? Are they also protected from liable suits? A study was conducted in representative midwest schools in order to determine the attitudes of principals and counselors in elementary schools. A two-page questionnaire was passed out to forty-five people with questions which pertained to the role of principals and counselors in cases of child abuse, and the nature of cases encountered. The results revealed observations of sixty-one cases of abuse. The general nature of the abuse was beating and malnutrition. Teachers made the majority of referrals. In twenty-eight of the cases, mothers performed the abuse and, finally, the majority of children remained in the previous environment with corrective or protective means.[48]

The maltreated child often shows no signs of physical abuse, as these are the last phases of the spectrum. Why should the law, if it is really aimed at protection and prevention, seek to correct the problem only in the last stages of the cycle? It would seem more logical to train those people who come into daily contact with the families in methods for detection of preliminary signs of abuse. These individuals should also be granted immunity to liability. The problem is more than just a medical problem. It is a medical-social-phychological-legal problem. Why should the law restrict itself to the medical aspect?

A final comment made by Monrad Paulsen is the final blow which will be aimed at the law, in general. He states:

> Reporting is . . . not enough . . . After a report is made, something has to happen. A multidisciplinary network of protection needs to be developed in each community to implement the good intentions of the law . . . The legislatures which require reporting, but do not provide the means for further protective action delude themselves and neglect children.[49]

Prevention and Protection

> The Battered Baby Syndrome, as one of the symptoms of family breakdown, is a telling argument for the need to reorganize the welfare services toward the positive prevention of family deterioration.[50]

It is the responsibility of society to investigate cases of child abuse to educate and to rehabilitate parental delinquents. There is a need for an integrated effort of all social agencies to fight the problem. Constructive laws should safeguard the rights of the abused child, and of the parents.[51]

The families of these children are usually already known to various social agencies at the time of the abuse. Files include allegations of assault; drunken, disorderly conduct; premarital pregnancy; truancy; shoplifting; and marital discord. There is great need for intensive help for the family as a whole.[52] The extent to which our society is willing to invest in broad social welfare service is quite low. Society is not willing to provide the adequate protective services required for both the child and the family involved.

Serapio R. Zalba has made some salient proposals which would aid in the prevention of child abuse. He suggests the introduction of preventive mental and social hygiene services at the most obvious points of familial stress (i.e., birth of the first child). He calls for more effective remedial efforts. The necessary essentials are more funds to man community based health and welfare services and the establishment of a more sensitive network for the identification of early abuse.[53]

The Committee on Infant and Pre-School Child has stressed the point that agencies must be provided with qualified personnel and funds in order that they may provide adequate protection. There must be legal authority to implement a prompt social investigation with permission to remove the child from the environment presumed to be dangerous. Assistance should also be offered to the family in order to promote more responsible behavior. The agencies of investigation and protective services range from private organizations (S.P.C.C.) to county and city departments of welfare, juvenile branches of the police, and the investigating sections of juvenile or family courts. According to the committee report, any program of protection must involve case finding, case reporting to authorized agency which can offer immediate protective service, and investigation of circumstances surrounding the abuse, and finally the maintenance of a central registry for each reported abuse. This registry would facilitate detection of repeated abuse and should be kept at the city or county department of health or welfare. The committee also recommends that the records be destroyed if innocence is proven.[54]

Helen Boardman described the results of a staff project at the Children's Hospital in Los Angeles in 1959. The purpose of the project was to develop effective means of protection for abused children. The plan was to strengthen family ties by means of a method of intervention which did not involve punitive measures against the parents. The eventual, successful procedure followed was the following:

1. If the examining physician suspected a case of inflicted trauma without an adequate explanation, the hospital social worker obtained a supplementary history from the parents and tried to evaluate the parent-child relationship. The social worker also tried to see if the parent expressed a need for help.

2. A full-time medical staff member then coordinated all the information and decided whether or not the case should be taken to the law enforcement agencies.
3. If a report was in order, the social worker, in a non-accusing manner, informed the parents of the impending action.
4. The social worker then called the officers to the hospital for an initial verbal report, which was followed by a written report.
5. The law then requested a juvenile court petition on behalf of the child. This request initiated further study of the child's situation by a probation officer and brought the child to the attention of the courts.
6. The probation officer worked in conjunction with the social worker to insure that medical and social planning were coordinated in the recommendations to the court.
7. The juvenile court was able to evaluate the need for protection for the child without sufficient evidence to bring criminal charges against a specific adult.

Other agencies will have to be consulted to find ways to help adults accept help. In the meantime, however, the hospital staff is taking action in an effort to protect the battered children on the basis of medical evidence.[55]

A new approach to reporting child abuse was studied in 1967 by Paull, Lawrence, and Schimel.[56] It was their belief that children were not necessarily better off with their parents. Their study was conducted in Milwaukee's Children Hospital. Previously, all cases were reported to the social services department of the hospital, which would in turn assume the responsibility for the investigation. This department had the central file for the statistics, and the investigators made an attempt to study the parents, to understand the problems involved as well as the personalities. A supportive, non-critical method prevailed. However, a new approach was required. A special committee was formed in the hospital. It consisted of one or more physicians, the administrator, and the social worker. The committee would review all cases of suspected abuse reported to it by staff physicians, it would report all cases to law enforcement agencies, as well as formulate recommendations with regard to social, medical, and protective measures needed for the child. When abuse was suspected by a physician, a signed form was sent to the chairman of the committee, with all pertinent family information included. The social workers would then interview the parents, and subsequently the social worker and the chairman conducted a parental interview. If and when sufficient evidence of abuse was obtained to provide a basis for planning and action, a committee meeting was scheduled. If legal action was decided upon, the case was sent to the district attorney's office and other agencies involved. Committee recommendations were included in this report. The committee form of reporting and acting has focused attention on the problem of abuse, has improved the rate of reporting, has created a direct line of communication with the staff, and finally, has improved communication between community agencies and medical staff.

In the case of the District of Columbia Children's Hospital, a study conducted in 1971 indicated that the director of the Social Services Department would submit a monthly report to the administration which summarized and named the cases of child abuse received by attending physicians. The director was also the liaison between the hospital and the Women's Bureau of the Metropolitan Police Department. Today, however, the reports go from the hospital directly to the juvenile court. According to police policy, the Women's Bureau could handle the cases or refer them to other agencies. Sixty-two percent of the cases reported to the Women's Bureau were subsequently referred to the Protective Casework Services. The authors of the study concluded that all families suspected of child abuse should be referred for protective services before the allegedly abused child is released from medical custody.[57] They closed by adding: "Skillful, patient and continuous casework aimed at strengthening the parent's ability to care for their children was the most successful approach . . ."[58]

The research conducted at the University of Rochester recommended a team diagnosis. When a parent is suspected of abuse, referral should be made to a medical social worker in an effort to gain assistance in the evaluation of social and psychological factors. The study should concentrate on the home situation, the parental attitude toward the abused child and the siblings, and the parent-child relationship. Information should be gotten from parental interviews and other community agencies. The interviews should be flexible, the parent should be allowed to speak freely, and a nonpunitive or judgmental approach should be applied. Past family hospital records should also be reviewed. Home visits by a medical social worker and a public health nurse, who knows the neighborhood, should be undertaken in order to evaluate the family as a whole. If the research points to the necessity of parental psychiatric care, and this suggestion is not accepted by the parent, the child must be removed and placed in an appropriate community and child welfare service.[59]

A model system utilizing the team approach is in operation in Colorado Springs, Colorado. There, a board of social workers, health and police officials, physicians, and prosecutors decides action in suspected instances of child abuse. The importance of proper liaison between the different agencies is stressed. And particular efforts have been undertaken to educate the public so that suspected instances are reported.

C. Henry Kempe and his associates have proposed the idea that one spouse be questioned with regard to the mate. Questions should include probes into any unusual behavior exhibited by the mate, child's behavior, and rearing techniques employed by the parents. Psychological tests, interviews with relatives, and further observations of parental behavior in relation to the hospitalized child are also quite revealing and can be used in preventive measures. Kempe feels if X-rays and other exams reveal abusive behavior, an objective report, supported with photographs and X-rays, should be sent to the hospital director, social services department, and the police department.[60]

There have been many controversies with regard to the most effective methods of prevention and protection from further abuse. Some authors argue over the wisdom of family division. They question the fate of the remaining siblings and the abused child's resulting insecurity. Others focus their attention on effective parental treatment. Men like Thomas Szasz question instead the right of society to force psychiatric guidance on battering parents. He feels that the rhetoric of "helpfulness" conceals the perennial conflicts and tragedies of human life and makes it appear that these conflicts could be resolved if everyone only showed a little good will.[61] Still others suggest group counseling as an alternative.

At the Gaithersburg, Maryland, symposium on child abuse, experts testified that in 80 percent of the cases in which authorities remove children from the home because they were physically abused, the children can be returned safely to the parents after the latter have received proper therapy. In most cases, it was felt, criminal prosecution of the parents is not necessary. In many cases, the parents need and want help themselves, but are afraid to request it, or do not know how to go about it, or do not find any at hand. They are themselves victims of society's general disregard for this problem.

The question many like to pose is: "What happens to a child once he is removed from his home?" Is his new environment that much better? Is life in an institution or a foster home, where several incidences of child abuse have been reported, but hushed up, such a great improvement? Many believe that with an *organized,* interdisciplinary approach of medical, psychological, and sociological personnel, supported by substantial financing from the state, the family as a unit can be rehabilitated. The aim of such an intervention should be the protection for the child, the prevention of further abuse, and the establishment of familial harmony. A serious commitment by society of funds, talent, and manpower for research and experimental interventions in this area is therefore imperative, if we want to tackle the problem of child abuse effectively.

Notes

1. R.C. McCrea, *The Humane Movement* (College Park, Maryland: McGrath Publishing Company, 1969), p. 136.
2. J. Caffey, "Multiple Fractures in the Long Bones of Infants Suffering from Chronic Subdural Hematoma," *American Journal of Roentgenology* 56, 2 (Aug. 1946): 163-73.
3. F.N. Silverman, "The Roentgen Manifestations of Unrecognized Skeletal Trauma in Infants," *American Journal of Roentgenology* 69, 3 (March 1953): 413-27.
4. C.H. Kempe, F.N. Silverman, B.F. Steele, W. Droegemueller, and H.K. Silver, "The Battered Child Syndrome," *Journal of the American Medical Association* 181, 1 (July 1962): 17.

5. F.N. Silverman, "The Roentgen Manifestations," pp. 413-27.

6. "The Battered Child," *Newsweek,* Vol. 71 (July 3, 1968).

7. *The Washington Post,* Thursday, Nov. 9, 1972, H2.

8. Henri C. Raffalli, "The Battered Child," *Crime and Delinquency* 16, 2 (1970): p. 140.

9. Lester Adelson, "Homicide by Starvation," *Journal of the American Medical Association* 186, 5 (Nov. 2, 1963): 458-60.

10. Elizabeth Elmer, "Identification of Abused Children," *Children* 10, 5 (Sept.-Oct. 1963).

11. Raffalli, "The Battered Child," p. 143.

12. Helen Boardman, "A Project to Rescue Children from Inflicted Injuries," *Social Work* 7, 1 (1962): 43-52.

13. L.B. Silver, William Barton, and Christina Dublin, "Child Abuse Laws— Are They Enough?" *Journal of the American Medical Association* 199, 2 (Jan. 9, 1967).

14. Kempe et al., "The Battered Child Syndrome," pp. 17-24.

15. L.B. Silver, C. Dublin, and R.S. Lourie, "Does Violence Breed Violence? Contributions from a Study of the Child Abuse Syndrome," *American Journal of Psychiatry* 126, 3 (Sept. 1969): 404-407.

16. Kempe et al., "The Battered Child Syndrome," pp. 17-24.

17. J.C. Holter and S.B. Friedman, "Child Abuse: Early Case Findings in the Emergency Department," *Pediatrics* 42, 1 (July 1968): 128-38.

18. J.C. Holter and S.B. Friedman, "Principles of Management in Child Abuse Cases," *American Journal of Orthopsychiatry* 38 (1968): p. 130.

19. Ibid., pp. 127-35.

20. Adelson, "Homicide by Starvation," pp. 458-60.

21. Ibid.

22. B. Simons, E.F. Downs, M.F. Hurster, and M. Archer, "Child Abuse," *New York State Journal of Medicine* 66 (Nov. 1, 1966): 2783-88.

23. J.D. Delsordo, "Protective Casework for Abused Children," *Children* 10, 6 (1963): 213-18.

24. Serapio R. Zalba, "The Battered Child," *Science Digest* 70 (Dec. 1971): 8-13.

25. Elizabeth Elmer, "Abused Young Children Seen in Hospitals," *Social Work* 5, 4 (Oct. 1960): 98-102.

26. Elizabeth Elmer et al., "Unsuspected Trauma with Injuries During Infancy and Childhood," *Pediatrics* 31, 6 (June 1963): 903-08.

27. H.D. Bryant et al., "Physical Abuse of Children—An Agency Study," *Child Welfare* 42, 3 (March 1963): 125-30.

28. "10,000 Children Battered and Starved—Hundreds Die," *Today's Health,* 43 (Sept. 1965): 24-31.

29. Bryant et al., "Physical Abuse of Children—An Agency Study," pp. 125-30.

30. Elizabeth Elmer and Grace S. Gregg, "Development Characteristics of Abused Children," *Pediatrics* 40, 4 (Oct. 1967): 596-602.

31. Ibid.
32. I.D. Milowe and R.S. Lourie, "The Child's Role in the Battered Child Syndrome," *Journal of Pediatrics* 65 (1964): 1079-81.
33. B. Simons, E.F. Downs, M.F. Hurster, M. Archer, "Child Abuse," *New York State Journal of Medicine* 66 (Nov. 1, 1966): 2783-88.
34. R. Galdston, "Observations on Children Who Have Been Physically Abused by Their Parents," *American Journal of Psychiatry* 122 (1965): 440-43.
35. Kempe et al., pp. 17-24.
36. M. Morris, R.W. Gould, and P.J. Matthews, "Toward Prevention of Child Abuse," *Children* 11, 2 (1964): 55-60.
37. Elmer et al., pp. 903-08.
38. Holter and Friedman, "Child Abuse: Early Case Findings in the Emergency Department," p. 128-38.
39. Kempe et al., pp. 17-24.
40. V.J. Fontana, "The Neglect and Abuse of Children," *The New York State Journal of Medicine* 64 (Jan. 15, 1964): 215-24.
41. Lester David, "The Shocking Price of Parental Anger," *Reader's Digest* 85 (Sept. 1964): 181-86.
42. Kempe et al., pp. 17-24.
43. Elizabeth Elmer, "Identification of Abused Children," *Children* 10, 5 (Sept.-Oct. 1963): 181.
44. Fowler V. Harper, "The Physician, The Battered Child and the Law," *Pediatrics* 31, 6 (June 1963): 901.
45. Silver, Barton, and Dublin, "Child Abuse Laws—Are They Enough?" p. 65-68.
46. Monrad G. Paulsen, "Legal Protection Against Child Abuse," *Children* 13, 2 (Mar.-Apr. 1966): 42-48.
47. Elizabeth Elmer and J.B. Reinhart, "The Abused Child," *Journal of the American Medical Association* 188, 4 (April 27, 1964).
48. Dean E. Rochester, M. Ellis, and Sam C. Sciortino, "What Can the Schools Do About Child Abuse?" *Today's Education* 57 (Sept. 1968): 59-60.
49. Silver, Barton, and Dublin, "Child Abuse Laws—Are They Enough?" p. 65-68.
50. Cynthia Walton, "The Battered Baby Syndrome," *New Statesman* 72 (Sept. 9, 1966): 348.
51. V.J. Fontana, Denis Donovan, and Raymond J. Wong, "The Maltreatment Syndrome in Children," *New England Journal of Medicine* 269, 26 (Dec. 26, 1963): 1389-94.
52. Walton, "The Battered Baby Syndrome," p. 348.
53. Zalba, "The Battered Child," pp. 8-13.
54. Committee on Infant and Pre-School Child, "Maltreatment of Children," *Pediatrics* 37 (1967): 377-82.
55. Helen Boardman, "A Project to Rescue Children From Inflicted Injuries," *Social Work* 7, 1 (1962): 43-52.

56. Dorothy Paull, R.J. Lawrence, and Beverly Schimel, "A New Approach to Reporting Child Abuse," *Hospitals* 41 (Jan. 16, 1967): 62-64.

57. L.B. Silver, C. Dublin, and R.S. Lourie, "Agency Action and Interaction in Cases of Child Abuse," *Social Casework* 52 (March 1971): 164-71.

58. Silver, Dublin, and Lourie, "Agency Action and Interaction in Cases of Child Abuse," p. 170.

59. J.C. Holter and S.B. Friedman, "Principles of Management in Child Abuse Cases," *American Journal of Orthopsychiatry* 38 (1968): 127-36.

60. Kempe et al., "The Battered Child Syndrome," pp. 17-24.

61. Thomas Szasz, "Justice and Psychiatry," *Atlantic Monthly* 222 (Oct. 1968): 127-32.

Other References

"Battered Child Syndrome," *Time* 80 (June 20, 1962): 60.

"Saving Battered Children," *Time* 85 (Jan. 8, 1965): 43.

"When They're Angry," *Newsweek* 59 (April 16, 1962): 74.

"The Battered Child," *Newsweek* 71 (July 3, 1968): 68.

"Cry Rises From Beaten Babies," *Life* 54 (July 14, 1963): 38-39.

"10,000 Children Battered and Starved-Hundreds Die," *Today Health* 43 (Sept. 1965): 24-31.

"Battered Child Syndrome," *America* 116 (Feb. 18, 1967): 236.

"The Maltreated Child," *Medical Journal of Australia* 2 (July 17, 1965): 130-31.

"Experts Say Most Teen-Age Slayers Were Abused as Children," *The Washington Post* (Thursday, Nov. 9, 1972), p. H2.

"Rise in Child Abuse Cases Reported in West Germany," *The Washington Post* (Thursday, Nov. 9, 1972), p. H2.

"State Child Abuse Bill Urged," *The Washington Post* (Wednesday, Nov. 29, 1972), p. D1.

11 Child Injury in West Jerusalem
Susan Harlap and Israel Drapkin

Introduction

The battered child syndrome was first brought to medical attention by Caffey,[1] Silverman,[2] and Kempe.[3,4] Inhumanity to babies and small children is so disturbing that most people, even professionals, react to it with disbelief and denial. Only when Kempe, after ten years' fruitless efforts, deliberately adopted this shocking term, did he succeed in breaking through this universal emotional defence-mechanism into the consciousness of his colleagues and the public. Later he broadened his definition of Child Abuse, describing the Battered Child Syndrome as "only the extreme form of the whole spectrum of non-accidental injury and deprivation." Twenty percent of the babies he investigated for "failure to thrive" were not ill, but deprived.[5]

In view of the traditional Jewish warmth among adults of both sexes towards young children, many Israeli health workers deny the existence of the battered child syndrome and attribute cases of obvious neglect exclusively to parental ignorance and poverty. However, in every country where the syndrome has been sought (United States, United Kingdom, Scandinavia, Germany, Holland, Italy, Hungary[6]) it has been found. In Israel, Glazer and Levine[7] and Shvil and Shapira[8] have reported classical cases of the battered child syndrome and Prof. A. Russell's interest in the subject led to the foundation of the Society for the Protection of the Child, a multidisciplinary body which is studying the problem from many aspects. Dr. F. Noam[9] has for some years been intensively treating problem mothers in a slum area in Jerusalem and H. Zmirin[10] has made a careful study of a similar group.

Do we have child abuse and child battering in Israel? What is the size of the problem? Where and how should we seek it? This paper is an attempt to answer some of these questions and also to get a general picture of the size and nature of the problem of child injury in the Jerusalem area, whatever its cause;

Supported by a grant from the Research Committee of the Faculty of Law of the Hebrew University to the Institute of Criminology of that Faculty.

We thank Dr. S.A. Loria who received the hospital case records, and who contributed many of the ideas expressed in this paper. We thank also Professor A.M. Davies for permission to use the material of the Jerusalem Perinatal Study; Mrs. R. Prywes (R.N.), Mrs. N. Samueloff (R.N.) and Mrs. H. Rossman (R.N.) for their great assistance with the records of the Jerusalem Perinatal Study; the Archivists of Hadassah Hospital, Sharei Zedek Hospital, and Bikur Holim Hospital for their assistance in tracing files, and Dr. Friedman-Mor, Dr. F. Noam, and Dr. M. Amir for much useful information and advice.

for to the *victim* it is immaterial whether he is maimed for life by battering or because his neglectful or simply careless parents allowed him access to a boiling kettle, a bottle of poison or an unbarred window, when he was too young to understand their dangers.

This study attempts to evaluate childhood injury qualitatively, quantitatively, and in relation to the population at risk, in order to obtain demographic material comparable to that from other countries. For this purpose we have taken advantage of the Jerusalem Perinatal Study, which since 1964 has been collecting data on all children born in the Jerusalem district and during a three and one-half year period recorded particulars of all their hospital admissions.

Little is known of the variations in the prevalence of child abuse in different countries and cultures. Most of the demographic material is from the United States[11] and appears to be related to the battered child syndrome exclusively: data from fourteen states having statutory reporting suggests an average of nearly forty cases per million population annually, while similar data from four U.S. cities showed rates ranging from 40-140 cases per million. On this basis one would expect 100-400 cases annually in Israel. Several American numerator-based studies have described the characteristics of abused children and their abusers: children under four and the prematurely-born are particularly at risk. The syndrome has not been found to be associated with any particular racial, religious or socioeconomic group, though cases coming before the courts or reported to welfare agencies tend to be biased toward low socioeconomic status. In the United Kingdom, though cases reported to the N.S.P.C.C.[12] were entirely from lower social classes, the general impression[13] is that the syndrome is due to a personality disorder, not restricted to any social class.

This study attempts to ascertain:

1. The prevalence of childhood injury (under five years) leading to hospital admission and, in particular, the age-specific expectation of injury in each of the first five years of life.
2. The causes of such injuries insofar as it is possible to determine them.
3. The demographic characteristics of the different subgroups of injured children, in particular where injury was associated with neglect or gave rise to a suspicion of battering.

As regards battering, all injuries under one year are suspicious, particularly bone fractures and head injuries. Subdural hematoma, which may occur without external bruising or skull fracture if the baby is violently shaken or thrown,[14] has frequently been implicated, and unless promptly detected and treated may maim the child for life.

Once the child is mobile, it is difficult to differentiate between accident and battering; however, a discrepancy between the degree of injury and the occurrence which allegedly caused it may afford a clue as may the latter's inappropriateness to the child's age. Only a radiological skeletal survey revealing signs of multiple old fractures, chipping of the bones, epiphyseal displacement or subperiosteal hemorrhages at different healing stages[15,16] can give incontrovertible evidence of whether the child was injured once only, probably accidentally, or many times through battering. Unfortunately this examination seems to be rarely done in Jerusalem at present. In the absence of objective evidence of this nature our estimate can only be tentative.

Material and Methods

This study makes use of the computer-stored data of the Jerusalem Perinatal Study.[17] Since 1964, a file has been opened for every baby born to residents of West Jerusalem (the pre-1967 Israeli sector), comprising demographic and other data abstracted from birth certificates and labor-ward records. To this basic file, a record-linkage technique adds details of deaths, congenital malformations, and other data relating to pregnancy and early childhood.

Between January 1, 1966 and June 30, 1969 all admissions to hospital of the study's children were recorded and it is these data which form the basis of the present study. The information available from the computer-stored file includes the coded diagnoses, dates of admission and discharge, lowest hemoglobin, weight on discharge, and details of death. For the cohort of babies born in 1966, there is a complete record of hospital admissions from birth to a mean of three years (2½ to 3½ according to the month of birth); for 1967 to a mean of two years and for 1968 to a mean of one year. The cohorts of babies born in 1964 and 1965 can only be studied between the ages of two to five and one to four years respectively, but they afford useful information on the pattern of injury in later infancy.

All children who had been admitted to hospital with diagnosis of injuries, burns, and neurological disorders were identified from the computer-stored file. Details were sought not only of the episode of trauma, but of all other hospital admissions of the children concerned. Additional information was added from the archives of the Jerusalem Perinatal Study, and from a search of the children's inpatient files in the three hospitals, though the latter could not always be found.

Most of the neurological cases, which were clearly due to congenital abnormalities or birth injury, were excluded from the study at an early stage. A few were retained for further study but very few were included in our final calculations. Children with major congenital malformations were excluded, as were those whose trauma was clearly irrelevant (perinatal, hemophilia, osteogenesis imperfecta, etc.).

Evidence of neglect or battering was sought as follows:

Neglect

1. admission to hospital with gastroenteritis on more than one occasion or with bronchopneumonia on more than one occasion.
2. weight below the lowest limit of normal for age, according to the Wellcome Trust Working Party Classification[18] with allowance for low birth weight according to Drillien's tables.[19]
3. anemia: a hemoglobin of less than 8 gm/100 ml on one occasion or under 10 gm/100 ml more than once (excluding cases of hemolytic disease or prematures in their early months).
4. rickets, scurvy, etc.
5. an episode of poisoning in addition to trauma.
6. more than one episode of trauma (this could also be indicative of battering).
7. failure to bring the child to hospital on the day of the injury.

Battering

1. known cases, where the diagnosis was made and recorded by the clinicians.
2. probable cases, where there was strong evidence such as:
   a. denial of trauma in the presence of severe injury
   b. discrepancy between the severity of the injury and the way it was alleged to have occurred.
   c. age incompatible with self-inflicted injury
   d. autopsy evidence, etc.
3. possible cases where similar evidence existed but was not so strong.

Demographic Study

The population-at-risk was assumed to be the 29,245 babies born from 1964 to 1968 who survived the first twenty-eight days of life.

Results

Two hundred and ninety children were admitted to a hospital because of trauma during the three and one-half years from January 1, 1966 to June 30, 1969. Ninety were suffering from burns, 35 from the results of traffic accidents, and 165 from other injuries. All but four were under five years of age.

Table 11-1 shows the rates of hospital admissions due to trauma per 1,000 children in each of the first five years of life. Burns are rare in the first year and rise to a peak in the second, when they represent nearly 60 percent of all trauma; thereafter they decrease. Traffic accidents are seen from the third year of life and increase in prevalence in subsequent years; by the fifth year they account for 30 percent of trauma. In the first five years of life 1.7 percent of all children will have been admitted to hospital because of trauma.

Nature of Injuries. Of the 200 children with injuries other than burns (classified in the case of multiple injuries under the most serious) 55.5% percent were suffering from head injuries; 21.5 percent from fracture of long bones, and 23 percent from other injuries. The head injuries were mostly fractured skulls and concussion; while the majority appeared to make good recoveries, a few were left with permanent neurological damage or with abnormal EEGs.

Cause of Injuries Other than Burns. At least 17.5 percent of injuries were due to traffic accidents. For the remainder the information is scanty and in 43.5 percent of the cases we do not know the cause; in many cases the file merely stated the nature of the child's injury, with no information as to how it happened, and in some cases the file could not be found. Where the alleged cause was mentioned it was usually very briefly: "fell from bed" "fell from 2nd floor" or just "fell." Over 35 percent of the injuries were attributed to falls, of which 10 percent were from a considerable height—from windows up to the fourth floor or from roofs. Another 8 percent of the cases were attributed to a fall from bed or other low furniture. Among these there were a few where the degree of injury seemed incompatible with the small distance fallen or with the age of the child. Another 17.5 percent were due to miscellaneous and unspecified falls.

Table 11-1
Childhood Injuries in West-Jerusalem by Age

Age	Cohort Studied Born	Number of Children	Burns	Rates per 1000 Traffic Accidents	Other Injuries	Total
under 1	1966-68	17,766	0.2	–	2.0	2.1
1 and under 2	1965-67	17,507	2.5	–	1.8	4.3
2 and under 3	1964-66	17,316	0.8	0.5	1.8	3.1
3 and under 4	1964-65	11,479	0.4	0.7	1.2	2.3
4 and under 5	1964	5,559	0.5	1.6	3.2	5.4

Misadventure.   A few cases could be described as unavoidable misadventure. We were on the lookout for injuries during the three days (June 5, 1967 to June 7, 1967) when Jerusalem was under bombardment, but found none. (It is however possible that during that emergency records were kept less carefully than usual; also children may have been treated in casualty stations and sent home.) One child was subsequently injured by a hand-grenade, two children were badly bitten by dogs, and two fell off their own bicycles (which we have not included among traffic accidents).

Traffic Accidents.   As far as it is known (some entries merely state "traffic accident") only two children were passengers in cars involved in an accident. The majority were run down by a variety of vehicles ranging from a tractor to motor cars, motorcycles, and bicycles. One of the victims died.

Burns.   Ninety children (31 percent of all those injured) were suffering from burns which were sufficiently severe to require admission to the hospital. Most had grade II burns and a few grade III, often involving a quite extensive percentage of body surface. The vast majority were scalds due to hot fluids. Many required skin grafting shortly after the incident and several children had to be readmitted for further plastic surgery later. There were four deaths (4.4 percent). Of the burns, 8.9 percent had already occurred during the latter months of the first year, 61 percent in the second year, and thereafter the frequency decreased rapidly with age.

Demography of Childhood Injuries.   Rates of admissions for injuries in various demographic subgroups were studied, by relating the children admitted in 1965-69 to the population of children born alive in 1964-68 who survived the first month of life. All types of injuries were more common among boys (12.5/1,000 compared with 7.2 in girls), among children born into large families (16.2 in seventh or later born, against 6.5 in first-born children), and among those whose father's occupation was of low social status (13.3 in manual workers compared to 6.4 in professionals and white-collar workers). Rates for all groups of injury were considerably higher among the children of mothers of Asian or North African origin (10.7 and 13.6 respectively) compared to those of Westerners (4.8) or second-generation Israelis (7.8), in keeping with the standard-of-living differences between the groups. Nevertheless, injuries were not confined to any sector of society.

Neglect

Fifty of the 290 injured children also showed evidence of neglect according to the criteria stated in "Material and Methods." (See Table 11-3) Twelve had

Table 11-2

Childhood Injuries by Various Demographic Variables

(West-Jerusalem children born 1964-68)

Variable		Number of Babies	Rates per thousand			
			Burns	Traffic Accidents	Other Trauma	Total
Sex	M	15,019	3.4	1.3	7.7	12.5
	F	14,226	2.7	1.1	3.4	7.2
Birth weight	under 2.5 kg	1,823	2.2	1.1	6.6	9.9
	2.5 kg or more	27,422	3.1	1.2	5.6	9.9
Birth order	1	7,845	2.7	0.6	3.2	6.5
	2-3	11,156	2.6	0.9	5.7	9.2
	4-6	6,126	2.8	1.6	6.9	11.3
	7+	4,064	5.4	2.5	8.4	16.2
Social status	high	9,065	2.3	0.8	3.3	6.4
	medium	10,009	3.3	0.9	5.5	9.7
	low	10,171	3.5	1.9	7.9	13.3
Years of mother's education	9 or more	12,147	2.6	0.5	3.7	6.8
	0-8	12,564	3.0	1.3	7.2	11.5
	unknown	4,534	4.6	2.9	6.9	13.9
Birthplace of mother's father	Israel	3,690	2.4	1.1	4.3	7.8
	Asia	9,811	2.5	1.4	7.1	10.7
	North Africa	7,219	4.8	1.7	7.1	13.6
	West	7,736	1.7	0.5	2.6	4.8
Arabic	—	720	9.7	—	11.1	20.8
Number of previous child deaths	0	27,554	3.1	1.2	5.5	9.8
	1+	1,691	2.4	1.8	7.7	11.9
Total (including unknowns)		29,245	3.1	1.2	5.6	9.9

malnutrition by international standards[20,21], weighing less than the lowest limit normal for their age. However, since most of the accident cases were not weighed, it was only possible to assess weight-for-age in the minority of cases who had additional hospital admissions. Thus our findings are likely to underestimate the true proportion of underweight among injured children. Fifteen of the injured children had been in the hospital several times for gastroenteritis or bronchopneumonia: one child for gastroenteritis twice and bronchopneumonia four times. Five children had been burnt twice and another had a burn and concussion on separate occasions. There were thirty-four injured boys and sixteen girls with neglect (sex ratio, 64:32). Among children with burns, traffic accidents, and other injuries neglect was seen in 13, 20, and 19 cases respectively.

Suspected Battering

This was an extremely delicate assessment, made more difficult by scanty histories and missing files. The list of forty-one cases included three certain cases (of which one died), where the diagnosis was made by the clinicians, seven probable cases (of which two died) and thirty-one possible cases. All the certain and probable cases were first injured under one year, as were nearly two-thirds of the possible cases. If three-quarters of the "probable" cases and one-quarter of the "possibles" were real cases of child abuse, the estimate of the total number of cases would be about sixteen, which in relation to the number of children at risk, amounts to a rate of 0.55/thousand, in the first five years of life.

Demographic Associates of Injury With Neglect and Suspected Battering

Injuries with neglect were strongly related to standard of living. There was a six-fold difference in rates between first-born children and those born seventh or later; a four-and-a-half fold difference between high and low social status, and nearly a three-fold difference between children of mothers with a high school education and those of mothers with a primary or no education. Ethnic group differences reflected these trends—the rate of injuries with neglect being more than twice as high among children of mothers of Asian or North African origin compared to those of Western or second-generation Israeli mothers. For the suspected battering cases, the relation to standard of living was considerably less marked and the cases were not confined to any one social class, birth order or ethnic group. Both suspected battering and injuries with neglect were more common among males. Neglect was particularly common among injured children who had been of abnormally low birth weight (under 2.5 kg). Suspected battering but not neglect was more common among families in which there had been a previous child death.

Discussion

Childhood Injury

What is immediately apparent is that the rate of injuries among young children with an expectation of 1.7 percent in the first five years of life, is extremely high and constitutes a grave problem in itself. The most dangerous year of infancy is the second, because of the child's mobility, curiosity, and inability to understand danger. This is shown in the overall incidence of injury, but

Table 11-3

Injuries With Neglect, and Suspected Battering by Various Demographic Variables

Variable		Injuries With Neglect		Suspected Battered-Baby Syndrome	
		Number of Cases	Relative Risk*	Number of Cases	Relative Risk*
Sex	M	34	1.29	29	1.36
	F	16	0.71	12	0.57
Birth weight	under 2.5 kg	9	2.88	2	0.79
	2.5 kg or more	41	0.88	39	1.00
Birth order	1	4	0.29	7	0.64
	2-3	16	0.82	16	1.00
	4-6	17	1.65	10	1.14
	7+	13	1.88	8	1.43
Social status	high	6	0.41	7	0.57
	medium	11	0.65	16	1.14
	low	33	1.88	18	1.29
Years of mother's education	9+	7	0.35	10	0.57
	0-8	33	1.53	26	1.50
	unknown	10	1.29	5	0.79
Birthplace of mother's father	Israel	3	0.47	4	0.79
	Asia	20	1.18	16	1.14
	North Africa	17	1.41	15	1.50
	West	6	0.47	5	0.43
Arab	—	4	3.33	1	1.00
Number of previous child deaths	0	47	1.00	37	0.93
	1+	3	1.06	4	1.71
Total (including unknowns)		50	1.00	41	1.00

*Ratio of observed to expected numbers of cases based on null hypothesis of no differences in rates between different demographic groups.

particularly of burns. Traffic accidents are normally considered "misadventure," yet traffic accidents were most frequently associated with neglect.

The picture that emerges is, at best, one of widespread parental carelessness. It must be seen in the context of our very high rates of traffic and industrial accidents. This parental carelessness may also be part of the reaction against the overprotective Jewish family tradition in the Diaspora.

It is not hard to explain the marked relation of high risk of injuries to descending socioeconomic status, large families, and poor maternal education. It is hard to explain the preponderance of males in all groups of injuries even under one year of age, when temperamental differences between the sexes are not so marked.

The Battered Child Syndrome

In the controversy about "battered babies" it appears that both sides are right: cases do exist in Israel but they appear to be fewer than one would expect from the American literature. Because health-care personnel are not aware of child abuse, it is likely that many cases still go undetected. Our tentative estimate of the prevalence of the battered child syndrome, 0.55 cases per thousand live births or less than 20 cases per million population, is about half the lowest American estimate. This would give a yearly average of about three cases in Jerusalem and less than 50 in the whole of Israel. The problem is not, however, negligible when one considers that one of the "known" cases and two of the "probable" cases are dead. Detection is rendered more difficult by the fact that here, as in the international literature, there does not appear to be any clear-cut social or demographic distribution; consequently all injuries under one year must be viewed with suspicion. It must also be emphasized that this study is based on hospital data and does not include cases of possibly less severe ill-treatment which may be known to social workers, public health nurses and general practitioners.

Deprivation

Numerically, the victims of deprivation and neglect, which are a part of child abuse, present a much greater problem. Several studies have shown that Jerusalem has one of the highest rates of hospitalization in the world for children under one year; 18 percent of all children born.[22,23,24] Children of low socioeconomic status and whose mothers had scanty education have a greatly increased risk of hospitalization for gastroenteritis and bronchopneumonia, as well as for injuries. Many babies are admitted to the hospital in their first year of life because of "failure to thrive."

Additional material from the Jerusalem Perinatal Study shows that among children of normal birth weight who were free from major malformations and malignant disease, nearly 15 percent of those admitted to the hospital in their first three years of life weighed less than the lowest limit for their age.[25] Thus a minimum of 3.9 percent of the population were malnourished by international standards.[26,27]

Among the neurological cases which we excluded from this study were a small group of children with acquired brain damage which appeared to be due to an episode of severe dehydration in their first few months; this should be avoidable when medical help is sought promptly. Also several children admitted to the hospital for assessment of psychomotor retardation were grossly underweight and appeared to be suffering from environmental deprivation. Most of these children were probably victims of deprivation or neglect.

We do not know to what extent such cases of childhood deprivation are due to parental inadequacy or social underprivilege, but it is clear that urgent social intervention is required in certain sectors of society. It may be relevant to put forward a few practical suggestions:

1. Intensive propaganda for prevention of accidents in the home is required in the Infant Welfare Centres and through the mass media.
2. The parents of every child admitted to hospital for injury should be interviewed by a social worker both to afford support at a time of great distress and to ascertain the family circumstances which led to the accident and how they can be mitigated in the future. In addition, her training in assessing interpersonal relations might enable her to detect and draw attention to the occasional abnormal parental reaction compatible with "battering."
3. Increased use of radiological skeletal surveys, especially for children injured under one year, would improve chances of detecting "battered babies."
4. A large-scale investigation and intervention program is required in the field of infantile deprivation.

Notes

1. J. Caffey, "Multiple fractures in the long bones of infants suffering from chronic subdural haematoma," *Amer. J. Roentgenol.* 56 (1946): 163.
2. F.N. Silverman, "The roentgen manifestations of unrecognised skeletal trauma in infants," *Amer. J. Roentgenol.* 69 (1953): 413.
3. C.H. Kempe, F.N. Silverman, B.F. Steele, W. Droegemuller, and H.H. Silver, "The Battered Child Syndrome," *J.A.M.A.* 181 (1962): 17.
4. R.E. Helfer and C.H. Kempe, *The Battered Child* (Chicago: University of Chicago Press, 1968).
5. C.H. Kempe, "Paediatric implications of the Battered Child Syndrome," *Arch. Dis. Child.* 46 (1971): 28.
6. B.F. Steele and C.B. Pollock, "A psychiatric study of parents who abuse infants and small children," In R.E. Helfer and C.H. Kempe, *The Battered Child,* (Chicago: Univ. Chicago Press, 1968).
7. I. Glazer and S. Levine, "The Battered Child Syndrome," *Harefuah* 77 (1969): 55.
8. I. Shvil and E. Shapira, "The Battered Child Syndrome, *Harefuah* 78 (1970): 248.
9. Noam, F. personal communication.
10. Zmirin, H. (unpublished manuscript).
11. D.G. Gil, "The incidence of child abuse and demographic characteristics of persons involved." In R.E. Helfer and C.H. Kempe, *The Battered Child* (Chicago: Univ. Chicago, Press, 1968).

12. A.E. Skinner and R.L. Castle, "78 Battered children-a retrospective study," N.S.P.C.C. London, 1969.

13. S. Isaacs, "Neglect, Cruelty and Battering," *Brit. Med. J.* 3 (1972): 224.

14. A.N. Gutkelch, "Infantile subdural haematoma and its relation to whiplash injuries," *Brit. Med. J.* 2 (1971): 430.

15. J. Caffey, "Some traumatic lesions in growing bones," *Brit. J. Radio.* 30 (1957): 225.

16. F.N. Silverman, "Radiological aspects of the Battered child syndrome," In R.E. Helfer and C.H. Kempe, *The Battered Child* (Chicago: Univ. Chicago Press, 1968).

17. A.M. Davies, R. Prywes, B. Tzur, P. Weiskopf, and V.V. Sterk, "The Jerusalem perinatal study. 1. Design and organization of a continuing, community-based, record-linked survey," *Israel J. med. Sci.* 5 (1969): 1095.

18. Editorial. *Lancet II*, 1970, p. 303.

19. C.M. Drillien, *The Growth and Development of the Prematurely Born Infant* (Edinburgh: Livingstone, 1964).

20. Editorial, *Lancet II.*

21. Joint F.A.O./W.H.O. Expert Committee on Nutrition, *8th Report,* No. 447, Geneva, 1971.

22. T. Bentwich, "The background of infant hospitalisation in the Jerusalem area, with special reference to social and medical factors," M.D. thesis, Hebrew Univ., Jerusalem, 1970.

23. S. Harlap, A.M. Davies, M. Haber, N. Samueloff, H. Rossman, and R. Prywes, "Ethnic group, immigration and infant morbidity in West Jerusalem," *Proc. 2nd Symposium on Society, Stress and Disease,* Stockholm, June 1971.

24. A.M. Davies, "Preventive medicine in Israel," *Prev. Med.* 1 (1972): 121.

25. S.A. Loria, (unpublished manuscript).

26. Editorial, *Lancet II.*

27. Joint F.A.O./W.H.O. *Report.*

12

The Child as a Sex Victim: Socio-Legal Perspectives
LeRoy G. Schultz

Victimology has received relatively minor attention in American criminology, and where scant attention has been paid it has revolved around victim-compensation policy. The American correctional system likewise has not paid realistic concern to restitution to victims, either as a condition of probation or through prison wages.[1] Only recently has corrections, sociology, and social work indicated a strong interest in victimology, victimogenesis, and victim welfare.[2] Part of our difficulty in doing research on victims, treating them or establishing policy regarding them, is the lack of any hard data on victims and even the incidence of sex victimization. In 1972, there were 46,430 criminal acts of forcible rape in the United States, and 47,507 other types of sexual offenses, these figures representing a 70 percent increase since 1967.[3] The incidence of child sex victimization in the United States is most difficult to accurately measure. There is no central or national recording system for sexual offenses against children and what sparse data are available vary the offense nomenclature so greatly that uniform reporting is impossible. Legal charges against a sex offender transgressing against the child may run from "forcible rape" to "peace disturbance," yet both involve the same type of violent sexual behavior but were labeled differently to accommodate the plea bargaining process in common law countries. Estimates have been made of 4,000 cases of child sex victimization in large urban areas annually,[4] a national average of 5,000 cases of father-daughter incest,[5] and 200,000 to 500,000 cases of sexual assaults on female children ages four to fourteen years.[6] In one large city with advanced victim services, 24 percent of all sexual assaults were on children under age fourteen.[7] Estimates of sexual assaults on young males are almost non-existent. One victim project reported thirty boys received emergency room treatment, yearly, for sexual assault in a large city.[8] It has been further estimated that approximately 50 percent of all crime is not reported to law enforcement agencies,[9] suggesting that the incidence of sex offenses against children is much higher than the official statistics indicate. It is possible also that the sex victim will be treated by a family physician or social worker in private practice, and therefore, no public record is available.

Victim Typology

Child sex victims may be placed upon a continuum from totally accidental victimization at one end, involving little victimogenesis, to seductive partner at

177

the other end, with extensive victimogenesis. In between the ends are various categories identified by the degree of consent the child gives to the sexual act(s), and her eligibility to give legal consent. Many child victims consent to the sex offense, intentionally or unwittingly, or offer only passive resistance, and in many child victimization relationships the victim and offender are in a symbiotic relationship or they form a cooperative dyad. The degree of consent, the type of child sex victim-offender relationship is important to know since it shapes the victim's, as well as society's, attitude toward the sexual offense and toward the offender, and it will affect the victim's willingness to legally testify against him and possibly generate subsequent guilt feelings. The type of therapy a child sex victim may require appears related to where he is situated along the victim continuum with important factors centered around the degree of physical force or violence employed by the offender and the intensity of the victim-offender relationship *prior* to the sex offense.

In past sex offense research, female victims were described as having a "collaborative" role in the sexual offense in 7.8 percent of 330 court cases,[10] as "non-objecting" in 40 percent of 1994 court cases,[11] as "encouraging" the offender in 66 percent to 95 percent of all sexual offenses,[12] as fully "partici-pating" in 60 percent of 73 court cases,[13] and as "seducers" of their offenders in 185 court cases.[14] While victim precipitation, cooperation, seduction or the "Lolita syndrome" present problems for the legal agencies in assessing degrees of guilt and punishment for the offender, therapists may be called upon to deal with the child as a sex-delinquent or character disorder.[15] In general, physical force and violence on child victims plays a small role in the offenses, for example, 4 percent of 333 court cases,[16] and this is related to the fact that most sex offenses against children are committed by persons they have a relationship with prior to the offense, such as a family friend, a neighbor or teacher,[17] so that physical force is unnecessary to the success of the offense. In the research by Gagnon, 1.9 percent of the child victims sustained a forced act of either vaginal, or oral penetration and an additional 2.7 percent a general violent attack on the child's whole body.[18] By far, the major form of sexual behavior expressed between offender and child-victim is exhibition of sexual organs, genital and non-genital petting or fondling, consensual oral genital or oral anal contacts, or attempted penetration of the vagina without force.

Effects of Victimization

The effect of victimization upon children has been exaggerated in the earlier literature, partly due to a naive misunderstanding of the role of sexuality in the development of children, misunderstanding the average child's adaptive capacity and a Victorian belief that sex must leave permanent trauma for the innocent child. Generally, sexual assaults of children do not have an excessively unsettling

effect on personality development[19] nor a serious effect on his/her later adult
adjustment.[20] Of the offended children where violence and penetration were
involved, physical damage[21] may involve sex organ damage, tears or rupture,
possible hemorrhage, general body damages such as abrasions, bites or bruises
broad ligament laceration, veneral disease, vulvitis, or pregnancy. These types
of problems can be treated promptly and efficiently in the clinic, hospital or
properly equipped office if adequately staffed.[22] Psycho-social after-effects
of the sexual offense against the child are not so readily assessed as the physical.
Possible negative or traumatic effects are related to the amount of violence
employed by the offender, the type and depth of the child's relationship to the
offender, and the family, society, and "significant others" reaction to the
offense. Immediate reaction in the child may range from simple fright, much
like when a child encounters something new and unpleasant, to vomiting and
hysteria and panic. Some children will react without fear or guilt and some may
report the offense as stimulating and erotic.

In a British research project, 43 percent of 82 victims indicated no overt
disturbance after the sex offense when seen by diagnosticians, 16 percent
appeared unsettled with resultant behavior problems, 14 percent required therapy
and 6 percent required confinement in a correctional institution.[23] In general
the best recovery is made by the child who was sexually assaulted without physical violence by a stranger.

The child's relationship to the offender is very important in understanding
the offense dynamics and its effects upon the victim. Most victimized children
are seeking out or allow affectionate behavior from their offenders, many feel
kindly and lovingly towards them, and perhaps have long-term relationships
established with them, sometimes over a period of years with a pattern of frequent sexual behavior. This gratification of the child's love needs from her
father over time is particularly significant in cases of incest where a daughter
will refuse to place criminal charges or testify against her father for fear of being
responsible for parental separation or divorce, the loss of the father or her love
supply, or seeing him sentenced to a correctional institution, or out of oedipal
guilt. Young female victims are sometimes blamed by their mothers for breaking up the family, particularly when the family was held together by the classic
sexual three-way process. The same holds true for the young female adolescent
victim who manifests strong resistance to placing charges against her "steady"
boyfriend or lover.

In many instances, young victims engaged in behavior that was seductive or
affectionate, but were naive about its potential as a sexual stimulus and once
the offense was committed, felt betrayed, shocked, and a generally negative
reaction. Many victims appear dismayed to find, post-offense, that the offenders'
behavior was in direct response to cues they gave. The child victim also may
feel guilt if she reports some gratification from the offense, being the object of
love and attention from an older person whom her family and society all of a

sudden condemn. In the older child having invited the offense may take one of two directions. First, partial involvement in victimogenesis may actually minimize the traumatic after-effects or, second, post-offense symptoms may be accentuated as a result of guilt feelings. If the child victim feels she precipitated or helped stimulate the sexual event, she may feel guilty that society has chosen to prosecute only one-half of the criminal relationship. The young adolescent victim may wonder about her reputation or marriageability. If the sexual offense involved considerable physical violence, the victim may display hysteria, shock, or disabling feelings of hostility towards her offender(s) or a grief-like reaction.[24] Her self-confidence may disappear as she questions what she did wrong or what precautions she did not take against victimization. She may question her possible victimization again or if she will develop a normal interest in sexuality.

By far the greatest potential trauma to the child's personality is caused by society, its institutions, and the victim's parents as a result of (a) the need of the court to use the child victim for the prosecution of the offender and (b) the need of the victim's parents to prove to themselves, other family members, neighbors, and significant others that the victim was free of any victimogenesis and that they were good parents. Naturally, we expect society to react severely to forced child-adult sex relations, and such interpretation is bound to insure the unlikeliness of escaping the trauma produced by the definition and interpretation.

In the administration of justice in common law countries, the suspect has the right to trial and to confront and cross-examine those who charge him with an offense. Child trauma occurs as a result of the courts' need to have the child victim repeat the details of the sexual offense several times, to police, warrant officers, prosecutors, and a jury of twelve adults, sometimes with the suspected sex offender present.[25] This places what is perhaps in the child's mind a short-lived traumatic event with few permanent consequences, out of proportion to its importance to him, and forces the child to reorient his ideas toward a confusing adult interpretation of the offense, its new importance, and the victim's role in punishing the offender. Most police, sheriffs, and prosecutors have no training or education in non-damaging methods of interviewing children and tend to use adversary approaches appropriate for adults which are successful in gaining convictions.[26] The suspect's lawyer or defense attorney has the duty of defending his client with every tool at his command, and he may contribute or induce emotional trauma, by attempting in open court to show the victim is incompetent, malicious, seductive, a consenting "Lolita" or brought false charges for various personal reasons.[27] The dilemma here is the need to protect the child from the potential trauma induced by the legal court proceedings, but at the same time convicting and rehabilitating the offender. This dilemma can be reduced by using special interrogation methods and professional interviewers as will be discussed later. If law enforcement agencies and courts can not eliminate the trauma induced by repeated testifying, then non-reporting of the offense may be the best choice in terms of the child's welfare. In addition, if most American correctional institutions have no effective rehabilitation programs, the rationale for reporting the offense to police is weakened.

It is clear from research on child sex victims that it is not the sexual act *per se* that creates trauma, but the parent's behavior toward the child victim on discovery of the offense, and how parental behavior affects the child.[28] Parents may overreact, become hysterical, physically attack the offender in front of the child, physically attack the child victim, berate, belittle or punish the victim, demand, under threats, that the child inform court and police officials that the sex offense was not provoked by the victim, or parents may threaten court officials unless the offender is sentenced instantly. The British research indicated that 26 percent of the parents of sex victims engaged in post-offense behavior which aggravated the child's situation or exploited the child's situation for their own social benefit.[29] As rapidly as possible following the offense parents will need help in accepting the offense in such a way that horror, panic, and fright are not communicated to the child so as to create trauma where perhaps none existed before.

Case. The case involved an 8-year-old female sexually molested by a 67-year-old retired male in a public park. The offender had removed the victim's under clothing and was apparently preparing to make penile-anal contact, when a passerby interrupted and called police. Medical diagnosis indicated no penetration. The enraged father of the victim charged into the court social worker's office and demanded that the offender be "put away for life or I'll beat the shit out of that pervert myself. Ain't nobody going to ruin my daughter like that and get away with it." The court social worker, sensing potential child trauma, began deconditioning the father's negative effects on the child by empathizing with the father's need for vengeance, but also showing that the victim's welfare was now top priority and how his behavior was contributing to damage to the victim. Considerable time was allowed for ventilating the father's hostility toward police and courts in an unchallenging atmosphere. When he began settling down, the social worker gently informed him of his possible role in creating trauma and how he was thinking only of his need for retaliation. Simple instruction was given on how to play the offense down, what to talk about in front of the victim, that little damage actually occurred, the adaptive nature of most children, and guidelines for preventing a second victimization were given. The father left the office more in control of himself, with insight on his behavior's effects upon his daughter.

Most single instances of sexual trauma, unless reinforced by court testifying or parental overreaction, produce few permanent consequences, and this fact should be exploited early on behalf of the child victim.

Treatment Implications

Once the child victim has received medical attention for the physical aspects of the offense[30] he/she should be referred to a professional person who has skill in interviewing children. This may be a pediatrician, psychiatrist, social worker, psychologist or nurse, depending upon manpower resources in a given area or hospital staff. Those professional staff skilled in processing cases involving the "battered child" or child abuse may be most prepared here. The professional involved will be faced with helping the family decide on the desirability or non-desirability of reporting the offense to the police. A refusal to report the offense to police may be based upon the reluctance of the young victim to repeat the details of the offense to others, a desire to avoid any publicity or social stigma, potential revenge from others, or a belief by victim, parents or professional that the incident created so much emotional disturbance that accurate recounting or recall of the offense details is unlikely. The pros and cons of these various issues will need to be assessed and discussed with the victim and family in an effort to help them make their decision. The decision centers on what the potential effect will be if the child files charges and is required to testify, as against the safety of the community of potential victims if the offender is not prosecuted and remains at large. If the family and victim decide to bring charges against the alleged offender they should be instructed in this process, and in select cases, a professional should accompany them to the police/sheriff's department and warrant office to at least prevent any further interrogation beyond what the victim can safely tolerate. The family and victim should be instructed to report the incident, once they have made the decision, as soon as possible, as various countries, states, regions, and jurisdictions, have time limits for the reporting of some sexual offenses. Some introductory effort should be made by the professional to make reasonably sure the offense is not the product of the child's imagination or being reported out of spite or retaliation or other falsity.[31] Instruction should be given to parents and child to preserve any physical evidence, particularly blood, fecal, urine or semen stained clothing, rugs or bed coverings as well as fingernail scrappings, plus hairs and fibers. Photographs of general body damage may be required.

Regrettably, in some states or jurisdictions, the child victim may be forced to testify against the offender without the victim's consent, and the victim may be placed in detention until the trial. This situation prevails where the prosecutor feels the offender poses a dangerous threat to the community and the victim's testimony is required for conviction, consent notwithstanding. Such rare situations require close supervision by professionals in the mental health field and juvenile detention, as the potential for trauma is substantial.

In some instances, the child victim must be placed in detention or foster home because the parent is the sexual aggressor or the parent is charged with child neglect or abuse, or for having contributed to the delinquency of the child.

If the court of jurisdiction requires the child's testimony the professional should prepare him for the court experience, easing to the extent possible anxieties created by the anticipated legal proceedings. This may be done through the psychotherapist's traditional treatment tools of role playing, mock trial or behavior rehearsal technique.

Case. The case involved an 11-year-old female who while a patient in an urban hospital was approached by a man posing as a physician during patient visiting hours. The man told the patient he was a physician assigned to her case and proceeded to masturbate the patient both vaginally and anally. He then dropped his pants and asked the victim to masturbate him. She refused. Then, he masturbated himself to orgasm with the semen falling on the victim who laid terrified in bed. The child was reported as hysterical, unable to converse clearly with chronic sobbing and feelings of shame and "being dirty".

Four local hospitals had reported this suspect as responsible for 32 sexual offenses against children over a two-year period and the four hospital administrators were concerned to have this type of offense stopped once and for all, as it was causing considerable difficulty in normal hospital routines. The family's social worker, however, questioned if the victim could sustain the potentially trauma-producing effects of the court process. The parents were insistent on ridding the community of the offender as a civic duty. A pre-trial treatment plan was deviced by the social worker to decondition the potential traumatic effects of testifying by the behavior rehearsal method.[32]

The social worker's office was converted into a simulated court room by moving the furniture around. Other social workers played the role of judge and prosecutor, the social worker handling the case played defense counsel of the offender. Each role-player went through the types of questions that would be asked, but they were asked in very non-threatening styles as each role player knew of the child's sensitive areas. In troublesome areas the child was verbally helped with verbalizing answers. Two additional mock trials were held in the privacy of the social worker's office, where questions were repeatedly put to the victim in a non-threatening manner, with her mental health interests uppermost, with warm sympathetic accepting actors. By the third mock trial (third week) the victim was responding comfortably to questions the defense would raise as to her role in the offense, her morals, chastity and character, and a general re-living of the whole sexual assault, and the social worker felt that the victim could now appear in open court and testify without the fear of trauma. With her family support and a professional at her side, she did testify very well with no trauma, and the offender was given a lengthy sentence. Praise was given the victim by both judge and prosecutor after the trial.

Efforts should be made by the professional handling the case to speed up or slow down the legal proceedings in the interest of victim welfare, prevent delays, insuring privacy in court proceedings if possible, and standing ready to assist the victim throughout the entire court process.

Treatment will be primarily of the supportive type. Parents will need supportive but firm assistance in taking a constructive and non-damaging attitude toward the offense, its social repercussions, the possible effects upon the victim, and the role they can play in the reduction of trauma. They may need instruction and direction on "playing down" the significance of the offense. Many child victims are seeking affection not given by the family or are seeking substitute attachments to compensate for insecurity in the family. Such parents may need advice and direction on overcoming maternal affection-insufficiency. Parents will need an opportunity to ventilate feelings with a supportive professional, particularly if there is guilt about parental contribution or negligence.

Child victims may need assistance in precise understanding of what happened, in simple anatomical sexual terms, and ventilation of feelings of anger, guilt, and helplessness with a sympathetic and supportive professional.

Many child victims are from homes and families that are disorganized and lack adequate supervision. Some will require sex education not provided by the school or church. Some will have been socialized within homes and neighborhoods with sex codes different from that reflected in law; others will indicate poor impulse control related to deprivation, rejection, and maternal inconsistency. These later may be the main problem for social work focus and the whole range of traditional protective services of correction and prevention. Incest cases pose a special problem for the family in that the victim may have developed a strong affection for her father over a long period of time.[33] Courts and social agencies are quick to separate the family members with little preparation for the child's loss of the source of her affection.

Marked efforts at preventing a second victimization, or another family member being victimized, should be made through educational measures that are realistically geared to the child's needs and intellectual level, which avoid creating more fears and anxiety. Particular avoidance should be made of lengthy description of sexual pathology or "dirty old men" generalizations which compound the problem further. The relative harmlessness of certain types of sexual behavior for the victim, exhibitionism for example, should be reinforced and a feeling that the child can share his sexual ideas and experience with open-minded parents may prevent concealment of damaging experiences. If the offender is acquitted, the child should not be branded a liar.

Policy Problems

Most children probably have the strength, stability, and home support which enables them to endure the temporary stress of repetition of the details of the offense before a police officer, prosecutor or jury if accompanied by a professional, but for a select few the court proceedings are themselves the chief traumatic event. There appears no effective way of determining which children can sustain the court process and its possible long-range effects. Fortunately, the cases in which repetitive testimony is required are few. Approximately 80 percent to 90 percent of all criminal defendants plead guilty without a trial in the United States[34] so that the child's testimony or appearance in court is not required. In this majority of cases, the child will be spared all but the police, warrant office and grand jury experience. It is the court experience with its adversary nature that poses the greatest potential for trauma. Where violence was employed by the offender, he may not want to risk a jury trial, particularly in states where the jury determines guilt and sets the sentence, and he has an advantage in bargaining for a lighter sentence by pleading guilty. It is when the issue of victim participation or seduction arises that defendants may demand a trial in order to impress the jury with victimogenetic factors, particularly in the case of victims over age fourteen.

The fact that as many as 50 percent of sex victims or their parents do not report the offense to legal authorities may be the resultant of the child's contributory behavior or that parents feel the police and court experience will be damaging. The result is that many, perhaps dangerous sex offenders are not apprehended. If the latter situation prevails there is a need for reform in the methods of child interrogation following the offense. The mental health of the victim may be in the hands of untrained police officers, sheriffs or court personnel.

Since most counties in the United States have at least one trained professional, the child welfare worker attached to the county or regional welfare office, he may be the most practical resource for the professional task of interviewing the child victim. It would appear more practical to teach the social worker a legal perspective than to teach police and prosecutor a mental health orientation.[35]

One country, Israel, has a policy where a professional person interviews the child victim under age fourteen and decides if the child's mental health will be effected by reporting the details of the offense in open court.[36] If he decides that the court experience would be harmful to the child, the social worker may be cross-examined in court *instead* of the child. The defendant cannot be convicted on the evidence of the social worker, youth worker or probation officer, unless supported by other evidence.[37] Naturally, this procedure breaks the fundamental rule of the inadmissibility of hearsay evidence and deprives the accused of the right to cross-examine the accuser in common law countries. The problem centers around a balance between justice to the child and to the offender. In divorce proceedings, the social consequences to the dependent children involved are taken into consideration and perhaps this concept can be extended to sex offenses against children, although the analogy is far from exact for obvious reasons. Although the welfare and interests of the child-victim and offender seem to clash head-on, neither's legal rights can be abridged. The Israeli law, therefore, cannot be transplanted to many other countries because it would violate basic rights of the accused to face his accuser, the right to cross-examine, the right to exclude hearsay, and the right to equal protection of the laws. In addition, Israel has a rigid sex code and a negative attitude towards sexuality, stemming from her religious heritage, which itself may instigate the trauma.

Guidelines for Interviewing

Much of what follows is based on the author's experience in interviewing sex crime victims over a seven-year period, and is not suggested as rigid format. Modifications in content and style are determined by the situation, the child's personality, and the interviewer's skills. Constant effort must be made, to the extent humanly possible, to prevent over-identifying with the assaulted child.

An appointment should be pre-arranged with the victim and parents in their home at a non-school hour. Having the interview in the victim's home has the advantage of providing a familiar relaxed atmosphere and places no burden of travel to a strange, perhaps frightening office or building. The purpose of the interview should be stressed in compatible language to the victim and his parents. My own experience has been that if the child has been informed by his parents that he has nothing to fear, i.e., they endorse the interview, and to cooperate with the social worker, then much has already been accomplished. The victim and parents should always be interviewed separately, safely out of hearing and viewing distance of each other. The presence of another person may induce bias, distortions or omissions in the victim's version of the offense and its consequence. It is wise to tape record the interview with the victim. One's manner and choice of language should be natural and appropriate to the child's age, intelligence, and social class. For example, slang or childish terms, if understood, may be appropriate. Reasonable neutrality is basic and the interviewer should avoid prematurely taking sides, with or against the child, the child's parents, or the defendant. Some sex victims feel outraged, demoralized, defensive or outcast. Mutual trust and confidence may be established by sympathetic questions, encouragement and assurance, aimed at creating a feeling in the victim that one is interested in his/her current predicament and welfare. Ample recognition and sympathetic acceptance of the victim's opposition to the interview should be made by the interviewer. Some victims will welcome an opportunity to express their views freely, once the purpose of the interview is felt, without the atmosphere, fright or limitations of the police station or court.

The interview should begin with the consideration of the more objective, tangible, and physical elements of the offense, and after establishing a desirable degree of rapport, the interviewer can proceed to emotional considerations of the offense, within the limits of the victim's capacity to tolerate the discussion.

The interviewer must be alert to the possibility of disturbing the interviewing relationship by questions that are too abrupt, rapid or demanding. Conflicts, gaps, or mistruths should be clarified in a moderate, helpful, non-emotional manner.

If the case is processed through the courts, the professional should see as his function the preparation of the victim and his family for the court experience. He may seek to have the case moved up on the docket for early handling, may oppose unreasonable delays or adjournments, may request the case to be heard in chambers or that the public be excluded from the courtroom. He may discuss with the prosecution the advantages in bargaining for sentence or accepting a guilty plea. After the case is disposed of, the professionals' task remains to rehabilitatively minimize the damaging offense and court effects, should they persist.

Conclusion

1. Probably less then 5 percent of all child sex victims are assaulted through physical violence or vaginal/anal penetration, so that physical damage is minimal in most cases.
2. Most of the child-sex victims who would be traumatized by the court experience, indicated personality disturbances before the offense.
3. Most of the sexually assaulted children, where no violence was employed, were engaging in affection-seeking behavior, and did not perceive the offense at the time as traumatic.
4. Guilt in sexual victims is fairly absent, but may be engendered by parents, courts or community *after the fact.*
5. Most sexual assaults do not affect the child's personality development, particularly where neither violence nor court appearance occurred.
6. Where a court appearance is necessary to convict an offender who is dangerous to the community, and such court appearance results in mental or social damage, the child should receive victim compensation from the state or court. Courts should experiment with one-way screens and video taping to reduce possible victim trauma.
7. With the increase in sex education in elementary schools, reported victimization may decrease.
8. With rapid value change regarding sexuality in Western countries, what actually constitutes a sexual offense may change, particularly where the issue of informed consent is involved.
9. Urban communities require socio-medical services for sex victims, and trained professionals to provide help through the hospital, police station, and court experience.

Notes

1. L. Schultz, "A Compensation Policy for Sex Victims," in H. Gochros and L. Schultz, *Human Sexuality and Social Work* (New York: Association Press, 1972), Chapter 24.

2. W. Nagel, "The Notion of Victimology in Criminology," *Excerpta Criminologica* 3 (1963): 245-50; S. Schafer, "The Victim and his Functional Responsibility," *Criminologica* 5, 3 (1967): 25-29; L. Schultz, "The Social Worker and Treatment of the Sex Victim," in H. Gochros and L. Schultz, *Human Sexuality and Social Work* (New York: Association Press, 1972), Chapter 14; L. Lamborn, "Toward a Victim Orientation in Criminal Theory," *Rutgers Law Review* 22 (1967/68): 733-68.

3. *Uniform Crime Report,* Federal Bureau of Investigation, 1972.

4. American Humane Association, *Protecting the Child Victim of Sex Crimes* Denver, Colo: The Association, 1966), p. 2.

5. American Humane Association, *Child Victims of Incest* (Denver, Colo: The Association, 1968), p. 5.

6. American Humane Association, *Sexual Abuse of Children: Implications for Casework* (Denver, Colo: The Association, 1967), p. 10; H. Gagnon, "Female Child Victims of Sex Offenses," *Social Problems* 13 (1965): 191.

7. C. Hayman et al., "Sexual Assault on Women and Girls in D.C.," *S. Med. J.* 62 (1969): 1228.

8. Ibid.

9. A. Biderman, "Surveys of Population Samples for Estimating Crime Incidence," *Annals of the American Academy of Political and Social Science* 374 (1967): 16-13; C. Gorham, "Not Only the Stranger," *Journal of School Health* 36 (1966): 341.

10. Gagnon, "Female Child Victims," p. 176.

11. L. Radzinowicz, *Sexual Offenses* (New York: MacMillan, 1957), p. 83.

12. P. Gebhard, *Sex Offenders: An Analysis of Types* (New York: Bantam Books, 1969), p. 747.

13. J. Weiss, "A Study of Girl Sex Victims," *Psychiatric Quarterly* 29 (1955): 1.

14. B. Glueck, *Research Project for the Study and Treatment of Persons Convicted of Crimes Involving Sexual Aberrations* (Albany, N.Y.: Dept. of Mental Hygiene, 1956), p. 296.

15. A. Freedman, *Therapy of Sexually Acting Out Girls* (Palo Alto, Calif: Behavior Science Books, 1970).

16. Gagnon, "Female Child Victims,"

17. T. Gibbons and J. Prince, *Child Victims of Sex Offenses* (Nell, London: Institute for the Study and Treatment of Delinquency, 1963), p. 11.

18. Gagnon, "Female Child Victims," p. 183; C. McCaghy, "Child Molesting," *Sexual Behavior* 1, 5 (1971): 16-24.

19. L. Burton, *Vulnerable Children* (New York: Schocken, 1968), pp. 87-161;

A. Yorukoclu and J. Kemph, "Children Not Severely Damaged by Incest with Parent," *J. Am. Acad. Child Psychiatry* 8 (1969): 606-19.

20. Gagnon, "Female Child Victims," p. 188.

21. G. Schauffler, *Pediatric Gynecology Yearbook* (Chicago, Ill: Interscience, 1958).

22. G. Lipton and E. Roth, "Rape: A Complex Management Problem in the Pediatric Emergency Room," *Journal of Pediatrics* 75 (1969): 859-66; American College of Obstetrics and Gynecology, *Suspected Rape,* Medico-legal Bulletin No. 209, 1970.

23. Gibbons and Prince, "Child Victims," p. 13.

24. A. Werner, "Rape, Interruption of the Therapeutic Process by External Stress," *Psychotherapy: Theory, Research and Practice* 9 (1972): 349-51.

25. F. Arntzen, "Can Children by Harmed by Police Interrogation?" *Our Youth* 23 (1971): 66-68.

26. C. Flammang, "Interviewing Child Victims of Sex Offenses," *Police,* Feb. 1972, pp. 24-28.

27. Note, "Complainant Credibility in Sex Offense Cases," *J. Crim. Law and Criminology* 64 (1973): 67-75; L. Meyers, "Reasonable Mistake of Age: A Needed Defense to Statutory Rape," *Michigan Law Review* 64 (1966): 105-36.

28. Gibbons and Prince, "Child Victims," p. 6.

29. Ibid., p. 14-15.

30. A. Trankell, *Reliability of Evidence: Methods for Analyzing and Assessing Witness Statements* (Stockholm, Sweden: Beckmans, 1972; J. MacDonald, *Rape: Offenders and Victims* (Springfield, Ill.: Thomas, 1971), pp. 209-231.

31. A. Lazarus, "Behavioral Rehearsal vs. Non-directive Therapy vs. Advice," *Behavior Research and Therapy* 4 (1966): 209-12.

32. I. Weiner, "On Incest," *Excerpta Criminologica* 4 (1966): 135-55.

33. C. Newman, "Pleading Guilty for Considerations: A Study in Bargain Justice," *Journal of Criminal Law, Criminology and Police Science* 46 (1956): 780.

34. Conference Proceedings, *The Extension of Legal Services to the Poor,* Dept. of Health, Education, and Welfare (Washington, D.C.: U.S. Printing Office, 1965), pp. 133-60.

35. D. Reifen, "The Sex Offender and His Victim," *International Child Welfare Review* 12 (1958): 109-13; *Law of Evidence Revision 57154.9 Laws of the State of Israel,* 1955.

36. D. Libai, "The Protection of the Child Victim of a Sexual Offense in the Criminal Justice System," *Wayne Law Review* 15 (1969): 977-1032.

37. See D. Reifen, "Court Procedures in Israel to Protect Child-Victims of Sexual Assaults." In I. Drapkin and E. Viano (eds.), *Victimology: A New Focus,* vol. III, *Crimes, Victims and Justice* (Lexington, Mass.: Lexington Books, 1974), ch. 6.

13

The Neglect of Incest: A Criminologist's View

J.E. Hall Williams

Introduction

Incest is one of the latest crimes to enter the English criminal law, dating only from 1908, although there is a long history of its recognition as an offense by the ecclesiastical courts, dating back to the Middle Ages. There was for some time a shared jurisdiction with the Crown courts, but this was for people of high rank only and did not survive after the Restoration. From 1661, throughout the eighteenth and nineteenth centuries, the Church courts continued to exercise jurisdiction. At the very end of the nineteenth century and in the early years of the twentieth century, there was some pressure to bring the matter of incestuous behavior within the reach of the ordinary criminal law. This pressure was at first resisted, successive Lord Chancellors advising against it, on the ground that to legislate about the subject would simply be to give it greater publicity and tend to multiply cases, and do more harm than good. However, by 1907 the Home Office view had changed, and it fully supported the abortive bill introduced in that year. The bill was reintroduced in 1908 as a private member's bill and was supported by Mr. Herbert Samuel who said that the Home Office had long been aware of the need for such legislation. The Lord Chief Justice also sent a telegram supporting the bill and the Lord Chancellor supported it too. The House of Commons passed it late on a Friday afternoon in June.

The Statistics

The criminal statistics for England and Wales show that between two and three hundred cases of incest become 'known to the police' every year. This must be a very small fraction of the total amount of such behavior. Of these 'offences known', nearly all are 'cleared up' because the identity of the offender is obviously known as soon as the offense is identified. Less than half the cases are prosecuted to conviction. Clearly considerable discretion is exercised by police and prosecutors in deciding whether or not to commence criminal proceedings. Of those convicted, about one-half to three-quarters are sent to prison

Reprinted by permission from *Medicine, Science and the Law*, 1974, January, 64-67. Also, by permission of the author.

Table 13-1

Classification of Indictable Offenses of Incest for 1971 and the Sentences

			Sentences		
Offenses of Incest	Number	Higher Courts	Number	Magistrates' Courts	Number
Known to the police	307 (cleared) up 286)	Conditional discharge	6	Supervision	2
		Hospital order s. 60,		Fine	1
		Mental Health Act 1959	3	Care	2
For trial	147	Probation	34	Committed	1
Convicted	140	Detention centre	2	for sentence	
		Borstal training	4		
		Suspended sentence	20		
		Imprisonment	70		
		Other	1		
Total			140		6

(Table 13-1). The length of sentence varies considerably, but there would appear to be a large number of sentences of three or four years imprisonment.

Such sentences make the prisoner eligible for parole, and it is in that context that information has been collected about the subject.

The Sample Studied

Sixty-eight cases are examined which were considered for parole by a panel over a two-year period (1970-71). These cases, of course, do not include the less serious offenses which the courts have decided to deal with by sentences of eighteen months imprisonment or less, or which are dealt with by a non-custodial sentence. They represent only the more serious cases of incest, and the sample was not selected by any scientific sampling method, so that caution must be expressed about the significance of the findings.

Results

The following points emerge from this rather limited study.

The Offender. The majority of the offenders were aged between 30 and 50 years, with a clustering round about 40. There were no women offenders. Approximately a quarter (24 percent) were reported to be of low intelligence, or mentally below average, or subnormal. Over a quarter (26 percent) had previous convictions for sexual offenses. Thirty-one percent had previous convictions for other offenses. Nearly two-thirds (57 percent) had some previous convictions for sexual or non-sexual crimes. Forty percent of the offenders received sentences of 3 years, 23 percent received sentences of 4 years, thus making a total of 64 percent who received sentences of 3 or 4 years. Twenty-one percent received sentences of over 4 years. Twenty-one percent had a poor work record and only 7 percent were said to have fairly good prospects of employment on release from prison. Eighteen percent had a drink problem; while the offenders were mostly from the lower working class in urban areas, and from large families living in very poor and overcrowded conditions. Fifty-three percent of these cases were convicted of the legal offence of incest; 3.8 percent were convicted of indecent assault or attempted indecent assault; 22 percent were convicted of buggery; 27 percent were convicted of unlawful sexual intercourse; and 4 percent were convicted of rape. It is obvious from these figures that many offenders were convicted for several different legal offenses simultaneously.

The status of the relationship with the wife varied from case to case. In 16 percent of cases the wife was dead, divorced, or separated. In many cases marital relationships were under strain or there were sexual difficulties between husband and wife. Opportunity, and/or temptation, to commit the offenses frequently arose from the fact of the wife's absence from home temporarily, at work, on holiday, or in hospital.

The Victim. The victim was the offender's own child in 53 percent of the cases, while stepchildren were involved in 15 percent of the cases, and children of a common law wife in 6 percent. Sisters or brothers were involved in 9 percent of the cases, and nieces in 4 percent of the cases. The majority of cases involved only 1 child; 30 percent of the cases involved 2 children. There were a few with more than 2 children, and the victims were overwhelmingly female.

In a proportion of the cases the relationship had gone on for a number of years, sometimes with successive children. In 16 percent of the cases the relationship had continued for more than a year, and in nearly all cases it appeared to have been a consensual relationship. In 12 percent of the cases there was violence, or threats, or the person was known to have an explosive personality.

The offenses came to light by reason of pregnancy in 9 percent of the cases and by some other discovery including the wife's report to the police in 11 percent of the cases. There is need for more research here about the ways in which the offense comes to light. The age of the victims was mostly between 10 and 16 (60 percent); the average age was 12.5 years. Quite a few victims were under the age of 10, just as many were over the age of 16, even 20 and older.

Prognosis. There were very few cases where the offender could be released to go home to his family; mostly they were going to live elsewhere. Some 12 percent hoped for a reconciliation with the wife, and 4.4 percent had actually been reconciled. Thirty-five percent were reported as having no hope of reconciliation, or as being now divorced, or having a divorce pending. Nearly two-thirds (56 percent) were paroled but 24 percent were second review cases, i.e., they had been rejected for parole on their first application.

With regard to guilt and remorse, some offenders denied their guilt; some expressed remorse and said they had been chastened by punishment; some had been punished before; and a few could not see anything wrong in what they had done.

Comparison With Other Information

These findings appear to correspond closely with those of the German study by Dr. H. Maisch (1973), in several respects. He found a similar proportion of offenders charged with incest in the legal sense (51 percent) and he found that most cases were father-daughter relationships. The average age of the female incest victim was 12.3 years. Roughly two-thirds of his sample were between the ages of 9 and 16 years. The average age of the offenders was between 40 and 50 years, and they were to be found in the lower strata of the population, in large families in poor living conditions. Dr. Maisch's findings concerning the rather low proportion of offenders with previous convictions, and with previous records of sex offenses, do not tally with those reported here. He found 40 percent of the offenders were of low intelligence, and there was a high proportion of alcoholics. With regard to the role of the wife and mother of the victim he has this to say:

> Neither is the development of the victim's personality fully comprehensible nor can a measured judgment be passed on the 'incest situation' unless one considers the wife and mother, and her role in the management of the family.

He found a high proportion of disturbed family situations existing before the start of the incest. One-third of the mothers had suffered from physical illness, often affecting sexual relations. The wife's absence or illness had led to restricted sexual relations in 48 percent of cases. In 41 percent sexual relations had already broken down before the start of the incest. 'Incest', he concluded, 'is not the cause but the symptom or result of a disturbed family order'.

This present study also tallies at various points with the criminal statistics for England and Wales for the year 1971.

Conclusion

1. Incest is a very much neglected crime. It has attracted little notice from

criminologists, although anthropologists and sexologists have given it considerable attention.

2. It is interesting because of the role of the victim, the question of opportunity, the relationship with the spouse before discovery and afterwards, and
the general social and economic conditions in which it appears to thrive. Also
the question of the future of the family is often difficult.

3. The question whether, and if so in what form, it should remain punishable as a separate offense is one to which we should address ourselves (Wootton
1971, p. 33). Morris and Hawkins (1970) believe incest to be one of the next
candidates for reform, and certainly the harsh penalties in some jurisdictions
and in some English cases give cause for concern. It could be argued that all
protection needed is already available through the existing law concerning
sexual offenses of unlawful sexual intercourse (with girls under the age of 16);
intercourse without consent (rape); and the homosexual cases can be dealt
with by prosecutions for buggery and indecent assault or incitement to gross
indecency.

Professor Graham Hughes (1964) believes that the horror of the crime
requires that it should remain separately punishable as an offense, and he calls
for a revised definition to include stepdaughters and adopted daughters, and
limited to the ages of 16 to 21, or 16 to 18 in the case of a woman. The
penalties would be reduced to a maximum period of 2 years imprisonment.
Over the age of 21 the sister or half-sister would be protected from her brothers,
but the penalty would be a maximum of 12 months. The existing law relating
to statutory rape or unlawful sexual intercourse would be used for offenses
against persons under the age of 16. Applying this to our sample, only 17.6
percent of the cases would remain to be prosecuted as incest. Professor Hughes
believes that 'the incest situation is one which causes harm of an identifiable
kind which is a proper subject of criminal prohibition'.

It would seem, however, that the harm lies mostly in the relationship with
children younger than 16 years, and hardly ever with adults. It would also
seem to be largely a case where the family represents something of a social-
problem family requiring intensive casework. Admittedly it may be essential
to remove the father from the home and give time for the wife to decide about
the future. It is also essential to protect the victim from further offenses,
and any other children who may be coming up to an age suitable for sexual
relationships. Sentences of more than 3 years would appear to be quite unnecessary, however, and can only be imposed on a retributive or deterrent basis.
Parole after 12 months or 18 months is desirable in everyone's interest in nearly
two-thirds of the cases. If suitable arrangements for accommodation were
available it is probable that a higher proportion could be paroled.

4. The human problems surrounding incest are frequently problems
of the neglect of children and the failure to provide sufficiently for the
situation:

a. Where there is subnormality or low intelligence of the children and/or the mother;
b. Where there is a breakdown of the normal sexual relationship between husband and wife, or a pregnancy prevents it;
c. Where there is an absence of the mother from the home for a period, by reason of her going out to work, ill-health leading to her being admitted for hospital treatment, or her going on holiday.

The social services' department and the schools could possibly do more to prevent these situations becoming the occasions for incestuous behavior.

5. Further research is needed on the role of the victim, and the part played by the wife/mother in the whole situation:

a. Before discovery and during the period of the offense;
b. After discovery.

References

G. Hughes, *J. crim. Law, Criminol. Pol. Sci.,* 55 (1964): 322.

H. Maisch, *Incest.* London: Deutsch, 1973.

N. Morris, and G. Hawkins, *The Honest Politician's Guide to Crime Control.* Chicago: Chicago University Press, 1970.

B. Wootton, *Contemporary Britain.* London: Allen & Unwin, 1971.

Conclusions and Recommendations Adopted by The First International Symposium on Victimology Held in Jerusalem, September 2-6, 1973

I. What Is Victimology?

1. a. Victimology may be defined as the scientific study of victims. Special attention, however, should be devoted to the problems of victims of crime, the primary concern of this Symposium.
   b. Criminology is enriched by a victimological orientation.
2. Individuals, groups, organizations, nations, and societies can be victimized.
3. Focus should be expanded from the 'two-dimensional' person-to-person interaction to the three or multidimensional one, thus including the bystander and other relevant persons.
4. Lack of concern by a bystander at the scene of a crime is objectionable and, whether or not a criminal act or omission, should be educationally counteracted.
5. The bystander who attempts to assist a victim should be granted immunity for his reasonable acts and compensation when injured.

II. Victimization

1. Research on hidden victimization is needed.
2. A subjective feeling of victimization may not be accompanied by a sufficiently objective basis for society to take responsive action.
3. Victimization of and by groups is no less serious than victimization on a person-to-person level.
4. Certain forms of inadvertence or negligence which occur in industrialized society are as great a cause of victimization as intentional acts.

III. Causes of Victimization

1. Just as certain persons are thought to have high probabilities for committing crime, so also others may have the same likelihood for being victimized.
2. The victim may precipitate the crime.
3. A victimizer may be a person who has himself previously been victimized.
4. The administration of justice may sometimes use excessive punishment and thereby victimize the former victimizer.

IV. Prevention, Treatment, and Research

1. a. Ineffective means of preventing and controlling crime may cause unnecessary suffering to victims, offenders and society.

   b. Legislators, courts, and other authorities responsible for crime prevention and control should evaluate and renovate the organizations and services in this field in order to increase their effectiveness and reduce unnecessary human suffering.

   c. Victimology can lead to improvement of legal procedures, including sentencing, and thereby reduce recidivism and the risks of victimization.

2. Institutional procedures should be provided to protect the victim against unintentional, harmful consequences of the judicial process. A balance should be reached between the needs and rights of the victim and the defendant.

3. a. Some governments and state organizations victimize vulnerable groups, causing a danger of escalation to mass violence. Such practices are condemned and an appeal is made to the conscience of mankind to maintain and enforce a restraining vigilance.

   b. International control of this type of victimization is necessary.

4. The right of asylum should be strengthened in order to assist the victim of the state.

5. Governmental and non-governmental bodies should provide both emergency and prolonged medical, psychiatric, psychological, and social services to victims of crime, without charge.

6. a. Research is needed on the extent to which victimization may lead victims to become offenders.

   b. Research into victim probabilities could help society to prevent the victimization of vulnerable persons.

V. Compensation

1. All nations should, as a matter of urgency, give consideration to the establishment of state systems of compensation for victims of crime and should seek to achieve maximum efficacy in the application of existing schemes and of those that may be established.

2. All available means should be employed to disseminate information about compensation schemes and the participation of all appropriate bodies—governmental and non-governmental—should be secured in their implementation.

3. All existing compensation schemes should be investigated and evaluated with a view to extending their application, bearing in mind the respective requirements of the various communities in which they operate.

It is suggested that the following questions be given full consideration by all nations intending to set up compensation schemes or intending to modify existing schemes:

1. Should there be a maximum and/or minimum level for compensation?
2. What is the nature of the losses that should be recompensed? e.g. direct damage, loss of earnings, pain and suffering.
3. Should consideration be given to the victim's conduct at the time of the offense and/or to his general character in determining the question of compensation?
4. Should payment be by right and denied only for stated reasons by the court?
5. Should present-day schemes be extended to include crimes against property?
6. Should the state be entitled to claim reimbursement from the criminal and/or should the state be empowered to compel criminals to give part of their earnings to the state?
7. Should states set up compulsory insurance schemes for certain professions whose exercise relies upon an element of fidelity and trust in order to cover damage caused by one of their members, e.g. doctors, lawyers, accountants, insurance companies, members of stock exchanges?
8. Should compensation schemes contain opportunities for appeal?
9. Should bystanders attempting to aid victims be entitled to compensation for damage or losses suffered?
10. Should the victim be entitled to immediate partial compensation in order to tide him over initial expenses, the determination of the final sum to be made subsequently by the compensation board?
11. Should an accused person who is found not guilty be entitled to compensation for court costs incurred and/or for other losses?
12. Should a judge in a criminal trial be entitled to order compensation by the state concurrently with his verdict?
13. Should the office of ombudsman be set up to provide direct focus on the needs of the victim, with special concern for mitigating immediate trauma, prevention of further stress at the hands of society, as well as for offering treatment for victim-recidivists?

This Symposium calls upon governmental and other national as well as international organizations to disseminate as widely as possible the conclusions and recommendations reached in the course of its deliberations, with the hope of achieving thereby the reduction and alleviation of victimization.

Indexes

Name Index

Subject Index

List of Contributors

Neville H. Avison, Department of Criminology, University of Edinburgh.

Bruno M. Cormier, Clinic in Forensic Psychiatry, McGill University, Montreal, Quebec.

Vahakn N. Dadrian, Department of Sociology, State University of New York, Geneseo, New York.

Israel Drapkin, Institute of Criminology, Hebrew University, Jerusalem.

Russell R. Dynes, Department of Sociology, Ohio State University, Columbus, Ohio.

J.E. Hall-Williams, The London School of Economics and Political Science, University of London.

Susan Harlap, Department of Medical Ecology, Hebrew University, Hadassah Hospital, Jerusalem.

Pawel Horoszowski, Department of Sociology, Northern Illinois University, DeKalb, Illinois.

Chanoch Jacobsen, Technion, Israel Institute of Technology, Haifa.

Stuart Palmer, Social Science Center, University of New Hampshire, Durham, New Hampshire.

E.L. Quarantelli, Disaster Research Center, Ohio State University, Columbus, Ohio.

Stephen Schafer, College of Criminal Justice, Northeastern University, Boston, Massachusetts.

LeRoy G. Schultz, School of Social Work, West Virginia University, Morgantown, West Virginia.

Klaus Sessar, Max-Planck-Institute für Ausländisches und Internationales Strafrecht, Freiburg i.B., West Germany.

Emilio C. Viano, Center for the Administration of Justice, The American University, Washington, D.C.

About the Editors

Israel Drapkin, M.D., has been Professor of Criminology and Director of the Institute of Criminology at the Hebrew University of Jerusalem since 1959. Previously, he was director of the Institute of Criminology of Chile (1936-59) and professor at the University of Chile (1950-59). He has served as correspondent to the United Nations Social Defence Section since 1950, and as a United Nations expert both in Israel and at the Asia and Far East Institute for the Prevention of Crime and Treatment of Offenders (UNAFEI). He has been visiting professor at the Haile Selassie I University (Addis Ababa), Central University of Venezuela, the University of Pennsylvania, and the American University (Washington, D.C.). Professor Drapkin was the chairman of the Organizing Committee of the First International Symposium on Victimology held in Jerusalem in 1973. He has contributed articles to professional journals and is the author or editor of several books, including coeditor (with Emilio Viano) of *Victimology* (Lexington Books, 1974).

Emilio Viano, Ph.D., is Associate Professor of Sociology and the Administration of Justice at The American University's Center for the Administration of Justice in Washington, D.C. He is also a faculty member in the Independent Study Program of the City University of New York, and, during 1974/75, at the Institute of Criminal Justice and Criminology of the University of Maryland. During 1973/74, Dr. Viano was the project director of the special project, "The Humanities and the Police," funded by the National Endowment for the Humanities. Previously, he was on the research staff of the National Council on Crime and Delinquency in New York City. Dr. Viano is the author of several articles which have appeared in professional journals, and is coauthor of *Social Problems and Criminal Justice* (Chicago: Nelson-Hall, 1974); coeditor (with Israel Drapkin) of *Victimology* (Lexington Books, 1974); coeditor of a volume on police-community relations to be published by J.B. Lippincott; and editor of a book on criminal justice research to be published by Lexington Books. He also coauthored *Management of Probation Services* (vols. I and II) and *Decision Making in Administration of Probation Services,* published by the National Council on Crime and Delinquency, and *Evaluation of Atlanta-Fulton County Correctional Agencies and Development of a Consolidation Plan* (McLean, Va.: PRC Public Management Services, Inc., 1973).